SOVIET POWER: THE CONTINUING CHALLENGE

SOVIET POWER: THE CONTINUING CHALLENGE

James Sherr

St. Martin's Press   New York

Scholarly & Reference Division,
St. Martin's Press, Inc.,
175 Fifth Avenue, New York, NY 10010

First published in the United States of America in 1987

Printed in Hong Kong

ISBN 0–312–74873–6

Library of Congress Cataloging-in-Publication Data
Sherr, James, 1951–
Soviet power, the continuing challenge.
Bibliography: p.
Includes index.
1. Soviet Union—Defenses.   I. Title.
II. Title: Soviet power.
UA770.S48   1987   355'.033047   86–20342
ISBN 0–312–74873–6

Contents

List of Abbreviations

AA	Anti-Aircraft
ABM	Anti-Ballistic Missile
AFCENT	Armed Forces Centre
AFSOUTH	Armed Forces South
AFV	Armoured Fighting Vehicle
C^3	Command, Control and Communications
CC	Central Committee
CGF	Central Group of Forces
CGS	Chief of the General Staff
CMEA	Council for Mutual Economic Assistance (alternatively, COMECON)
Cominform	Communist Information Bureau
Comintern	Communist International
CPSU	Communist Party of the Soviet Union
DOSAAF	Voluntary Society for Cooperation with the Army, Aviation and Fleet
ERW	Enhanced-Radiation Warhead
FROG	Free Rocket over Ground (unguided tactical missile)
FRG	Federal Republic of Germany
GDR	German Democratic Republic
GK	High Command (*Glavnokomandovaniye*)
GKO	State Defence Committee (*Gosudarstvenny Komitet Oborony*)
GlavPU	Chief Political Directorate of the Soviet Army and Navy (*Glavnoye Politicheskoye Upravleniye*) (or Main Political Directorate/Administration)
GLCM	Ground Launched Cruise Missile
Gosplan	State Planning Commission
GRU	Chief Intelligence Directorate of the General Staff (*Glavnoye Razvedyvatelnoye Upravleniye*, alternatively Main Intelligence Directorate)
GSFG	Group of Soviet Forces, Germany
HQ	Headquarters
ICBM	Intercontinental Ballistic Missile
ID	International Department of CPSU Central Committee
IMEMO	Institute of World Economy and International Relations
INF	Intermediate Nuclear Forces
IRBM	Intermediate Range Ballistic Missile
ISShAK	Institute of the USA and Canada
KGB	Committee of State Security (*Komitet Gosudarstvennoy Bezopasnosti*)
KOR	Workers Defence Committee (Poland)
LWP	Polish People's Army (*Ludowe Wojsko Polskie*)
MAD	Mutual Assured Destruction

MFA	Ministry of Foreign Affairs
MfS	Ministry of State Security (GDR)
MGB	Ministry of State Security (KGB's predecessor, 1946–54)
MIRV	Multiple Independently-targetable Re-Entry Vehicle
MLRS	Multiple Launch Rocket System
MoD	Ministry of Defence
MRBM	Medium Range Ballistic Missile
MVD	Ministry of Internal Affairs (*Ministerstvo Vnutrennykh Del*)
NBC	Nuclear, Biological and Chemical
NGF	Northern Group of Forces
NKGB	People's Commissariat of State Security (MGB's predecessor, 1941–46)
NKVD	People's Commissariat of Internal Affairs (MVD's predecessor, 1917–46)
NSWP	Non-Soviet Warsaw Pact
NVA	National People's Army (GDR) (*National Volksarmee*)
OECD	Organisation for Economic Cooperation and Development
OEEC	Organisation for European Economic Cooperation
OMG	Operational Manoeuvre Group (*Operativnaya Manevrennaya Gruppa*)
ORMO	Voluntary Reserve of Civic Militia (Poland)
OVS	Combined Staff of Warsaw Pact
PKK	Political Consultative Committee of Warsaw Pact
PRC	People's Republic of China
PZPR	Polish United Workers Party
RSFSR	Russian Soviet Federative Socialist Republic
RVSN	Strategic Rocket Forces (*Raketnyye Voyska Strategicheskogo Naznacheniya*)
SALT	Strategic Arms Limitation Talks
SAM	Surface-to-Air Missile
SDI	Strategic Defence Initiative
SGF	Southern Group of Forces
SLBM	Submarine-Launched Ballistic Missile
SP	Self-Propelled
Spetsnaz	Diversionary Troops (literally, Special Forces)
SSBN	Ballistic Missile Nuclear Submarine
Stavka	General Headquarters (usually, Stavka VGK: HQ of the Supreme High Command)
TVD	Theatre of Military Operations (*teatr voyennyk deystriy*)
USSR	Union of Soviet Socialist Republics
VGK	Supreme High Command (*Verkhovnoye Glavnokomandovaniye*)
Voyska PVO	Troops of Air Defence (*Voyska Protivovozdushnoy Oborony*)
VPK	Military Industrial Commission (*Voyenno-promyshlennaya Komissiya*)
WPC	World Peace Council
WTO	Warsaw Treaty Organisation
ZOMO	Motorised Units of Civic Militia (Poland)

Throughout the book 'Socialism' refers to that variant of socialism recognised as legitimate by the CPSU.

Notes on the Contributors

Admiral Sir John Fieldhouse, GCB, GBE, was Chief of Naval Staff and First Sea Lord between December 1982 and October 1985 and is now Chief of the Defence Staff.

Dr Norman Friedman, formerly of the Hudson Institute, is a defence analyst.

Fred Halliday is Professor of International Relations at the London School of Economics and Political Science.

Malcolm Mackintosh, CMG, works at the Cabinet Office.

Dr Edwina Moreton is a member of the editorial staff of *The Economist*.

Helmut Sonnenfeldt is Guest Scholar, The Brookings Institution, Washington, DC.

Air Commodore E. S. Williams, CBE, MPhil, was Defence and Air Attaché in Moscow between 1978 and 1981.

Acknowledgements

The Institute which launched this study is committed to two propositions: that military power exerts a profound influence on the course and pattern of world politics; and that, to be properly understood – or effectively employed – military power cannot be divorced from the social and political context in which it operates. Unexceptional as these propositions might appear, they are under challenge from many quarters: from those who are more impressed with the limits of military power than with its utility; from those who believe that one can find security, or even salvation without it; but equally so, from those who would reduce security policy to military policy; and from those who believe it possible to understand war without understanding politics. The USSR's founders and its present custodians would find these views alien and not only misconceived. The subject of this study is the way the military instrument combines with others to advance the purposes of the Soviet state and its Communist Party; it is also about the philosophy which shapes those purposes and the striking continuity manifested over the years in the Soviet way of war and politics. 'The continuing challenge' is a very great power which owes her achievements not to accidents of history, but to her own dogged persistence. Deficient as she is by some measures, the USSR is rich in human as well as in material resources, and she has many cards to play. The USSR is a Superpower for all her faults, not half a Superpower as it is sometimes alleged.

This volume represents the culmination of an RUSI Main Theme study, 'Soviet Power and Prospects'. Out of a very full and rich assortment of lectures that structured the Institute's work, the small number presented in Part II have been chosen with an eye to gaps in my presentation, to approaches which contrast with my own, and to their obvious quality. Constraints of space have prevented inclusion of other contributions equal in quality, but we take comfort in the fact that many have now been published in the *RUSI Journal*, and we hope we will be forgiven by the authors concerned.

Scholars very properly set store by scrupulousness and care in research, documentation and expression. Scholarship, however, can also refine first order questions out of existence. I would not duck the charge that my effort in large measure has been one of interpretation, and I have not shied away from original, and occasionally controversial, points. But original thought is not autonomous. It must be stimulated, informed and disciplined. Thankfully, I have benefited from gifted and learned patrons, and the thoughts expressed here owe much to the inspiration of others. No informed reader will fail to note my intellectual debt to Malcolm Mackintosh, Peter Vigor and Christopher Donnelly. I gratefully acknowledge their assistance as well as their influence, particularly in the case of Malcolm Mackintosh, who commented upon this manuscript with care and insight. I have also benefited, as anyone properly should, from the writings of John Erickson and the work of Harriet and William Scott. Michael Howard, who in all his pursuits combines the historian's sympathetic imagination with a capacity for trenchant judgement, remains a model and not just an influence. Influence, however, is an intensely personal matter, and it occasionally takes a form that surprises the patron. The usual disclaimer in publications about guilt by association must certainly apply here: the judgements expressed in this volume are my own, and I accept full responsibility for them.

In more practical and equally personal ways, this study bears the mark of a thriving and closely-knit institution. Were it not for the perseverance and resilience of the staff of the RUSI, the author's temperament might have got the better of his purpose. Gratitude and no small measure of admiration are due to David Bolton and Brian Holden Reid for weathering and largely taming the idiosyncrasies of a headstrong, if diffident, performer. I should also like to single out Farooq Hussain, and Jennifer Shaw (now with Brassey's), for the warmth and firmness of their support – and Lieutenant Colonel Samuel Pope for many fruitful discussions over just as many liquid lunches. Finally, for 'well known reasons' (as *Pravda* might say), I salute Christopher and Elizabeth Wenner, Christopher Coker, Mark Almond, Thomas Stuttaford, Christopher Granville, Caroline Bolton, John Chipman, Jack Pole, Wilfrid Knapp, Maurice Keen and John Dunbabin (others are lodged in mind, but mercifully spared disclosure). My most considerable debt is to my parents, to whom the book is dedicated.

JAMES SHERR

Foreword

The existence of the Soviet Union as one of the Great Powers of the world since the end of the Second World War has been a central element of world affairs, of international relations and of the search for an acceptable balance in global power, not only for the West and the Communist countries, but also in the Third World. What has been far from clear during this period has been the nature of Soviet power and the motives of those who use it. We know, of course, the basic factors of geography, climate, population, economic resources and history in general terms, but we lack to some extent, at least, a new and updated analysis of the available evidence on which an objective observer can try to understand why the Soviet State and Communist Party have acted and act as they do. What, we have asked ourselves, makes the Soviet Union interpret a given situation in the way it does? What are its principles and its standards in policy-making towards the rest of the world? What are its aims and ambitions? How dominated are Soviet leaders by fear, or are they inspired more by hope of achieving their goals by the successful use of power? How Russian is Soviet power, and to what extent is it motivated by the short or long-term principles of Marxism–Leninism?

These are a few of the many questions about the Soviet Union that James Sherr tackles in this well-researched and valuable book. He starts with the assumption that in 1945 when the successes of Soviet arms had brought Russia for the first time for decades face to face with the traditional nations of Europe, as well as the United States and China, outside knowledge of the Soviet Union and understanding of its goals and intentions were very limited. The average non-political, non-governmental European or North American observer probably recalled that Russia for the last 200 years had been a ponderous and ramshackle Empire, ruled by absolutist regimes: a nation with little experience of parliamentary democracy, economic growth or scientific advances. The Empire had crumbled in 1917 mainly as a result of defeat in war, and been replaced by a Communist regime which tried to establish Marxism at home and initially, at least, promised to export it abroad – by force if necessary. Western observers remembered that under the brutal and absolute dictatorship of the Georgian Iosif Stalin, millions of Russians perished in concentration camps or as a result of purges and famine while Stalin pursued his strategy of building 'socialism in one country'. This was his alternative in that difficult period for Soviet power to the endless drive towards 'world revolution' associated with the name of Leon Trotsky.

Then, in 1939, came the Second World War, and in 1941 the German invasion of the Soviet Union. The Soviet Union became our ally, and we watched with rising admiration the Red Army's defeat of the invaders in defensive battles, followed by the massive Soviet counter-offensives which brought Soviet power, military and political, to the centre of Europe. For the first time we in the West actually saw the Soviet state in action, and on our doorstep. Some Westerners who were serving or prisoners-of-war in Eastern Europe experienced personal contact with the Red Army as it crossed into Eastern and Central Europe: others met Russian soldiers as the Allied forces linked up in Germany or Austria. Statesmen and other leaders negotiated with them, as the war drew to a close, on the future of the world in the wake of the defeat of the Nazis. Most of these contacts took place against the background of unbounded admiration for the Soviet Union and the Red Army. But none of them produced real communication between the Soviet Union and the West: none told us at that time what the Soviet Government wanted, what it planned to do in Europe or the Far East, or how the victory for which it had sacrificed so much, as Russia, the Communist State, entered the world arena as one of its Great Powers.

What the Soviet Union did do, in fact, is now history, and much of James Sherr's book draws its evidence from the events of the last four decades. As early as June 1945 Soviet leaders were warning their people that the victory over Germany did not mean the end of all struggles, and that conflicts with other opponents of the Soviet system remained to be fought and won. Stalin concentrated first on consolidating his liberating conquests in Europe and the Far East. He then launched 'probes' to see how the post-war situation might be used to benefit the Soviet Union, explaining in his classic letter to Marshal Tito in 1948 that 'the only reason why there are no Communist Governments in France or Italy is because the Red Army did not reach Paris or Rome in 1945'. Stalin set up the 'Cominform' in 1947 to coordinate Communist action all over the world under Soviet direction. He imposed a Soviet-dominated regime in Czechoslovakia in 1948, and tried to drive the Western Powers out of Berlin by means of the Berlin Blockade in 1948–49. He expelled one of his allies, Yugoslavia, for failing to toe the Soviet line, as well as supporting a major Communist rising in Greece.

In Asia, the Calcutta Conference in 1947, held under Soviet auspices, ordered the Communist Parties in a number of Third World countries into armed action to overthrow their governments and establish Communist regimes there. And finally in the Stalin era, the Soviet Union, having suffered setbacks in Europe and the Third World, encouraged or authorised the North Koreans to attack the South in 1950, believing, it seems, that South Korea was excluded from the defence 'perimeter' established informally by the United States for the protection of American and Western interests in the area.

Even more significant that these 'probes' – although they did much to lead to the foundation of NATO in 1949 – was the Soviet decision in the late 1940s to take a short cut to political and military parity with the United States which then had the monopoly of the atomic bomb and means for its delivery. The Soviet Union was already approaching possession of her own atomic weapons by 1948, and in that year took the decision to build a land-based strategic missile force capable, when it became operational in 1959, of delivering nuclear weapons to targets in North America. James Sherr correctly points out that it would be an oversimplification to attribute the Soviet Union's current Superpower status solely to its military power. I would submit, however, that for the Soviet leaders of the 1940s the advance to Superpower status involving the creation of military and strategic 'parity' (in the Soviet sense of the word) with the United States, had the highest priority in the Soviet allocation of resources at that time.

As the Soviet Union recovered from the devastation and the human and economic disasters of the Second World War, and the planned advance to strategic 'parity' with the United States proceeded, a richer, more powerful Soviet Union under more innovative and sophisticated leaders, sought in a variety of ways to expand Soviet influence in Europe, the Far East and in the Third World. The Soviet Union and its allies achieved some successes – in the Middle East, the Caribbean and South East Asia – and suffered setbacks – within its own Bloc in Eastern Europe, necessitating the use of force to restore Soviet control – and in relations with China. Several of these 'probes' tested Soviet skills and put the West and many Third World countries on guard. But the most fundamental watershed in Soviet policy came in 1969, in fact, when the Soviet Union believed that its armoury of land-based strategic intercontinental missiles (ICBMs), later to be reinforced by submarine-launched missiles (SLBMs) had reached 'approximate parity' with that of the other Superpower. The figures were, in fact, about 1400 Soviet ICBMs to 1054 in the United States. In other words, the Soviet Union had become an 'equivalent' Superpower with the United States. Negotiations to codify the strategic balance with acceptable 'upper limits' to strategic force deployments could therefore begin.

The Strategic Arms Limitation Talks (SALT) and the treaties of 1972 and 1979 went some way to convincing the Soviet leaders that the strategic nuclear balance was in a satisfactory state, and that effective arms control negotiations with the United States and NATO would probably become a continuing process. In Europe, negotiations led to the Helsinki Accord of 1975, and progress was made on East–West trade. This allowed the Russians to divert resources to their Theatre Forces, conventional and nuclear, and to their ocean-going Navy for wartime purposes and in support of Soviet politico-military activity in peacetime in various parts of the world. This dual process was slowed down and deflected into different channels in the early 1980s, partly by new defence policies and concepts of arms control and the military balance pursued by President Reagan, who believed that some of his predecessors had given away too much to the Soviet Union in arms control, in both strategic and in theatre weapons.

A new and younger leadership in Moscow from early 1985 faced these dilemmas and had to take, or consider, decisions on how to deal with a very different East–West strategic and military relationship from that in the heyday of *détente* and SALT. These Soviet leaders have to work out how the next stage in these relations can best be planned, including the achievement of Soviet goals in US–Soviet relationship, in Europe, towards China and in the Third World in the existing and forthcoming balance of power. In order to understand what Soviet thinking along these lines is likely to be, we have to absorb the historical evidence of Soviet policy-making. But we must also understand Soviet and Russian motives in choosing and pursuing their policies. That is what this book does so readably and convincingly.

James Sherr writes with a thorough knowledge of Russian and Soviet history, culture, economic resources and philosophy – both national and Soviet ideological. His study concentrates on the contemporary scene and methods of using their power which are relevant today. But his interpretations of Soviet motives are based on Soviet concepts of merging the age-old and intuitive traditions of Russian political and military thinking with those elements of Marxism which are acceptable to Soviet leaders who rule their country as a modern global Superpower. To put it another way, these motives and methods have to be relevant to political leaders who as Russian ideologists have added 'Leninism' to the 'Marxism' which they inherited from the early revolutionaries. Gorbachev now calls this 'integral socialism' in his latest pronouncements. These men have to apply this process in the environment of the latter part of the Twentieth Century, dominated as it is by the rapid growth in the number of new states, rival ideologies, including Moslem fundamentalism, high technology, and nuclear power, both civil and military.

James Sherr rightly stresses that really the first lesson we have to learn about Soviet decision-making is the primary role of 'rivalry' in their thinking. Everyone, every power, every other ideology in the world is a 'rival' to the Soviet system. In some cases, the Russians appear to believe, these 'rivals' actively seek the downfall of the Soviet Union or at least the weakening of its power by means which, in extreme cases, may include some form of military action – though not, by now, a full-scale nuclear attack on the USSR.

This concept of gearing up the country to cope with 'rivals' is central to Soviet policy-making and planning. The very Soviet system allows the Soviet leaders a persistence and flexibility in their dealings with their opponents on which elected governments cannot always rely. As James Sherr puts it: 'to the Communist Party of the Soviet Union, East–West cooperation makes sense only within the context of rivalry'. But the Soviet leaders do not accept ways of dealing with their opponents which are risky or unbridled. Moreover, they do not favour 'master-plans' for world domination with precise or even general time-scales any more. What they do accept and why, is, I believe, well described in this book: I therefore conclude this Foreword by saying: 'now read on. . . .'

MALCOLM MACKINTOSH

Part I

The Continuing Challenge

1 First Principles

We are convinced that sooner or later Capitalism will perish, just as feudalism perished earlier. The Socialist nations are advancing towards Communism. History does not ask whether you want it or not.

N. S. Khrushchev, *Tass*, 29 June 1957

'Without its military power, the Soviet Union would be of limited consequence in world affairs.' So concluded one well known study of this subject, and the view it expresses is one which is widely shared.[1] It cannot escape notice that the growth of Soviet military strength from the mid-1960s, and of the military instrument in Soviet policy, has coincided with declining economic performance, a loss of vitality, and a tarnishing of the Soviet image in other ways which diminish that country's international respect and appeal. It is, then, as a military power that the USSR must be understood – or so the received wisdom would have it.

For all that is true in this perception, it is the father of bad intellectual habits and temptations. One is a captivation with the details of hardware, numbers and performance to the exclusion of the military–strategic and military–political issues which render them significant. If the West's security depends on accurate assessments of the capabilities and fighting qualities of the Soviet Armed Forces, it hinges at least as much on an ability to grasp how Soviet strategists plan to match means to ends and how these forces fit into an overall scheme of policy. Above all, success in framing appropriate and durable security policies demands that we come to grips with the Soviet calculus of peace and war. Why, for example, has the USSR rejected the conventional wisdom that, in the nuclear age, armies exist solely 'for deterrence'? Do Soviet doctrine and force postures express a belief that nuclear war can be won, or at least waged as an instrument of policy? Has the USSR invested seriously in a capability to 'fight and win' such a war – and would this capability express an intention to launch one at the opportune moment, or solely to prevail in one should it be imposed upon her? At a time of *détente*, what explained the USSR's 'principled' rejection of Western notions of world order and of

3

a 'moderate course' in world affairs?[2] Why in those years did the Soviets display an interest in military solutions just when her adversaries had come to doubt their utility and legitimacy? Finally, to what do we owe the momentum of the USSR's military expansion at a time when she, to all appearances had reached a plateau of security and NATO's own efforts had slackened? There have been divergent and controversial answers to these questions. What is needed, however, is not an alarmist view of Soviet intentions, but an appreciation of the distinctiveness of Soviet perspectives. Moreover, we would do well to recognise in these perceptions the wisdom of a practiced, educated and highly expert military elite. The subject of the study from which our opening quotation is drawn is, appropriately enough, the challenge posed by Soviet military *thought*.

A study concerned with power as a whole cannot overlook a second pitfall of many Western approaches. That is the tendency to slight the non-military instruments of power and influence available to the Soviet Union – some of which are uniquely available to her and unfamiliar to ourselves. By some readings, Soviet leaders may consider them decisive. Marxism–Leninism has bequeathed 'democratic–centralist' political institutions and an intellectual bias toward the long-term view. Both afford the Soviet leaders a persistence and flexibility in their dealings which their bourgeois rivals cannot readily reciprocate. Elected governments are not at liberty to adopt the course of 'zigzag-retreat', let alone the line that 'all things come to those who wait'. Intangible weapons can be deployed to tangible effect – particularly when traditional policies are under attack, as in Europe, or political order is under threat, as in parts of the Third World. Soviet experience and organisational resources in propaganda, mass mobilisation and other 'active measures' are as much a part of any East–West contest as economic assistance and the more visible forms of power projection. In the Third World, their grasp of the syntax and grammar of revolutionary struggle often gives Soviet protégés the upper hand against opponents far better endowed in the conventional instruments of power. In spite of these assets, examples abound where Soviet clients have misjudged their potential and failed in their efforts. But assets these are, and any discussion of power is flawed if it excludes them. Far from political warfare and other active measures being by-gone techniques from times of weakness, they have grown in importance with military strength.[3]

For many, the overriding need of our time is not East–West rivalry, but cooperation. In a world where war remains possible and where it could have catastrophic consequences, this is a compelling appeal. But the urgency with which it is often voiced betrays complacency as well as despair: an assumption that the choice is ours to make and a conviction that only one or the other is possible. To the Communist Party of the Soviet Union (CPSU), East–West cooperation makes sense only within the context of rivalry. But rivalry does not make sense if it is wanton or unbridled. The Soviet leaders are ideological, but they are not ideologues. Marxist–Leninists are part of a rational political tradition: they subscribe to an ethic of consequences; they will be the last to allow principle to override self-interest.

Nevertheless, if we are to come to terms with the realities of Soviet power, we would do well to face up to the strength of the competitive drive in Soviet policy and its tenacity. Moreover, if we are to comprehend these realities accurately and not in caricature, we cannot afford to be distracted by straw men and false dichotomies. 'Masterplans' for 'world domination' are not at issue if we are to understand that the USSR sees itself as a contestant in a global competition and that it brings a strategic vision to the contest. 'Strategy', as Richard Pipes has observed, 'is not getting what one wants, but knowing what one wants and what it takes to get it'.[4] A tactician knows when to retreat; a strategist ensures that his retreats as well as his advances are in keeping with his purpose. A strategist has the ability to isolate the decisive question and subordinate all the others to it; the object is always the goal, not the game. The issue is not one of strategy *versus* flexibility, least of all ideology *versus* realism. To the contrary, the most consistent strand in Soviet conduct has been a ruthless and unsentimental rigour in matching means to ends.

The Soviets are not 'pragmatists' in the manner of those who allow the means to dictate the end. Much strategic discussion in the West revolves around the issue, 'what can be done with what we can afford'? In the USSR the question more typically has been, 'what must be done, and how do we set about affording it'? This approach is evident today in the organisation of the Soviet economy and the priorities imposed upon it. In the past it has been even more apparent in the privations withstood for the sake of collectivisation and the Five-Year Plans, and for victory in war itself: in a willingness to tolerate tactics wasteful of human life for the sake of strategic success; and to relocate, suppress, or liquidate individuals and entire peoples who either opposed or would not contribute avidly enough to this goal. 'He who wills the end wills also the means': in this sense, Soviet spokesmen are right to insist that these sacrifices have been necessary. But other societies have frequently altered their views of what was necessary in the face of far less adverse costs.

To speak of the primacy of competitive considerations in Soviet policy, we need not postulate a country free of anxiety, weakness and defensive concerns. For much of Soviet history weakness has been chronic and defensive concerns overriding; even in time of strength they will have first priority. The question is not whether these concerns are sincere, but whether the USSR is a status quo power. As Admiral Fieldhouse notes in the second part of this volume, 'defence is pre-requisite to any other activity'. The vulnerabilities of the Soviet Union have usually been the consequence of her ambition. Consistently in Soviet history, strength has whet that ambition, adversity has inspired reasonableness and prudence. That history seems to be a recurring tale of how vulnerabilities, rectified at great cost, return as ambitions expand and rivals respond. Nor does it follow that, because of their strategic approach, the Soviet leaders are without ambivalences and dilemmas. As *dialectical* materialists, the Soviets understand that dilemmas are the stuff of reality: they never tire of pointing out that 'the situation today is extremely complex'. An example of such complexity is East–West *détente* in Europe, a state of affairs brought about in large measure by bold and imaginative revisions of West German policy undertaken at the end of the 1960s. The pre-requisite, and pre-condition, for Willi Brandt's opening to the East in 1969–70 was an FRG confident of her position in NATO. The German's shrewdly calculated that the Soviets too would grasp this point and conclude that it would no longer further her interests to play the role of spoiler between the FRG and her Western allies. It was not so clearly foreseen, however, that the FRG's very successes would affect her interests and her diplomatic indentity. Fifteen years on, many fear that the FRG's future confidence in NATO will hinge on whether these allies continue to respect the nature of her ties with the GDR and the Eastern bloc. It may go too far to suggest that Moscow has thereby become the arbiter of what is acceptable in West German or Alliance policy. However, what was to have been the Soviets' constraint has become the West's constraint. For the future, well-judged concessions on our part will, as much as 'containment', continue to create dilemmas for Soviet policy. But the pertinent questions will always be, 'who understands his dilemmas clearly?', 'who is best equipped to turn them to advantage'?[5]

If false distinctions are easily conjured up, they are fairly easy to dispense with. The same is not as true for what has come to be called 'mirror imaging', because of the difficulty of getting into someone else's skin and staying in it. Nonetheless, if we are to size up, let alone influence, the challenges confronting our Soviet rivals, we must grasp what it is that matters to them. Internally, central planning is in the first instance a system of control and, secondly, a means of producing goods and services. Reforms will not be undertaken which strengthen the economy at the expense of the regime (as we shall argue in Chapter 2); departure from old 'forms and methods' is not likely to produce a convergence with Western thought and practice. Moreover, the USSR will seek economic benefits from the West to extend its freedom of action: the West will not easily 'lever' the Soviet Union into acquiring these benefits on terms which restrict it. In Eastern Europe, the preservation of the Soviet model is as much a matter of internal as of external security. The USSR will not, for the sake of *détente*, prosperity or social tranquility, buy into some kind of 'evolutionary' course which puts this model at risk (Chapter 3). Finally, the military system is geared to the provision of definite capabilities for defending the country and advancing policy objectives – not to the maintenance of some notional 'parity' with opponents (Chapters 4 and 5). In all of these areas, there are choices and trade-offs to be made, but not always those which seem reasonable from our perspectives. As people reared in their own society and their own traditions, the Soviets will not always be found trying to match Western strengths; rather to counter and compensate and, as we shall suggest in Chapters 5 and 6, to devise stratagems which aim for the weakest links in our own chain.

If there is any special pleading in this volume, it is that we take the Soviet view of the world seriously. To dismiss it as 'oriental despotism papered over with Marxist verbiage' simply reveals our own cultural blinders.[6] Underlying what we find unsettling in Soviet policy is a tradition of thought about man and society, order and change, war and peace. If in present-day Soviet conditions Marxism–Leninism has lost touch with its Utopian roots, it has not lost its powers of diagnosis and interpretation. Even as political conditioning, it has a far from nebulous importance. Lenin can be invoked in support of realism, patience and prudence as well as ferocity, fanaticism and ruthlessness. But he can not be invoked to sanctify what he never espoused: comity, reconciliation and a charitable acceptance of the world as it is. There is little point in speaking as if a choice had to be made between this ideology and a traditional 'Russian' understanding of the Soviet Union. As Lord Beloff long ago reminded us,

The marriage between a territorial or ethnic power-complex and an ideology (divine or secular) is no new thing. If the experience of Islam and of Arab rule offers the most striking parallel, there is perhaps a closer one in the inter-relations of the Counter Reformation and the Habsburg dynasty. For a crucial century of the development of modern Europe, it is indeed impossible to say where religious zeal and dynastic aggrandizement respectively begin and end. . . . It is clear that such alliances when once formed have normally proved extremely durable.[7]

However impressive Russia's strides between 1860 and 1917 towards a liberal constitutional order, it was the triumph of what Trotsky in his Menshevik days termed the 'Asiatic' streak in Russian Marxism, and the exile or liquidation of Russia's more liberal classes, which restored a clear continuity with an older Muscovite tradition. Rather than portray Marxism-Leninism as window dressing for 'old-fashioned Russian imperialism', we would do better to realise what each tradition reinforces in the other.[8]

Finally, we must be on guard against the temptation to dismiss the more esoteric or unpalatable pronouncements of Soviet policy-makers as 'mere rhetoric'. In the Soviet Union, as in any society, the relation between words, belief and action is a complex one. In Britain the mere use of certain terms – 'law and order', 'compassion', 'the arms race', 'social justice' – can reveal a highly ideological stance and message. In the Soviet Union the stilted, stylised vocabulary of public discourse serves even more elaborately as a communication code between factions and tendencies. But if Soviet thinking is to be understood in its own terms, so must the language and idiom of political and military thought. Expressions such as 'the correlation of forces', 'peaceful co-existence' and 'military doctrine' have precise meanings, not easily translated into Western terms. In the military sphere, it is worth noting that the restricted and specialist literature (such as the General Staff journal, *Military Thought*) reflects the more distinctive and discordant themes of policy as much as more public pronouncements. Indeed, the more authoritative the source, the more closed and select the audience, the more frankly these themes are articulated. As we shall have occasion to note in Chapters 4 and 5, there is an impressive correspondence between doctrine as enunciated in military publications, military programmes and observable conduct.

If Soviet terms are without palatable Western equivalents, even less is it the case that, behind the opaque language, Soviet debates resemble Western debates. As an ideology in power, Marxism–Leninism assumes a concrete form. Just as Parliamentary democracy lives in the institution of Parliament, so ideology in the USSR is kept alive in the institutions, mechanisms and procedures which mould that country's politics and its political class. Where the advocates of policies are appointed by those who make policy (the institution of *nomenklatura*) and grass roots are accountable to centre ('democratic centralism'), debates are apt to follow a very different course from those within a society where élite is periodically accountable to mass and policy-makers account to an electorate or to elected superiors. Whilst the Party leadership has more than once given licence to 'ordered ferments' in military discussion (such as that between 1953–59), it has never had difficulty in bringing such discussion to an end when it has heard enough. Compartmentalisation and secrecy further restrict the possibilities for raising questions, pursuing them, or comprehending them fully. From the mid-1960s, economists have been able to air controversial issues within their areas of competence (indeed, much of what we know of the economy's short-comings comes from their work), but it would be unusual, if not unheard of, for them to address the broader implications of the issues they raise. Indeed, Western specialists occasionally discover that they possess more knowledge of the workings of the Soviet system than the system's responsible participants: like the director of an industrial enterprise in the defence sector who had never even heard of the organisation which set his priorities because it did not interact with him personally.[9] The now celebrated episode in the SALT I negotiations in which General Staff representatives ordered Foreign Ministry officials from the chamber so that they would not overhear military–technical details released to the US delegation shows how far into the power structure this compartmentalisation of knowledge extends.[10] The system seems masterfully engineered to confine power to a like-minded fraternity and restrict participation to those it wishes to hear from.

A PHILOSOPHY OF POLITICS

Raymond Aron once observed that 'policy is always ambitious. It aspires to power because political action involves, in essence, a relationship among human beings, an element of power. Yet grand policy wants such power not for itself, but to carry out a mission'. For many, East–West relations illustrate the principle that rivalries motivated by ideology will be more intractable, and less susceptible to limitation, than those confined to what is customarily called 'reason of state'. Without ideological conflict to bedevil East–West relations, we might still find East–West rivalry, but, as Aron went on to say, in an ideologically harmonious world, 'state hostility does not imply hatred'.[11]

Another scholar of these matters, Martin Wight, noted that a revolutionary ideology 'has never for long maintained itself against national interest. Doctrinal considerations have always within two generations been overriden by *raison d'état*'.[12] Many in the West believe that the USSR has lost much of its missionary impulse as the Communist regime has matured, and therefore hope that our rivalry can become much more 'traditional'. Ideology, however, is more than a sense of mission. It is a way of making sense of things. It is diagnosis, interpretation, judgement: an image of the world, not simply a programme, ideal or 'master plan'. Marxism–Leninism is powerful intellectual conditioning, as ex-Communists who bear traces of it will admit. Long after the USSR loses its ideals, it is likely to retain its distinctive outlook and approach. Today, East and West remain divided in their grasp of what *is*, even if they have come to care less about what ought to be (a debatable point in itself).

For Marxists, and particularly for Marxist–Leninists, the basic reality of life is conflict. As heirs of Hegel and bedfellows of Darwin, Marxists envisage social relations as a dynamic process; by 'politics', they understand a struggle for power, driven by class interest. Thanks to a largely different intellectual heritage, the champions of liberal democracy are accustomed to regard stability as a norm – indeed, a highly desirable norm – along with consent, compromise, and evolution (change within stability); to us the art of governing is the ability to accommodate different interests or reconcile them to a general interest. The norm of stability even has its analogue in the strategic sphere: 'strategic stability' and the notion that *mutual* deterrence should be the common concern of all. From a Marxist standpoint, this is the perspective of the rogue turned gentleman. So long as classes exist, there will be contending and incompatible interests, not a 'general' interest; 'consent' will be a disguise for domination; 'stability' will be imposed. In politics the overriding question is Lenin's immortal *kto-kovo* (who-whom?): *whose* stability? *whose* order? The turmoil which is found in much of what we call the Third World does not take the Communist world by surprise; it is only to be expected (and, as we shall see, assisted where possible). From the perspective of liberalism or conservatism, it is unfortunate and at times perplexing; we often ask ourselves who has caused it.[13]

Quite clearly, a different view of ethics is at stake and not only of politics. For 'bourgeois' thinkers, the relation between means and ends is largely an ethical issue. For Marxist–Leninists it is a practical issue. 'The character of a war,' Lenin stated, 'is not determined by who the aggressor was, or whose territory the enemy has occupied; it is determined by the class that is waging the war'. Marxist–Leninists find themselves firmly within the 'just war' tradition. In the judgement of the USSR's international lawyers, the violence of the oppressed can never be termed 'aggression'. In the service of 'national and social liberation', war is always rightful, if not always prudent: so, for that matter, is espionage, subversion and terror. The astringency of this means–ends calculation is what drew Lenin to Clausewitz, who described war as a *tool* of policy: no different in moral status from negotiation, propaganda or foreign trade. 'War', according to Lenin, 'is the continuation of the policies of peace and peace the continuation of the policies of war.' The criterion which determines 'when to choose peace? when to choose war?' is effectiveness. A Leninist wants no part of methods which retard his cause, nor of 'amateur revolutionaries' who delight in producing gesture without positive result. Not for him the maxim, 'let justice be done though the world perish'.[14]

When Marxists speak of ideological rivalry, they take this to mean a clash between concrete, 'objective' interests, not ideals or convictions. In the end, men will be moved by material interest, not abstract principles. There are rare individuals (like Lenin himself) who will betray their class in the service of a principle, but a class will not betray itself, nor for that matter will a state or its official representatives. This being said, not everyone will be shrewd enough to grasp his own objective interest at any particular moment, let alone unfathom the true motivation of others. Internally, therefore, Leninists insist on the pre-eminence of the Party: a disciplined vanguard with a small directive element, possessing a 'scientific' insight into these matters. (In the fine print, 'dictatorship of the proletariat' has always meant 'dictatorship in the name of the proletariat', and the same is true for today's 'state of the whole people'). In diplomacy, the challenge is to 'get behind the words and phrases of the opponent to discover the real interests behind them'.[15] The principles of bourgeois statesmen are like Hobbes's baited hooks. 'Human rights' may be a genuine concern, but it is as a weapon of struggle that it becomes state policy. If electorates in North America or Western Europe are honestly aroused by it, it is a more potent and clever weapon for that. Leninists mistrust not only rhetoric but the world of appearances. Stalin once remarked that 'a diplomat's words must have no relation to action, otherwise what kind of diplomacy is it?'[16] He also characterised the difference between Roosevelt and Churchill in these terms:

> Churchill is the kind who, if you don't watch him, will slip a kopek out of your pocket! . . . And Roosevelt? Roosevelt is not like that. He dips in his hand only for bigger coins.[17]

In the eyes of Stalin's successors, foreign statesmen may not be so devious or so capable. But no less than he, they proceed from the premise that morality has no meaning outside the class struggle. They prefer a world where capitalists act like capitalists, where business can be conducted on the basis of hard bargaining and the 'correlation of forces'. (It certainly will not be conducted on any other basis: asked how they would respond to President Carter's decision to cancel the B-1 programme, Soviet arms negotiators replied that they were not philanthropists).

From what has been said, it should be clear that international relations as much as the civil variety, is seen to have a class character – or at least a class aspect. The notion of international politics as an activity confined to 'sovereigns', immune from interference in their internal affairs, is, by any strict Marxist reading, bourgeois legal artifice: an attempt to disenfranchise 'class' as a global political force. 'There is no greater nonsense', Lenin warned, 'than the separation of international from domestic policy'.[18] Today's world not only comprises states and their governments, but an international monetary and banking system, multinational corporations, the world Communist movement, terrorists, peace movements, Islamic fundamentalists and a Polish Pope. It is the interaction of all these forces, not just states and their governments, which makes world politics what it is; policy must therefore aim to alter the overall 'correlation of forces', not just the 'balance of power' between states. In principle, this may be clear enough. But as a practical undertaking, the task of being the representative of a class as well as the authority of a state has produced some very complex challenges for the Soviet régime. From Trotsky's 'no war! no peace!', to the *détente* of the Brezhnev era, the connecting threat in some 70-odd years of Soviet policy has been the attempt to resolve, or at least reconcile, the two.

On the morrow of the Bolshevik revolution, the dilemma was not appreciated for what it was. The Bolsheviks saw themselves as the vanguard of a revolutionary movement, international in scope, dedicated not only to the destruction of capitalist states, but states as such, and the divisions betwen proletarians which they erected. The Bolsheviks issued their Decree on Peace (in essence a declaration of war on governments), and Trotsky uttered his quip about walking over to the Foreign Ministry, 'issuing a few revolutionary proclamations and closing up shop'. In defence of revolution, the most fertile and productive portion of Russian territory was signed over to Germany at Brest–Litovsk (1918), whilst Bolshevik negotiators smugly told the Kaiser's representatives that they would deal with the German people over their heads. But as revolutionary bids were rebuffed in Central Europe, and foreign intervention became a factor in Russia itself, it became plain that the interstate order was not a spent force. It also became plain that the survival of the Bolsheviks themselves would depend on the fortunes of a territory and a people of which they were part.

In response to these predicaments, there emerged from about the time of the Tenth Party Congress in 1921 what has since become a hallowed distinction: that between state-to-state relations (the province of the Soviet government and its Foreign Ministry), and 'relations between peoples', or the 'social dimension' of international politics (the preserve of the CPSU, the Comintern and its successors). The Soviet government, it was stated, bore no responsibility for the conduct of its representatives when they donned their Party hats. In the regime's formative years, this distinction between an interstate order, with which it was necessary to co-exist, and a capitalist order, with which one was at war, produced confusions worthy of a Restoration comedy. As testimony to Lenin's boast, 'what we give with one hand, we take with the other', the Comintern in 1923 turned its hand to toppling the constitutional authorities of Weimar Germany, its class enemy, at a time when these same authorities constituted, as a government, an indispensable friend to the Soviet state in Europe.[19]

Stalin's advent to power and the policy of 'socialism in one country' put an end to these escapades. The premise of Bolshevik policy was now reversed. Hitherto, revolution in Europe was considered essential to the survival of Socialism in Russia. Henceforth, it was held that the key to world revolution would be the strengthening of Soviet power. The first mission of the Communist government was no longer revolution abroad. To the contrary, as Stalin formulated it, 'he is an internationalist who unreservedly, unhesitatingly and unconditionally is prepared to defend the USSR because the USSR is the base of the world revolutionary movement'.[20] In short, a Communist's first task was the advancement of the Soviet state interest, even to the detriment of the revolutionary cause in his own country. From that point to the present day, 'Stalinist' or 'orthodox' Communists have adhered to this catechism. Hence, 'loyal' German Communists rallied behind the Molotov–Ribbentrop Pact in 1939, Chinese Communists locked in civil war with the Kuomintang defended Stalin's wartime alliance with Chiang Kai-shek, just as Egypt's Communists would later defend Khrushchev's alliance with Nasser from the vantage point of Cairo's gaols. The ambivalences in Soviet policy, whilst not ended, were disciplined: today as well, when the interests of revolution conflict with those of the state, the state takes precedence.

Far from bringing Soviet foreign policy into line with bourgeois practice, Stalin's innovations made it possible to integrate the ideological weapon effectively into state policy. In the post-Stalin years, this policy has retained the dualistic character it always possessed. As expressed by a *Manchester Guardian* leader in 1955:

> Russia is in a strong position . . . because she can appeal in Asia to both governments and peoples. As a great power, she offers governments (who may fear their subjects) certain inducements to be her ally: as the champion of Communism she offers to the mass of the people (who may dislike their governments) a transformation of their lives.[21]

In the 1970s, the USSR's promotion of a collective security arrangement with Asian countries revealed the same duality. Whilst calling for non-aggression pacts and an end to foreign bases and alliances, the Soviets insisted at the time that non-interference

> does not represent an insurance policy for rotten régimes, does not confer rights for the suppression of the just struggle of peoples for national liberation and does not obviate the necessity of social changes.[22]

The essence of the present day policy of 'peaceful co-existence' is not the acceptance of ideological diversity, but the belief that ideological struggle can be confined to means below the threshold of war. In contrast to Lenin's policy of peaceful coexistence, which had a provisional character and was seen as only a 'breathing space' between wars, the present policy, launched at the Twentieth Party Congress in 1956, holds out the prospect of avoiding war altogether, thanks to the revolutionising effect of nuclear weapons on world politics. War, however, remains possible if no longer inevitable. Hence, there must be no diminution of the capabilities of the Armed Forces: indeed, if war *is* avoided, it will be thanks to the manifest might of the Socialist camp. But in nuclear conditions, war has become unattractive, and the expectation, therefore, is that Imperialism will accept reverses rather than turn to armed conflict. In this particularly, today's 'peaceful coexistence' departs from Lenin's and Stalin's. What has not changed is the nature of the policy – 'a special form of the class struggle in the international arena' – or its purpose: the destruction of Imperialism.[23] In the ideological sphere, 'peaceful coexistence' is a call to arms. As stated by the Czechoslovakian Communist Party newspaper, *Rude Pravo*, 'in the ideological field there can not be any conciliation even if it is striven for by the opponent'.[24] Cooperative measures to avert war and the sharpening of struggle short of war are two sides to a common policy, which Khrushchev once described as 'escorting the capitalists to the grave with an arm around their back'.[25]

The policy of *détente* proceeds from identical principles. It is a formal and principled restatement of the distinction between interstate and international relations; moreover, the legitimacy of the distinction is to be endorsed by the opponent. Cooperation between states with different social systems is not to be confined merely to avoiding war, but widened to include the resolution of territorial disputes, the reunification of families, trade, culture, and scientific–technical cooperation. But, as Brezhnev put it, '*détente* does not in the slightest way abolish or alter the laws of the class struggle'.[26] The SALT agreements, the Helsinki accords, the treaties normalising the status of Berlin and the GDR illustrate the *détente* process at work. But the 'support' of the national liberation struggle overseas, or of 'progressive' and 'peace loving' forces in Western Europe is not at variance with *détente* and has nothing to do with interstate relations as such.[27] This is not to say there is no relation in the broader scheme of policy. As an article in *World Marxist Review* put it,

> It is becoming increasingly clear that the fight to extend the scope of *détente* and the fight for social and national liberation are, in effect, two battle fronts of a single, ever-widening revolutionary offensive.[28]

What Khrushchev said after his summit with Kennedy in 1961 is a 'principled' position of Soviet policy today: 'as Prime Minister of the Soviet Union I could promise Kennedy many things, but as First Secretary of the Communist Party of the USSR and leader of the world Communist movement, my hands are still free'.[29]

Today, as much as in 1921, Soviet policy proceeds along two axes. State-to-state relations are conducted through a Ministry of Foreign Affairs, and 'social relations' through the Central Committee's International Department, the linear descendent of the Comintern, and possibly the crucial organ for foreign policy making as a whole.[30] In today's Europe, Foreign Ministry officials put their case against INF modernisation or SDI to their opposite numbers in NATO; simultaneously, representatives of the International Department and its offshoots 'aggravate the contradictions' in the enemy camp. Inevitably, ambivalences arise. In interstate terms, the USSR suffers a setback if GLCM and Pershing II deployments are completed; in social terms, the price may be worth paying if deployment undermines the cohesion of NATO. Will the potential gain to the correlation of forces warrant the setback to the balance of power? Between 1983–85 the Politburo seemed paralysed by the issue, as between 1979–1983 Washington and Brussels often seemed oblivious to it. These ambivalences reside in the nature of the problem. In the matter of execution, there is a division of labour, not a clash of policy 'interests'. As a hand would become useless if its fingers had wills of their own, so a multifaceted policy would collapse without the coordination and cohesiveness of its constituent parts.

A PHILOSOPHY OF HISTORY

Marxism–Leninism is not merely a philosophy of politics; it is a philosophy of history. Far from being aimless and open-ended, conflicts between classes and states are held to follow scientific laws towards a certain and ascertainable end: the destruction of Imperialism and the triumph of Socialism on a world-wide scale. Put so artlessly – which is precisely as Soviet spokesmen put it – the proposition seems almost designed to sow disbelief. Do they really believe it? Adversity of the kind known to the CPSU has often been the midwife of millenarian thinking, and the Soviet regime has not been the first to combine a long-term Utopian vision with an unsentimental shrewdness about its day-to-day affairs. Combining the vision with the shrewdness, we are left with a less ingenuous approach to events: history is on our side, but it is not already decided; an unequal contest is still a contest.

For the Soviet public relations establishment, it is the 'objective' inevitability of change, not the assertiveness of the Soviet Union, which explains the West's setbacks in its former strongholds of influence. In that curious Marxist inversion of language which describes as 'history' what has yet to occur, Georgiy Arbatov, Director of the Institute of the USA and Canada, describes this process as 'historically unavoidable'.[31] Genrikh Trofimenko, similarly, argues that *détente* collapsed largely because the USA scapegoated the USSR for difficulties in the Third World which were of its own making. Trofimenko, however, also affirms what leading authorities assert with greater bluntness: the 'right' of the USSR to 'support the struggle of the peoples for their social and national liberation'.[32]

For the critics of *détente*, the sticking point was this 'right', not the reality of struggle or of change. It was not the triumph of the MPLA in Angola which put *détente* in question, nor for that matter an inter-state dispute like the October 1973 war, but the contributions of the USSR and its allies to these enterprises. In the Arbatov–Trofimenko scheme of things, other powers are regarded as actors in history, the Soviet Union as its agent. Others must justify their interventions in the language of law, security and interest, but the USSR is free to fan the flames of revolution and dismiss all that follows as 'the natural course of events'.

So much for the uses of a philosophy of history. What of its actual influence? From one perspective, the Soviet philosophy of history would seem to be the author of our worries; it would be difficult to account for Soviet ambition without it. Britain and the United States became global powers, if not 'in a fit of absent-mindedness' as is sometimes claimed, at least without herculean effort. The means were to hand; justification and ideology followed. In the Soviet Union, ideology preceded the means, and the means were acquired through great sacrifice.

Perhaps the principal influence of a belief in 'laws of social development' is to complicate Soviet calculations. As history's beneficiaries, is it better to give history a push or take the view that all things come to those who wait? A second dilemma compounds the first. However fleeting the present, it has its own imperatives. Your opponent may have a terminal illness, but if he is advancing on you with a gun, he is still a man with a gun. As a practical matter, the second dilemma usually resolves the first. The Soviets have built up strong instincts against 'adventurism'; they will not thow away long-term gains in the future which matters by wanton presumption in the here and now, whose discomforts one can usually survive. For this reason, the West ought to be thankful for the USSR's historical perspective. The USSR's philosophy of history disciplines her philosophy of politics. It reinforces those factors which make her preferred mode of conduct the policy of low risk: the proverbial hotel burglar in search of the proverbial unlocked door. Unlike the National Socialists in the 1930s, the Soviets will not storm up to the crown suite and smash the door down. Hitler was riled by resistance; the Soviets grow more reasonable in its presence. If Adolf Hitler were in power in Moscow, Tito would have been crushed in 1948 and Romania overrun in 1968. Instead, in 1948 Stalin purged 'fraternal' parties in Eastern Europe who were loyal to him, and Brezhnev in 1968 fell upon Czechoslovakia which was keen to conciliate, but which, unlike Romania, could not defend herself. In short, not in spite of, but largely because of their Leninist conditioning, the Soviets are responsive to the currency of power politics. It is no accident that they have survived longer than Germany's Nazis. If one deals with them in these terms, one can live with them for a long time, perhaps forever.

Unfortunately, as these examples reveal, not everyone has the wherewithal to deal with them. As Malcolm Mackintosh has noted,

> When an area in the world can, without danger or opposition, be occupied militarily by the Soviet Army for any length of time, then its transfer to the Communist camp can be carried out swiftly and relatively efficiently, without regard for world public opinion.[33]

Given the way the USSR has treated the miniscule and powerless throughout her history, the question arises as to how she would respond if a convincing counterpoise were no longer presented by her principal rivals. If the ground seemed to be yielding before her, would she read the hand of history in it? Should the time arise when the balance of power – or of perception – moved so far out of kilter, it is not impossible that the USSR would take history by the hand rather than wait on events. An even greater incentive to decisive action has been the need to prevent history turning against the Soviet Union in areas of paramount importance (thus, Hungary 1956, Czechoslovakia 1968, Afghanistan 1979 and Poland 1980). The 'irreversibility' of Socialism is basic to the legitimacy of every Communist regime: no less so if everyone understands that the irreversibility is contrived. An Emperor without clothes must have confidence that his subjects will never expose him.

THE PAST AS ALIBI

If the 20th century may be deemed the century which has elevated change into a tradition, not the least conspicuous example of this has been the speed and thoroughness with which states have reassessed, and in some cases overhauled, their diplomatic identities and hierarchy of interests. Britain, as a state whose character and prowess once owed much to a cultivated aloofness from the affairs of the European continent, has not only come to accept the permanence of continental commitments in this century, but within a swift span of years has graciously divested itself of Empire, opting first for a 'special relationship' with the United States, and now strenuously asserting her credentials as a member of the European club. France and Germany, who long exemplified the adage, 'learning nothing and forgetting nothing', have since 1945 made reconciliation and *entente* their first priority, thereby discarding much of the ballast of their past. Japan's metamorphosis out of militarism requires no comment. In each case it is a picture not only of facing new facts but of anticipating them sprightly.

In contrast to this record of co-opting, seducing and transforming rivals, the USSR's approach to the outside world presents a dreary, ponderous and relentless continuity. No doubt her attitude towards the bogey of 'encirclement' proceeds from strong and severe precedent. It can certainly be justified, but so on similar grounds could a revival of the German policy of *Mitteleuropa* be justified. The world today presents a contrast between those who have emancipated themselves from their experience and those who have become encased in it. Whatever its impact on the course of history in the world, the Marxist–Leninist catechism of rivalry, struggle and *kto-kovo* has retarded history in Russia.

Messianic universalism seems to march in step with a grim determinism born of hubris, insecurity and pride. The vanguard of revolution and progress, like the archetypal conservative, seems to opt for the devil it knows and can manage rather than the opportunities which it might not.

Indeed, in today's world, the USSR often seems less like a

revolutionary power than a representative of the pre-1914 era, not a world apart in manner and instinct from the Germany of Kaiser Wilhelm II. In latter day Imperial Germany, politics as well was understood as a struggle for supremacy, and there also could be found a view of history at variance with Western liberalism. There are echoes of 'Germany will be heard' in Gromyko's boast that no problem in the world today can be solved without reference to the USSR (a boast which, incidentally, only reiterates what Molotov stated in 1946).[34] Thus, in addition to reproaching others for failing to give the country its due as a revolutionary power acting in accordance with history's iron laws, the USSR also claims the rights and perquisites of a Power of the old school. No longer is she simply the embattled germ of a revolution which one day will rise up to destroy the bourgeois order; she is also a co-equal which, by virtue of her place in that same order, has earned a right to shape it. Today's uneasiness about Soviet global pretensions recalls Earl Grey's query to Bethmann–Hollweg: 'what do you *need* a blue water navy for?' As much as a clash between ideologies, present day East–West rivalry is a clash between a world which derives 'right' from interest and a world which derives 'right' from power itself.

PRIMACY OF PARTY OR REASON OF STATE?

The USSR presents a picture of Party control of every civil institution, including 'civil government' itself. We have already noted the position of the Foreign Ministry (controlled by the Politburo, monitored by the International Department). The same holds true for every other institution, with departments of the Central Committee assigned to monitor state ministries concerned with agriculture, industry, education, culture, and as we shall later discuss in some detail, the Armed Forces. One may ask why, if this is so, it matters. Whatever the convolutions of the Soviet political structure, to many these examples only suggest that in the USSR the CPSU is that institution which defines the State interest.

For good or ill, one cannot leave it at that. On any number of occasions, 'reason of State' would have encouraged different measures from those which the Soviet authorities adopted in deference to Party requirements. As we have already suggested, the Party's internal position in the USSR has from the start ruled out a security policy in Europe, East and West, which might really have capitalised on the

USSR's post-war prestige, secured the positive influence over Western Europe which she has always considered her due, and eased America back into cosy isolation. With such a policy, is it too fanciful to imagine Europe's statesmen saying, 'the whole point of collective security is to keep the Germans down, the Russians content, and the Americans out'?

Internally, the maintenance of a system of collectivised agriculture is not only a hobbling economic inefficiency, but also a manifest source of *external* weakness. The fact that so large a proportion of hard currency reserves are hostage to Western grain imports reduces what is left for importing 'high-tech' and other technologies with military potential, aggravates economic relations with the East European satellites, and presents a curious picture to those 'struggling' forces in the Third World enjoined to view the USSR as their model for overcoming dependency upon the capitalist West.

Where internal and international requirements compete, the Party is the fulcrum upon which they pivot. It is impressive, however, to what degree they complement one another and what a seamless web they can become in the perception of Soviet leaders. As 'peaceful co-existence' was the corollary to the New Economic Policy, so the Five-Year Plans were to 'socialism in one country', the 'Zhdanovshchina' to Tito's expulsion from the Cominform, and Khrushchev's 'thaw' to the ending of Stalinist isolation. It is disputed whether the *détente* of the 1970s and the crackdown on dissent which followed represented two sides of one policy or a struggle between two; but a relationship between them is commonly accepted. There can be few countries where citizens so uninformed about the outside world are so quickly affected by a change in the international line. Lenin's view that 'there is nothing more nonsensical than the separation of international from domestic policy' still applies.

In conclusion, the Party may be the shield of the state or its albatross, but its interest is paramount.

2 Foundations of Power: Resources

The results of production should increase more quickly than expenditure upon it.

D. F. Ustinov, July 1984

The economy must become economic.

L. I. Brezhnev, March 1981

The Soviet Union will survive its economic difficulties, but it is unlikely to surmount them. Twenty-five years ago, such a prognosis would have astounded many. In the wake of Sputnik a large number of observers, sympathetic and hostile, were convinced that the USSR's technical and scientific prowess, and the planning system which underpinned it, posed a profound challenge to the West's values, institutions and international standing. A fresh listening to the 1960 Kennedy–Nixon debates is enough to rekindle the exaggerated sense of urgency then felt that Communism represented the wave of the future, as its adherents had prophesied.[1] Today it is commonly held that the Soviet economy is an albatross – an albatross in the form of heavy military outlays, hard currency imports, and a lengthening backlog of consumer demands. It is widely accepted that this system 'has nothing to teach us'. Indeed, the fashion in many quarters is to ponder whether the West possesses the discipline and finesse to 'manage' the USSR's decline – or perhaps accelerate it. Several questions motivate this discussion. Is Western conventional wisdom a better guide to reality today than it was twenty-five years ago? What precisely is at fault with the Soviet economy, and to what extent is improvement possible? What are the implications of economic strain for Soviet power, internally and externally? Can outside pressure play a role in influencing the course of events?

The backdrop to any assessment is, inescapably, the formidable size and productive capacity of the Soviet economy (by CIA estimates 60 per cent larger in GNP than Japan's). Over the fullness of time, in spite of revolution, civil war and world war, performance relative to competitors has not been lacklustre: compared with 1913, when *per capita* GNP stood at 24.6 per cent of the US level, the 1984 ratio was 46 per cent.[2] On the other hand, the mere fact that in that time she has overtaken at most one of some 20 countries that outranked her in per capita terms is enough to establish that her record is less than spectacular. Whatever the verdict on her previous achievements, the decline in her performance over the past 15 years has been marked and far-reaching.

THE AGENDA OF DIFFICULTY

The well-known part of the story is the secular decline of growth rates from the heady levels of the 1950s (some 6 per cent per annum), as factor inputs (land, labour, raw materials) have levelled off.[3] Calls for innovation and for productivity related 'intensive' growth have been to little avail. Production targets have been consistently underfulfilled from the Ninth Five-Year Plan (1971–75) onwards. Estimated GNP growth declined from 3.7 per cent in 1971–75 to 2.6 per cent in 1976–80, and again to 1.9 per cent in 1981 (although it must be said that 1982 and 1983 have shown some improvement – up to 2.6 per cent and 3.7 per cent respectively – the CIA's estimate for 1984 is a lacklustre 2.5 per cent).[4] Investment growth rates, whilst also declining, continue to exceed the rate of overall economic growth: whereas fixed investment amounted to 25 per cent of GNP in 1970, it absorbed 34 per cent of GNP in 1983.[5] The task of maintaining existing production levels has therefore come to consume a higher and higher share of national output.[6] Tradeoffs between different sectors of the economy have also become more expensive and more painful in their consequences.

For one thing, the shape of the economy is becoming more primitive. Primary and extractive industries (now accounting for over 50 per cent of gross social product) are displacing manufacturing industries in relative importance, as investment is harnessed to the tasks of developing energy resources, ore and mineral deposits. This trend is costly. In the Soviet manufacturing sector it costs 0.7 million roubles in capital investment to increase production capacity by one million roubles, but it costs four million roubles to achieve the same result in the extractive sector. One result of this diversion of investment is under-mechanisation and a shortage of labour: almost one half of workers in industry are consigned to unmechanised tasks.

A second result is an overburdened infrastructure: fewer resources available to expand electrical generating capacity or to repair and extend railway lines. From the late 1970s, production of lifting equipment and railway rolling stock has actually dropped in absolute terms.[7] Whilst uncertainty about the volume and growth of defence spending is unlikely to be resolved unless the Soviet regime changes its character, few would dispute that the military's traditional claim on resources has been a major burden on the civilian economy. Whether the share of GNP devoted to defence is 13–14 per cent or some other figure; whether growth was 4 per cent a year throughout the 1970s, or for only half that time, military expenditure has been a major contributor to the investment squeeze.[8] By the mid-1970s stipulated military needs could only be financed by cutting investment in the productive base as a whole.[9]

A third contributor to the investment imbalance is agriculture, long the Achilles heel of the economy. During the time of Stalin agriculture was impoverished by conscious decision, as the human and material resources of the countryside were squeezed to finance industrialisation. Twenty-five years of exploitation have since been repaid by thirty years of largesse, but with dismal result: a situation which Professor Marshall Goldman of Harvard has likened to trying to cure a half-starved baby by overfeeding in old age.[10] At present, the agricultural sector accounts for 27 per cent of total investment; additionally, the burden of holding retail food prices at 1962 levels consumes a further $50 billion per annum in subsidies.[11] Each spurt in investment has for a time been halfway successful in boosting harvests and production, but policy to date has failed to grasp the nettles of productivity, variety, distribution and responsible land use. The paucity of infrastructure (storage facilities, railways, roads), over-cultivation of land, underproduction of fertilisers and farm machinery both reflect and contribute to these difficulties. In spite of massive investment and attention, in the 1980s 50 per cent of potatoes and 60 per cent of citrus fruits grown on state or collective farms spoil before reaching market; private plots, accounting for four per cent of arable land, supply 25 per cent of total output (30 per cent of meat and dairy products and 40 per cent of fruit); and the bill for overseas imports consumes as much as 45 per cent of hard currency earnings.[12]

Demographic developments have become equally disconcerting and perhaps even less susceptible to remedy. The four Union Republics which provide 80 per cent of the work force (RSFSR, Ukraine, Latvia and Estonia) face sharply declining birthrates relative to the less advanced populations of the USSR. Put more starkly, 85 per cent as many Russians will enter the labour force between 1986–90 as will retire from it; over the same period 300 per cent as many Turks, Uzbeks and Tadzhiks will enter the labour force as will retire from it.[13] What makes this an economic problem, and not simply a nationality problem, is the fact that the declining areas possess 85 per cent of the country's industry, 82 per cent of its electricity, and equivalent proportions of related infrastructure.[14] Whilst it may have become commonplace in Western Europe and the United States for Turks or Mexicans to move north in response to economic opportunity, the Turkic populations of the USSR show no such proclivity. Were this not all, the new sources of energy lie in regions devoid of infrastructure *and* population. Although the energy problem can be surmounted at a price, it seems certain that the imbalance between infrastructure and population will aggravate economic problems and in so doing worsen nationality problems as well.

As the workforce is shrinking, its stamina and morale may also be suffering. In the 1950s standards of public health in the USSR, and of public health care, were flaunted to 'non-believers' as one of the system's prime attributes.[15] Within a swift span of years, however, life expectancy and infant mortality have assumed Third World proportions: inferior even to Albania's and roughly on a par with Malaysia's. In the last quarter of the 20th century, the USSR may be just about the only country in the world where health standards are actually falling. Alcoholism, pollution (through misuse of pesticides and careless dumping of waste); shortages of proteins and dairy products (diluted milk, denatured baby formula); the siphoning off of drugs and anesthetics into the illegal second economy all take their toll. The level of safety in the workplace can be inferred from the fact that 20 per cent of the rise in death rates for men in their late thirties arise from 'accident'. (The USSR, with one-tenth as many motor vehicles as the United States, has just as many traffic fatalities). In a country where anything so conspicuous as reducing food subsidies courts trouble, cut backs in the health sector may seem a safer bet (in 1977 7.7 per cent of GNP was devoted to health care, down from 9.5 per cent in 1955; in comparison, proportions in the United States over the same period rose from 8 per cent to 11 per cent).[16]

A greater source of social frustration would appear to lie in the ossification of social mobility. In Soviet conditions this fact is very significant. The ethos of Soviet-style socialism has been opportunity. From the onset of the first Five-Year Plan, if not before, social equality has not only been sidetracked, but foresworn as the object of policy.[17] To this day the USSR is without a progressive taxation system. A 'universal' old age pension did not exist in principle until 1956, and not until 1965 was it extended to the peasantry and made universal in practice. But even in times of privation, idealism could sustain itself thanks to the prospect that talent and motivation would be identified and promoted. It is this era which is drawing to a close and, with it, the peculiar mixture of promise and peril which long characterised Soviet life. Not only has the élite closed itself off to interlopers (some 70 per cent of officer cadets at the Odessa High Artillery Military School are sons of active duty officers)[18]; but, on the evidence, skilled workers have become downwardly mobile members of society. In 1940 the salaries of engineering and technical personnel were over twice those of ordinary workers; by 1980 the differential had narrowed to 14 per cent. Thanks to under-mechanisation, one-third of youths with specialised secondary school qualifications end up doing unskilled work.[19]

Paradoxically, the relative unimportance of money in Soviet society compounds these difficulties. Those things which confer privilege (quality shops, education, flats and health care) are acquired through privilege in the first place; they cannot be had for money.[20] To some extent the private 'second economy' (accounting for as much as 25 per cent of GNP) circumvents the formal, official pecking order, but there as well, influence rather than money is what confers wealth. The economic downturn has only intensified the self-rejuvenating qualities of élites and multiplied the ways in which others are shut out. Under Socialism, the USSR has born out Marx's prophesy for capitalism: the proletarianising of an ever larger element of society. It has also stood Marx on his head, by transforming itself from a classless society into a caste society (if at the same time gratifying Lenin's hope that the intermediate stage of class society might be bypassed). The corruption, cynicism and disillusionment which now proliferate should not mystify us.[21]

REAL EXISTING SOCIALISM

This tale of woe is, from one point of view, a catalogue of imbalances: between primary and advanced industry, between high-yield and low-yield investment, between increased demands and ageing infrastructure, between resources and population, between money and the supply of goods. It also has the appearance of a self-inflicted injury. The commitment to maintain or increase expenditure on arms, agriculture and energy has drained investment from the manufacturing base on which all of these priorities depend. Neglect of incentives and of light industry in preference to 'priority' investment is perhaps the major obstacle to securing a return on this investment. Put in this way, management of the economy seems to have been grossly at fault. But there may be powerful grounds for saying that the command economy, is the culprit, rather than the management of it. If so, the problems we have surveyed must be seen as symptoms rather than causes 'more' and 'better' are apt to be palliatives, not cures. To many economists the cause of the difficulty lies in an institution, central planning, which *cannot* achieve balanced growth and innovation in a mature, sophisticated economy no matter how well it is managed.[22] Diversion of resources into light industry, for example, cannot solve the incentive problem as, without market pressures, there can be no guarantee that factories will produce what consumers wish to buy.

The basic and most idealistic justification of central planning is that the economy should be run for the benefit of society as a whole. (As we have seen, the establishment of such a system in the USSR also fulfilled two more specific objectives: internally, securing a monopoly of power for the CPSU; internationally, 'socialism in one country': the creation of a state powerful enough to enable the revolution to survive in a world of states).

Whatever its ostensible purpose, the elimination of the market and the creation of a command economy has one clear consequence: the 'who', 'what' and 'how' of economic relations is determined by planners, not by those who produce and consume. It is the structure of the system which demands this, not the unimaginativeness or selfishness of those involved. An enterprise director cannot do what *he* considers best for society since, without the market's signals, he cannot know what this is. He may know the difference between a tractor which works and one which does not, but he cannot know how many tractors are required, what sort of tractors to build, and where they are most needed.

If the centre were omniscient, none of this would matter. But in the Soviet Union, there are 12 000 000 products, 25 000 enterprises and a conceivable infinity of transactions. Therefore, we should *not* expect the centre to be omniscient. Soviet economists estimate that with state of the art computer technology, ten years of work would be required to produce each one-year plan. Until this state of affairs comes about,

plans will be the outcome of a long-term process, not easily altered
after they are drafted; and planners will have no choice but to make
rough approximations and search for performance indicators which
are easy to monitor. (Thus, the 12 000 000 products are 'aggregated'
into 48 000 'positions'). These tools of the trade may make planning
possible, but they do not necessarily produce what is needed by Soviet
society.

A GORDIAN KNOT?

As the quotations at the opening of this chapter suggest, the Soviet
authorities are not unaware of the seriousness of their own problems.
Nor have reforms been meagre or lacking in ingenuity. To minimise
supply difficulties, increasing numbers of enterprises have been
grouped into production associations. To bypass ministerial
demarcation lines, several territorial production complexes have been
set up. The July 1979 package of reforms cleared several obstacles to
'direct relations' amongst enterprises; it also gave teeth to a 1974
decree making delivery contracts binding. The July, 1983 'Andropov'
experiment has built upon the more sensible of these measures, also
reviving some of the decentralising features of the aborted 1965
reform: most interestingly, a wage norm based on 'normative' rather
than 'quantitative' (piece-work) indicators, thus, (it is hoped)
promoting innovation and productivity.[23]

The results of these measures will for some time be inconclusive, if
only because parties to an experiment must still depend on the larger
part of the economy which continues to operate according to
traditional principles. But it is clear that there are certain features of
the economy which these reforms will not change. 'Normative value
added', whilst preferable to quantitative value, still is not *market*
value: salaries continue to reflect the (it is to be hoped better
informed) judgement of planners, not real needs and opportunities.
By the same token, prices remain *administered* prices, also determined
by planners rather than markets. Administered prices may accomplish
a variety of ends, but not the balancing of supply with demand (for
social reasons, meat is cheap so there usually is no meat); nor will they
reflect real alternatives and scarcities (hence the metal content of
Soviet machinery is 25 per cent greater than in their American
equivalents,[24] and energy consumption per unit of GNP is almost twice
that in Western Europe).[25] Enforcement of delivery contracts is vital

in principle, but in Soviet conditions difficult to achieve in practice. If milk produced in a collective farm spoils in transit because the train transporting it lacks refrigerated rolling stock, who is at fault: the farm manager? the train supervisor? the repair shop? or the ministry which sets production quotas for refrigerated railway stock? If the port of Murmansk is blocked up for weeks and mackerel arrives spoilt, is it wrong that the crew be given its bonus for so many fish caught, or that the dockers be paid for so many tons unloaded?[26]

The obvious objective of the recent reforms – and the hardest nut to crack – is building quality and innovation into a performance indicator. This will not be the first time it has been tried, and the observations of one former planning official are worth quoting at length:

> When sales revenue is a chief success indicator affecting incentive funds, the enterprise can raise the indicator by buying more expensive inputs. . . . Similarly, if the enterprise switches from total sales revenue to net value of output as its performance indicator, it will select products with a high cost of processing, thus increasing net value added . . . [In] instances when Soviet planners have stipulated a revised set of leading economic indicators, and tied incentive funds to them, other indicators have moved in undesirable directions. . . . Planners found that, once again, only direct regulation could bring an improvement for any individual economic indicator. This sequence, rather than some wish by planners to turn the clock back . . . was, in my view the chief cause of the retreat from the 1965 reform.[27]

These examples suggest that de-centralisation in itself will not substitute for the market's rewards and penalties, or for genuine consumer sovereignty. Given this state of affairs, one would expect to see the country's leadership showing greater interest in markets and their expansion. But the more 'reformist' amongst the élite have either stopped short of introducing real market conditions (Kosygin) or have been oblivious to the need for them. Andropov's June 1983 speech, setting out his reformist agenda, criticised 'irrational trial and error methods' and spoke of restoring 'economic order' on the basis of discipline, hard work and sanctions. The now familiar formula – seeking 'new forms and methods of management' – a coded attack on Brezhnev's 'stability of cadres' means that the old are to be replaced by the young, the incompetent by the competent; it also signifies departures from outmoded routines and the unsettling of vested interests. But it does not amount to introducing market forces. On evidence (to date limited), Gorbachev, like his patron, has shown a strong interest in the East German reforms, which strengthen the centre (the State Planning Commission) and enterprises at the expense of intermediaries (ministries) – rather than the Hungarian reform, which strengthens markets. He, too, has combined searing indictments of economic performance with calls for the rejuvenation of cadres and administrative housecleanings. As Central Committee Secretary for Agriculture between 1978–85, Gorbachev was bound to have been largely responsible for the limited measures undertaken in support of private plots. But equally, he has been associated with calls for 'more and better' Party and State supervision (which, as Alec Nove points out, is at variance with more economic choice and responsibility).[28] We can only speculate as to why such ambivalence or hostility to markets persists.

In the first instance, there is nothing in the ideological and intellectual upbringing of the Soviet leaders which would make them partial to markets. From the perspective of the Soviet élite, 'Socialist construction', centralisation and Five-Year Plans have been responsible for raising a backward country to a world power. As they would tell the story, the USSR would long ago have been crushed but for these measures. To officials and *apparatchiks* obsessed with this legacy of backwardness, the West is advanced because it is the West, not because it is capitalist. Inefficiency, sloth, poor productivity are the residues of Russia's past, not a result of Socialist methods. Moreover, markets are anarchic, selfish, based on short-term gratifications (profit); 'plan' implies rationality, order, discipline. Russian workers are lazy and must be directed; peasants are untrustworthy and must be supervised. It would be excessive, even in today's permissive times, to return to Stalin's methods, but Lazar Kaganovich, Moscow Party boss in the 1930s had the right idea: 'when the manager walks into the enterprise, the ground should tremble!' If these are the premises and prejudices of Soviet leaders, much as faults in the system will be criticised, the system itself will not be held at fault.

A second side to this issue is managerial culture. Virtually extinct in the Soviet Union after over 60 years of Socialism is the linchpin of capitalism, the entrepreneur. (To the extent he survives, he is apt to make the illegal 'second economy' his habitat.) The Soviet manager is a bureaucrat and operator, not a venture capitalist or risk-taker. He is expected to be resourceful, not to show initiative. On balance, he will want uncomplicated planning targets, better communication, greater predictability and greater dependability of supply. Those who advance in this environment are men with an instinct for securing supplies, mobilising resources, finessing statistics, cultivating connections and 'working the system'. At the apex of the managerial hierarchy are men like the late Dmitriy Ustinov or Leonid Smirnov (head of the Military–Industrial Commission) with outstanding organisational competence, but with talents not necessarily suited to free market conditions. In time a system with the market's penalties as well as freedoms might well breed a different managerial prototype. But initiative will not be invoked by reform or fiat. The Soviet Union is not an 'initiative' society.

No doubt, the most fundamental factor working in favour of the present system is the fact that the regime is politically hoisted to it. There is an obvious side to this reality and a less obvious one. Most would agree that the professed *raison d'être* of the CPSU is the creation of a society 'of a new type'; the basis of its claim to infallibility is that it stands in the vanguard of this process. Whilst it can plausibly introduce a hybrid reform with de-centralising features, it cannot dismantle the machine it has created without repudiating itself. Whatever the economic benefit, the political repercussions of steps such as de-collectivisation would be far more unsettling than those brought about by the limited de-Stalinisation of the 1950s. But such implications are only part of the problem. Replacement of plan by market is in itself a surrender of power, since it means the elimination of planners. At present, Soviet agriculture, and therefore the day-to-day lives of Soviet peasants, are regulated by hundreds of thousands of officials and 33 ministries.[29] If production and exchange were henceforth to be determined by those who produce and consume, what functions would their former controllers then perform? What powers would the state still possess over those thus emancipated? (In the Soviet state more, perhaps, than in the United Kingdom, but that is not the issue.) In the United Kingdom, an employee can be dismissed from his job unceremoniously, but he cannot be prevented from working elsewhere, nor can his employer throw him out of his house. But in the USSR the state which employs him is the sole employer and is the same state which determines whether he have a house or not. It is not the KGB, 'indomitable' as it is, which makes the Soviet Union a totalitarianism society, nor even the CPSU's monopoly of political power, but the fusion of political and economic power. Monopoly of power – Stalin's first justification of the planning system – will probably be its last defence.

In political terms, the worry in carrying out free market reform may be less that the reform fails than that it might succeed. For the present, the firmest barrier against change from below are controllers in their hundreds of thousands. This is a large élite as élites go, conscious of its privileges and its place, and possessing real instruments of power over those who would challenge it. The leadership may purge the apparatus, but it dare not eliminate it, and it is not about to take an axe to itself. When all is said, this is why the alternative *we* think most rational for the USSR is the least rational and the least likely to emerge.

Is the inescapable conclusion, therefore, that the régime finds itself between the devil and the deep blue sea? It would be a bold conclusion, considering that the USSR is a country with a large, trained industrial workforce, a vast scientific–technical establishment and infrastructure, and leaders who possess enviable prerogatives to chop, change, reform and direct. It may smack of undue determinism to suggest that only this system's replacement will achieve anything and that its renovation will achieve nothing. Given present realities (namely, a system which creates problems for itself), it stands to reason that there will still be wise as well as foolish investment decisions, good as well as bad planning techniques, clumsy as well as ingenious incentives. The contrast between Poland and the GDR in these respects illustrates how telling such nuances can be. In the Soviet Union as elsewhere, what matters is how well people manage their dilemmas and not just whether they solve them. Like many issues which determine the course of history, the challenges of keeping pace in strategic competition, holding down grain imports, maintaining energy production and earning a hard currency income may be decided at the margin. If Gorbachev expects to untie the Gordian knot, he has over-estimated his powers. But it is an open question whether his policies will loosen it sufficiently to keep his country in the competition. For political and strategic purposes, that is the question that matters.

TRADE, TECHNOLOGY, DEPENDENCY

Four sets of questions define the subject:

(1) Does foreign technology play an important role in alleviating Soviet economic difficulties? Does it perform sufficiently better

than Soviet equipment to warrant the hard currency expended upon it?

(2) Is imported technology also effective by international standards? Has it reduced gaps between the USSR and Western countries?

(3) Is the technology which reaches the defence sector better utilised than in the civil economy? Is it more successful in reducing lead times? (a question we take up in the following section)

(4) Do we not, in supplying technology to the USSR, make it easier for her to free resources for military purposes? Does 'business as usual' make the trade-off between guns and butter easier than it would be if embargoes were more comprehensive and controls more strict?

The Soviet Union has had its love affairs with Western know-how, but it has also mistrusted it and even, on occasion, taken the view that foreign technology, like foreign ways generally, had little to offer. The First Five-Year Plan (1928–1932), the years 1941–47 (Lend–Lease and reparations) were both periods of considerable technology transfer from West to East. The revival of interest in what can only be described as a strategy of import led growth began in the late 1950s as uneasiness over the optimistic, autarkic assumptions of the Khrushchev period increased. Soviet interest in foreign technology therefore has not been a response to *détente*, but to perceptions of internal need, and increases in trade flows have not always coincided with greater political relaxation.[30] This is not to say that the USSR has not sought political dividends from economic ties. In her relations with Western Europe today, she would appear to seek them and, indeed, to enjoy some.[31]

However severe the gap between the Soviet Union and the West in technological know-how, this, one must reiterate, is secondary to the fact that the Soviet system makes poor use of the know-how at its own disposal. Housing is inefficiently heated because volume of construction is a more important planning indicator than fuel efficiency, not because the Soviets cannot do better.[32] Soviet society is poorly computerised, not because the RADA computer is inadequate, but because user–producer cooperation is poor, and Soviet managers have an interest in concealing the data on which computers depend. John Kiser relays the example of a West German order for advanced medical equipment, judged in its prototype form to be fully competitive with anything else available. Once transferred to series production, so many defects emerged as to make the consignment unusable.[33] (Indeed, some Soviet planners have speculated that it might be advantageous to license Western factories to produce Soviet equipment which would then be exported to the USSR.[34]) The question which therefore arises is whether the Soviet Union is better at diffusing the benefits of foreign technology than of its own.

To produce an impact on economic growth, the benefit would need to be considerable. In common with most command economies, the USSR 'under trades'. As a share of GNP, Soviet foreign trade amounts to about five per cent. (Trade with OECD countries amounts to only 1.6 per cent.) Of this total, food and food related products account for 28 per cent. When we look specifically at machinery imports from the West, we find that at their peak in the mid-1970s, they amounted to some 5–6 per cent of equipment investment.[35]

As a technology importer, the USSR possesses certain intrinsic advantages. Centralisation of foreign trade decisions (determined jointly by the State Planning Commission, *Gosplan*, and the Ministry of Foreign Trade) avoids duplication of purchases and enables strategic decisions to be taken concerning priorities in the economy as a whole. As a monopoly, the Soviet Union often has considerable leverage over foreign sellers. (Three separate negotiating teams were sent to each country tendering offers for the Urengoi gas pipeline, as a result of which the FRG, much to her surprise, found herself underbid at the end of the day.)

On balance, Soviet liabilities would seem to be a match for these assets. One is the separation of the foreign trade organisation (the negotiator and purchaser) from the end user, and the resultant disjunction between a planner's priority and a shop floor requirement. If as in pluralistic societies, individual enterprises were free to scan the market place themselves, they might duplicate purchases but, in the aggregate, would also spot more opportunities than would a relatively small number of foreign trade officials. Secondly, the Soviets' penchant for canvassing exhaustively for the best and cheapest may succeed in these objectives, but at the cost of enormous delay between the time when applications are approved and machinery actually installed. There is no small irony in this, as applications to purchase foreign technology in the first place will only be approved if the relevant Soviet machine building ministry cannot produce something of the appropriate standard and quantity in the time required. Perhaps it is true that the foreign trade organisation's tortoise-like negotiations outpace the snail-like progress of Soviet machine building, but it cannot be a thrilling race.

Once installed, there tends to be an awkward 'fit' between Western machinery and its Soviet factory environment. If Soviet equipment is not always of an adequate standard, Western equipment is often over-sophisticated for Soviet purposes, demanding much by way of supporting technologies which in the USSR simply do not exist. American studies suggest that US equipment in the Soviet Union operates on average at 60 per cent of its normal effectiveness.[36] The process of adaptation is not only difficult, it is also costly. Far from freeing resources for other priorities, some have suggested that each rouble of imported equipment requires an average of five roubles in investment support. In the view of at least one authority, these costs lead Soviet foreign trade organisations to *prefer* importing standard items over hi-tech equipment. But, another response to this problem has been a shift to acquiring integrated, turnkey projects.[37]

In spite of these obstacles, the evidence suggests that imported equipment yields high benefits. Philip Hanson, perhaps the leading expert in this area, has assessed the impact in these terms:

> The scale of these imports is small in relation to the Soviet investment programme. Their impact, both direct and indirect, on the level and growth rate of Soviet production is significant, but appears to constitute only a modest source of Soviet economic growth. There is evidence that the rates of return on hard-currency expenditure in this field are high.

These results may testify to the attributes of the equipment acquired and the proficiency of foreign trade organisations in tailoring purchases to real needs. They would also confirm that the integration of this equipment into Soviet industry receives considerable attention:

Significantly, however, Hanson adds: 'It does not necessarily follow that Soviet utilisation and diffusion of imported technology is highly effective by international standards'.[38] Once the standard of comparison shifts to international performance, then the system's obstacles are telling. As we have seen, the Soviet approach to acquiring foreign technology is defensive: biased towards thoroughness, a careful weighing up of alternatives, and an avoidance of risk. The result is often a hesitation in buying new technologies until they are proven, and a pace of negotiation which is both fatiguing and maddening to Westerners caught up in it. If the Soviet Union were 'catching up and overtaking' a stationary object, Soviet practice would make sense, but the process itself is a continuous one, and the

competitor is a moving target. Speed, not judiciousness, is therefore of
the essence. 'In general, it is hard to locate a major new technology
developed in any country for which the USSR was among the earlier
foreign purchasers of machinery or know-how.'

> Relatively late Soviet purchasing of plastics, synthetic fibre and
> compound and concentrated fertiliser technology is implied in
> the belated chemicalisation drive. . . . The Soviet acquisition
> of computers has been relatively late. . . . Soviet commercial
> acquisition of other major technologies, such as numerically
> controlled machine tools and offshore oil drilling has been relatively
> late. And so on.[39]

By the time a new process or machine appears in the USSR, it is
invariably on the point of obsolescence in the exporting country.

This pattern may be resistant to change. The Soviet institutional
structure produces decisiveness once decision is taken; it is not one
which produces decision quickly. The USSR is also bound to remain a
society where penalties for error will outweigh the rewards for well
judged gambles. But our most serious uncertainties about Soviet
abilities would seem to arise from the nature of diffusion itself.
Diffusing knowledge and acquiring it are as much an art as a science,
processes influenced by variables which cannot be measured as much
as by those which can. Two variables which can at least be specified are
the recipient's skill and his receptiveness. In this respect, it does not
bode well for the USSR that decisions pertaining to technology
imports and decisions pertaining to economic reform have moved
along independent tracks. Acquisition of foreign technology has
usually been an alternative to reform, not a complement to it. The
Soviets may rob themselves of their own best potential in this way.
Studies also bear out that people are the most effective disseminators
of know-how, and that hardware just dropped on the doorstep is the
least effective. The barriers which the USSR erects in the name of
security to communication between Westerners with knowledge to
disseminate and Russians who can benefit is perhaps the most blatant
of its self-imposed handicaps.[40]

Lead times, however, are only one economic factor relevant to
East–West competition. The potential of Western imports to free
Soviet investment resources is not insignificant. The six Urengoi
pipelines, constructed to large extent with West European pipe and
compressors, will increase natural gas production by seven to nine per

cent per annum, whilst the single export pipeline will add $8 billion per annum to hard currency earnings.[41] The project will alleviate the USSR's internal energy problem, ease the burden of supplying its CMEA clients and ensure continued funding for meat, feed grains and industrial equipment. Without the pipeline, or with great delay in its completion, one could see that it would be difficult for the USSR to carry on with business as usual. Precisely because the trade-offs are so clear, this particular project puts the right questions into focus. For the sake of this exercise, it matters little that, as a Soviet planner, I fail to narrow the gap between my compressor technology and yours; nor does it concern me that one rouble of imported Western equipment requires five roubles in investment support: if the six roubles I invest produce fifty roubles of output, how have I injured myself? Where trade-offs are at issue, rather than innovation, modernisation or know-how, the only question which matters is 'opportunity cost': resources which would otherwise be expended on equivalent Soviet equipment and, particularly, the question of investment versus overall return. The question of trade-offs therefore promises to remain a live issue in East–West (and no doubt West–West) relations.

This stock taking leaves us positioned inconclusively between alarm on the one hand and complacency on the other. Depending on circumstances, technology transfer can have dramatic or indifferent effect, but there is no clear-cut formula to hand. The potential will depend on what is transferred (not just, how advanced? but also, how compatible?); and on how it is transferred (is the end user a resourceful user? is know-how to accompany hardware? is the information flow to be continuous? is the effort to be concentrated in a particular sector or dispersed in dribs and drabs across many?) Finally, it will depend on the customer's purpose (a direct boost to production or indirect benefits?) The Soviets, as shown by declining equipment orders since 1976, have themselves become more careful in weighing the balance, and have lost much of their earlier enthusiasm, as Brezhnev made clear to the Twenty-Party Congress of 1981:

> We must go into the reasons why we sometimes lose our lead [in a technology] and spend large sums of money on purchasing abroad equipment or technology which we are fully able to make for ourselves, often indeed at a higher quality level.[42]

The hyperbole in Brezhnev's statement is less significant than the disillusion it reveals: Brezhnev, after all, was the figure most closely associated with the strategy of import led growth. The Soviet Union is too dependent and too much part of the world economy to return to hibernation, but another period of infatuation may have come to an end. For the future, technology transfer will remain a way of managing Soviet dilemmas, and perhaps ours, but it is not the key to our problems, nor the solution to theirs.

In sum and in conclusion, Western technology is not the good fairy of the Soviet economy. Soviet leaders will continue to consider Western imports worth the price on balance – but there *is* a price to pay and a balance to be drawn. To mix the metaphor, Western trade has been a sedative, not a tonic; it has acted as a brake on reform, not a stimulant. But what of those areas – strategic and ascertainable – where the West's contribution is of timely and material benefit? Can embargo be a useful instrument to protect lead times or influence Soviet policy? In specific instances the answer to either question may well be yes, but as a general proposition, three considerations must dampen anyone's enthusiasm for economic brinkmanship with the Soviet Union:

(1) When directed against industrial economies, sanctions invariably stimulate the creation of new capabilities. In some instances, the long-term benefit to the victim may be worth the short-term price, but it is a question which must be faced. 'Hurting' the Soviet Union is not enough. Will the consequences of hurting her be in her interest or in ours?

(2) Sanctions and embargoes throw the Soviet regime back upon what it does best: enforcing a state of siege, imposing military discipline on production and mobilising society along wartime lines. If there are to be sacrifices and belt-tightening, the Soviet leaders love nothing better than a backdrop of international threat to add pathos and realism to the drama.

(3) In the battle of wills, as well as the battle of resources, the Soviet Union has cards to play. Adversity is the regime's natural habitat, and in dealing with its own populace its one moral trump. Within the Soviet Union embargo is apt to strengthen unity. In the West, as we have seen, it is apt to promote disunity.

DEFENCE AND THE NATIONAL ECONOMY

The Soviet defence economy, it is often alleged, is a separate economy. There are, indeed, impressive reasons for characterising it as such, but only the most committed proponent of this view would wish to deny that the defence effort and the scientific–technological base on which it rests can be entirely insulated from the problems we have surveyed here. An important question for assessing military effectiveness is, 'if separate, how separate?'

But the prior question is how insulated the civil economy can be from defence considerations in the Soviet Union. Oskar Lange once characterised the Soviet economy as 'a *sui generis* war economy'.[43] The clear implication of this is that a fully autonomous civilian economy may not exist. Without doubt, civilian production exists. In a much quoted statement, Brezhnev once asserted that civilian production accounted for 42 per cent of the output of defence industry itself.[44] An obvious implication of the continuity between peace and war and between internal and foreign policy referred to in Chapter 1 is that there is less meaning to the civilian–military distinction in the USSR than elsewhere. If the law of life is struggle, the 'bottom line' in economic activity as with any other, is the contribution it makes to that struggle, and no sector can simply opt out of it, even if it can be shown by some other criteria that doing so would improve matters. More fish would be caught and fewer would rot if the Soviet fishing fleet, operating under 'civilian' ministries, did not circumnavigate to perform intelligence gathering for the Soviet Navy. Yet, by Party–State criteria, this represents an intelligent use of scarce resources (as does use of the merchant, fishing and oceanographic fleets to furnish 70 per cent of the Navy's supplies at sea).[45] The inroads of the military into 'civilian' domains are a basic fact of Soviet life, regarded as entirely normal by the population. From pre-, para- and reserve military training in schools and factories, to 'voluntary' contributions of food and material to the Armed Forces, to dual-purpose transport and the hardening of industrial plant, it is difficult to find an aspect of production in which military and security considerations do not in some way impinge. The Merchant Fleet (*Morflot*), for example, contains its own Military Sections charged with military training, and its vessels (equipped with gas masks and radiation detectors) are designed for prompt conversion to naval auxiliaries.[46] How many other countries have a ministry of Civil Aviation headed by a Chief Marshal of Aviation and a state airline under control of military intelligence?[47]

The Soviet military mind may admire US technology and regret that the Soviet GNP is only 50–60 per cent the size of its opponent's, but when surveying the way the US economy is organised, an officer of the

Soviet General Staff must ask himself how much of that GNP has any practical use. Consider the statistics in Table 1:[48]

Table 1

	USSR 1970	USSR 1980	USA 1979
Steel (million tons)	85.9	148	123
Metal-cutting Machine Tools (thousands)	202.2	216	65.2
Metal-forming Machine Tools (thousands)	41.3	57.1	30.5

The ever-present reality in the West – industrial 'restructuring', the whittling away of heavy industry and the growth of ever more exotic services – is not a model that automatically commends itself to imitation. In Chapter 4 we look at how Soviet society organises itself for war. What is important to emphasise is that war is the ultimate purpose for which Soviet society is organised. Butter, eggs, refrigerated goods trains are all desirable things to have, but they are not the test of an economy in Soviet eyes. Leaders of the military establishment do not, any more than their civilian colleagues, define their economy by its defects. This is not to say that they are not aware of them. In Soviet eyes, 'priority' – the essence of the defence economy – is both a response to defect and a great source of strength. Before considering precisely what 'priority' means, let us examine who determines it, who polices it and who benefits from it.

Standing behind the defence economy is a system of views entitled 'Soviet Military Doctrine'. Soviet Military Doctrine (which we discuss more fully in Chapters 4 and 5) would reject as a lunatic heresy the idea that there could be one set of assumptions governing defence production, a second governing the training and control of troops, a third for military strategy, and a fourth for the politico-military policy of the state. War, like policy its master, is a *purposeful* act. Defence budgeting and procurement do not move along different tracks from defence policy as a whole.

The inevitable complement to coherence, given the range of issues and concerns which must be addressed, is complexity. Soviet decision-making in this sphere (as in many others) combines what to a Western mind might seem incompatible: hierarchy and consultation, centralisation and a wealth of horizontal communication links, flexibility and ease of communication at the top, along with compartmentalisation and secrecy below. A staple feature of Soviet bureaucracy is overlapping responsibility (particularly at intermediate levels): in part a natural consequence of size and complexity, in part a way of ensuring consultation and coordination; it is also the Party's tried and trusted technique of divide and rule. The final and most important feature of the system is Party primacy. Party involvement in a question does not create jurisdictional disputes, but resolves them.

Below is a 'bare bones' outline of the principal actors in defence policy and their principal economic responsibilities. It should be noted that controversy surrounds the membership of some of these bodies and that there is no certainty about their precise relations to one another. Finally, in Soviet bureaucracy as in any other, there are perils in drawing too firmly the lines between policy, advice and implementation, but I introduce these distinctions here in order to keep confusion within bounds.[49]

Policy-Making Institutions

CPSU Politburo

Supreme policy-making body for all aspects of Soviet life. Approves the military (along with economic) plan. Considers budgets, aggregate resource levels, numbers of weapons. Extreme centralism and bureaucratic conservatism which characterise the USSR often plunge it into detailed consideration of procurement policy, but not on a continuous basis.[50]

Defence Council of the USSR (Sovyet Oborony SSSR)

Brings together the top political leaders, the military and the military–industrial establishment. Its re-emergence in the late 1960s[51] reflected (1) need for more continuous and effective Party–military consultation, (2) demands of the Armed Forces on the civilian economy and the need for greater coordination, (3) need to ensure that strategy and, ultimately, policy governs the application of increasingly complex technology: improve the 'fit' between procurement, deployment, force structures and policy.[52] Approves doctrinal formulations, weapons programmes, and draws up overall plan for Politburo ratification.

Ministry of Defence and its Chief Military Council
If the Defence Council is charged with 'leadership of the country's defence', the Chief Military Council is charged with 'leadership of the Armed Forces'. Along with the relevant directorates of the MoD, it furnishes financial and other guidelines to the General Staff for its detailed planning.

General Staff
The 'brain of the Army', perhaps the central force in long term planning, procurement and the organisation of research and development. Adjudicates resource disputes between individual services and acts as a clearing house for individual service proposals. If not the sole, then the principal source of military advice to the Defence Council, whose Secretariat is believed to be headed by the CGS, Marshal S. F. Akhromeyev.

Supervisory Institutions
(1) *Central Committee Secretary for Defence Industry* (G. F. Romanov until June 1985)* and *CC Department for Defence Industry* (I. F. Dmitriyev): Whereas the Defence Council is the chosen instrument for ensuring Party control over military policy, the Secretariat is the Party's vehicle for supervising defence industry. (The Secretary himself may have broader responsibilities.) The Department's 100 'responsible staff' members have considerable powers over the ministries they oversee. Works closely with:
(2) *Military–Industrial Commission (VPK)* (head L. V. Smirnov): A working commission of the Council of Ministers, but in the first instance of the Defence Council. Its chief may also be responsible to the CC Secretary for Defence Industry. The VPK is thought to have broad inter-branch prerogatives for coordinating research and development, securing resources for defence production and enforcing the 'military priority' throughout the economy. It is the VPK which draws up detailed contracts for production ministries, legally binding on all parties. It also plays a key role in technical evaluations.

Advisory Institutions
(1) Academy of Sciences: The leading force in basic research, and occasionally brought into mission-orientated research by the VPK

---

* Now Lev Zaykov.

and production ministries. Prominent individuals from the Academy act as consultants to the CC Secretariat, Politburo and Defence Council. Its social science research institutes may on occasion provide alternative policy assessments. (The Ministry of Higher and Secondary Education also contains research institutes which conduct defence work).

(2) State Committee on Science and Technology: A science policy agency attached to the Council of Ministers. Works closely with GRU to determine the requirement for promising foreign technologies.

Production Ministries
The Defence Industry Group is formed by at least nine ministries. (There are at least an additional nine which are military-related.) Each ministry controls a vast empire of research institutes, design bureaux and production enterprises. In their tasks they are answerable to the VPK, the Central Committee and the Deputy Chairman of the Council of Ministers for Defence Production. The nine ministries of the so-called Defence Industry Group are listed below.[53]

Aviation industry	(Aircraft and helicopters; airbreathing missiles)
Defence industry	(Conventional weapons)
Electronics industry	(Electronic components)
General machine building	(Ballistic missiles, space equipment)
Machine building	(Munitions)
Medium machine building	(Nuclear weapons)
Means of communication	(Telecommunications equipment)
Radio industry	(Electronic components)
Shipbuilding industry	(Ships and naval products)

What does 'priority' mean in the defence production sector? The simple answer is more and better. In concrete terms, priority refers to a variety of measures designed to insulate defence production from resource scarcities and the distortions of the planning process. These include:

Personnel: Salary differentials 20–30 per cent over comparable civilian work tend to siphon off the better qualified. As the most prestigious sector of the economy, the military sphere is also likely to attract the most ambitious and competent engineers, scientists and managers. Nor surprisingly, a large proportion of the top leadership have backgrounds in military industry. The similar career patterns and long personal acquaintance of men like Brezhnev, Ustinov, Smirnov, Serbin (former head of the CC Department of Defence Industry) and Alekseyev (head of the MoD Armaments Directorate) maintain a consensus sympathetic to defence requirements.

Capacity: The celebrated 42 per cent allocated to civilian production attests to the extent of excess capacity enjoyed by the defence sector, compared with the straitened circumstances of other industries. The other side of this coin is an impressive 'surge' capability on hand when the need arises. Similarly, manpower and budgets in weapons design bureaux do not vary with the production cycle. This allows for a continuous stream of models and prototypes: the USSR does not face NATO's proverbial problem of holding together a design team in peacetime.

Autarky: Coordination between enterprises from different sectors and ministries is notoriously poor in the Soviet Union. Hence, autarky in production is everyone's aspiration, but an unachievable (and unaffordable) one. Defence ministries, however, come far closer to this ideal.

> The Aviation Ministry . . . produces sheet aluminium, magnesium alloys, shaped metal products, plastics, and rubber products. Commonly used components such as instruments, machine tools, rivets, nuts and bolts, instead of being produced efficiently by a single supplier are manufactured by all branches of defence industry; missile electronics, for example, are produced by the Ministry of General Machine Building.[54]

Resources: The Ninth Five-Year Plan (1971–75) stipulated that light industry would grow more quickly than heavy industry; nonetheless, the opposite took place.[55] In Soviet conditions, this is not unusual. 'Priority' means that when the unscheduled but proverbial shortages arise, the Armed Forces receive the ration promised and others go without. Whereas cost is a definite factor taken into account in plan *formulation* by the Defence Council and Politburo, it is not allowed to become a disrupter of plan *fulfilment*. The arbiter over these matters would appear to be the VPK, which is empowered to commandeer resources where required, and whose work programmes carry the force of law.

Customer accountability: In defence, the customer is the Armed Service and the military representatives (*voyenpredi*) of its armaments directorate. Seconded to each enterprise and design bureau, they are empowered to reject, at factory expense, production which is not up to standard. Unlike the civilian quality control inspectors of the Department of Technical Control (OTK), whose salary arrangements link them effectively to their enterprises, the *voyenpredi* are in every sense the agents and servants of their respective services. Their fortunes depend entirely on how effectively they wield the bludgeon at their disposal; in fact, a military representative may be gaoled for accepting shoddy goods.

A second customer prerogative is choice. Weapons design bureaux, usually bearing the names of their founders (Tupolev, Korolyev), possess something akin to a corporate identity, as well as clear incentives for entrepreneurial behaviour. The system is one which breeds product specialisation, whilst also ensuring overlap in broad areas of competence. The result may be alternative proposals at the start (e.g., Mig-15, Yak-25) or reinsurance when things go awry in mid-course. When the Nadiradize design bureau, specialising in solid fuel missiles, ran into trouble with its SS-13, the Chelomei bureau, despite its maritime orientation, was able to redirect the SS-11 programme to the anti-Minuteman counterforce role.[56]

In their ensemble, these practices and privileges afford the defence sector a considerable degree of protection from the vagaries of the economic system. They also draw upon the system's attributes: an ability to mobilise talent and resources, coherence of policy and direction; the ability of the centre to support and remove obstacles; and the possibility of combining strategy with flexibility. In 1959, two years after the launching of the world's first ICBM, the civilian airport of Kiev, the USSR's third largest city, was without a paved runway.[57] This may say as much about priority in the USSR as anything else.

For all the truth of these points, and for all the striking contrasts, military production would appear to function more as a favoured section of the economy than as a separate one. The weaknesses which strike the economy as a whole – scarcities, changeovers from design to mass production – are, even in the defence sector, the principal constraints on what can be produced and how. Although the USSR supplies the US with 33 per cent of the latter's titanium, supply scarcities and limitations in manufacturing capability dictated producing the Mach 2.8 Mig-25 out of conventional steels (although a titanium version was successfully flown and tested).[58]

Soviet design and procurement philosophy displays a prudence and conservatism which reflects well known Soviet constraints, but also an ingenuity in the face of shortages and stringencies that characterises Soviet performance at its best. Scarcities, pressures of time, and the often rudimentary skills of workers and equipment operators dictate a search for 'minimal' rather than exotic technology, and a penchant for working along proven lines. Rather than strive to apply the most advanced technology available, the Soviet designer is conditioned to ask, 'what is the simplest solution which will do the job'? Simplicity need not always mean economy, but it has traditionally created a bias towards the single-purpose system, which allows concentration on point-design performance, as opposed to the multipurpose system common to Western inventories, which demands complicated and sophisticated design solutions. It also implies an abhorence of 'gold plating', with its inevitable expense, reliance upon outsiders and hence, delay. As Andrey Tupolev once put it, 'the country needs aircraft like black bread. You can offer pralines, cakes and so on, but there's no point – there aren't the ingredients to make them out of'.[59] Soviet design philosophy also rises to the system's innate strengths: an economy which finds quantity as cheap as quality is expensive (hence long production lines and low unit costs) and a procurement system effective at bringing together operators, designers and technologists. A Soviet tank may not be comfortable to ride in compared with a NATO tank, but it is reliable, easy to repair, and built quite deliberately for a particular kind of terrain, support system and warfare.[60]

Soviet weapons reveal a greater degree of 'design heredity' than their Western counterparts, with each new generation incorporating many of the technologies of the preceding one. (Indeed, old and new models may be in production simultaneously, as was briefly the case with the T-54, T-62 and T-72). The risk of project failure may thus be minimised, but performance as well as know-how may suffer. As one former tank designer put it, 'in time, simplicity can become primitiveness'.[61] The incremental approach has also been known to produce an impressive degree of evolution within a given generation, with each system pushed over time to its workable limits. Some 15 improved variants of Mig-21 emerged over a 25-year period, to impressive effect: the latest models possessing almost double the range and payload of the first.[62] The rigidities and continuities of the planning and design process may constrain ability to deal with the unanticipated and often press purpose built systems into unlikely roles. Thus the Mig-25, designed originally as a high altitude interceptor of the B-70, found itself adapted, upon the demise of the B-70 programme, for high speed reconnaissance and air defence.

This occurred despite the system being, from a Western perspective, singly ill-suited for its new air-defence role: inadequate in range, mobility, acceleration, and with engine components which were likely to melt when operated at full power.[63]

Other examples of mid-course diversions (the SS-11) have been moderately successful, and some (the SS-20, which started out life unsuccessfully as the three stage SS-16 ICBM) have been conspicuously so.[64]

Needs on occasion are identified which call for a sharp break with previous practice, or for a new genus of weapon altogether (such as the ICBM, Galosh ABM, particle beam weapons). The appearance of such systems, often in advance of any Western equivalent, usually generates flurries of excitement, yet early versions tend to possess rudimentary capabilities, and effective variants may take considerable time to emerge as the component technologies are brought up to standard. First in the world to deploy an ICBM, it took the Soviet Union ten years longer than the United States to develop a reliable guidance system; it has also taken 25 years to develop a quiet nuclear submarine, and having set the pace with anti-satellite weapons, the USSR may already have fallen behind the United States in this field. Nevertheless, as Stansfield Turner, former CIA Director, once summarised it.

> With brute force techniques . . . they do achieve about the same end result as we do with much more sophisticated techniques. For example, they will put multiple computers in a system, each of much less sophistication than the one we put in ours.[65]

Whilst it is no doubt true that the heaviness of early Soviet ICBMs and the 'dirtiness' of their warheads stemmed from crude propulsion and guidance systems, all that matters is that they accomplished what they were designed to.

Finally, how does the priority system, designed to deal with *internal* weaknesses, facilitate the absorption of foreign technology? It would be prudent to assume that the GRU, in collaboration with its clients, is effective at identifying needs and diverting what it purloins to the right places. We can also speculate that at least some 'non-negotiable' transfers are brought off more rapidly than those which go through the lugubrious procedures maintained by various State bodies and foreign trade organisations. But it is questionable how much the priority system helps the USSR absorb foreign technologies rapidly. To be sure, differences in scale and degree beyond a certain point can become differences in kind. But there are two further factors which weigh against the optimal absorption of what is made available. Secrecy and restrictions on communication between scientists and engineers are so stultifying that many reportedly are discouraged from undertaking defence work. (Zhores Medvedev's attempts to spell out the injury thus caused to scientific–technical advance landed him in a mental hospital.) The second is the complexity and sophistication of modern weapons systems themselves: each containing a sufficient number of different component technologies to ensure that progress, by and large, remains incremental rather than revolutionary. As Thane Gustafson has summed it up, 'the day when the simple invention of the stirrup changed the nature of warfare has vanished'. Finally, as in civil production, the critical variables will be the what and the how. Indeed, in this sphere, as in others, the simple transfer of equipment can be positively deleterious. (In one case recorded by Medvedev, the process of 'reverse engineering' – that is, copying – became a 13 year ordeal.) These considerations hold out some hope that, while the problem of maintaining lead times will remain serious, it will remain a manageable problem, much as it has in the past. To reiterate, a Soviet economy restructured to make best use of its own human and material assets would be more of a threat to the West than one which became exceptionally adept at acquiring the West's secrets. How then, on balance, is the Soviet effort to be assessed?

(1) The Soviet ability to achieve breakthroughs is often overrated. More impressive is the ability to make incremental improvements to existing capabilities and, over time, satisfy new requirements which are identified.

(2) As in the civil sector, the gap in know-how may be less than the gap in the technological level of what is produced; often a conscious decision is made to forego the most advanced option. The stringencies built into the economy are serious disadvantages and salutary disciplines: Soviet designers are the last to confuse the most advanced solution with the most effective one. Where a need is identified, the USSR has repeatedly shown an ability to produce to the technical standard *adequate*.

(3) We should not too complacently write off Soviet quantitative superiorities as the mere offset for technological backwardness. There is an element of 'mirror imaging' in this perception. The Soviet emphasis on mass armies is based on its history and geography, as well as considered judgements on the nature of future war in Europe. Quantity, essentially, is not seen as a compensation for weakness in technology.

It has, in contrast, been Western orthodoxy to cling to technological superiority as a substitute for what is often taken to be an unbridgeable quantitative gap. In the process the West may have sold itself a weapons portfolio which it lacks the means to produce in quantity. Soviet orthodoxy has always considered technology as multiplier, not as substitute. Given present quantitative disparities between East and West, incremental performance improvements do provide something to worry about. Rather than ask whether a NATO tank remains superior to a Soviet tank, the relevant question is whether it remains superior to four Soviet tanks.

(4) This may be the inescapable question for the foreseeable future so long as NATO procurement policy is predicated on highly trained work forces, scarce materials and sophisticated machine tools. The Soviet emphasis on simple materials and technologies ensures in contrast long production lines, low unit costs, and an ability to turn spare capacity over to military production with a minimum of retraining and re-tooling. The fact that the USSR produces two to three times as many machine tools as the United States is not without significance.

By way of postscript to these observations, some have discerned in the latest Soviet systems a greater introduction of new technology than is normally the pattern: a reflection, perhaps, of greater design confidence, but just as possibly the expression of worry about the pace of technological change in the present decade. It is difficult to conceal the suspicion that in Soviet eyes a new technological era is dawning, with consequences for military science as far-reaching as the ballistic missile and nuclear weapon, and the 'revolution in military affairs' which they unleashed. It is not so much the Western origin of new component technologies as their gestation in the West's civilian sectors which must pose the most vexing questions for Soviet policy makers and their orthodoxies. The priority system which has raided and impoverished the civilian economy for military benefit may in retrospect turn out to have been the scourge of military and civil progress alike. There are radical implications in these challenges, and Marshal Ogarkov's departure in 1984, as well as his return to favour in 1985, may not be unrelated to his keen awareness of them. A closer look at this challenge will be afforded in Chapter 5 but suffice it here to say that the military's vested interest in the established planning system, long a fixed point on the compass, may be changing.

CAN THE FUTURE BE MADE TO WORK?

It is clear that the Soviet economy is at an impasse, but we have tried to suggest that it is not at the abyss. As one looks to the future, there would appear to be margins of manoeuvre and debate. There would seem to be four types of players contesting the board and two axes on which the game pivots: conservative – transformist (a safer term than 'radical'), and centraliser – de-centraliser (a safer term than 'liberal'). With Chernenko's departure from the scene, it may appear that the *immobilistes* have lost their final defence. But if Gorbachev fails to meet the considerable expectations he has aroused, we may find there is plenty of rebound in the conservative cause. What, then, are the likely options between now and the end of the century?

Muddling Through – the Coalition of Conservatives and Centralisers

Analogy: Brezhnev, 1968–1982
Problems to be tackled by additional restructuring and 'administrative' reforms (some on the East German or Czechoslovak pattern), greater levels of investment in yet more priority areas, exhortation and other *ad hoc* remedies; a blind eye to the 'second economy' rather than a policy for it; consensual pattern of decision-making maintained and élite interests nurtured.

Consequence: The odd success as the more sensible reforms of the 1970s take root, but nothing sufficient to arrest the gradual listing of the economy; continued demoralisation of the workforce, but little threat to stability as élite maintains its cohesion against society; however, minority factions in élite becoming more forceful in demanding strategy versus drift.

Prospects: Possible as a short-term measure, but increasingly implausible for the longer term as the cracks become wider and resources for papering them over become more scarce.

Evolutionary Change – the Coalition of Conservatives and De-centralisers

Analogy: Kosygin–Brezhnev, 1964–68
Conscientious but 'experimental' introduction of Hungarian-style measures, with isolated centres of the economy turned into laboratories of reform; a limited legalisation of the 'second economy' on the East European pattern, and greater support for the consumer and for private farmers. Reluctance to displace planners, jurisdictional disputes 'resolved' by compromise; consensual decision-making and propitiation of the élite.

Consequence: Easing of supply problems in agriculture and boost to consumer satisfaction, but momentum lost as planners obstruct, managers become frustrated and disputes over prerogatives are fudged.

Prospects: A pattern which may evolve out of the failures above; its failure, however, could produce a turning of the tables and the triumph of:

Discipline and Reform: More Power to the Centre – the Coalition of Transformists and Centralisers

Analogy: Andropov, 1982–84, Stalin, Peter the Great, Gorbachev, 1985– ?
The 'big boot' approach to Russia's problems, with technocratic fine-tuning. Large turnover of personnel at the centre, but its prerogatives strengthened: a search for 'the best and the brightest'. A streamlining of 'transmission belts' between the centre and direct producers, coupled with the more consistent application of the better 1970-style reforms. Openness to experiment, debate, and admission of error, but ruthless enforcement of 'democratic centralism'. Administrative apparatus filleted to eliminate incompetence, lethargy and bottlenecks. Greater reliance on police methods (to concentrate the mind), falling most heavily on workforce (alcoholism, absenteeism), but also on managers and provincial officials.

Consequence: Boost to production and idealism: idealism counterbalanced by fear and threatened by worsening privation as attacks on 'corruption' begin to bite; growth partially nullified by a worsening of distribution problems as the second economy is rolled back. Eventual likelihood of a new equilibrium establishing itself as a new élite does and as police methods lose their novelty; in absence of market-style reforms, balance of incentives apt to remain negative. A mid-term solution, but not a long-term one.

Prospects: A strategy which will secure the backing of the younger, more creative and more frustrated members of (or aspirants to) the élite, as well as the Armed Forces and KGB; a strategy with greatest prospects of survival over an extended period, although its potential will depend on how quickly the regime recognises the 'second economy' to be a 'necessary' and 'non-antagonistic' contradiction in a Socialist society.

Discipline and Reform: Survival of the Fittest – the Coalition of Transformists and De-centralisers

Analogy: None as yet

A more consistent, competent, ruthless and less 'hare-brained' Khrushchevism. Hungarian-style reforms introduced, but comprehensively: markets function and managers make decisions unless planners say otherwise (at present few decisions can be taken unless planners authorise them). Administrative axe falls most heavily on the centre as its size is pared down; economic axe falls most heavily on the less efficient, as unemployment and bankruptcies make their first appearance.

Consequences: In the short term, unsettling effects for state and society alike. Survival into the mid-term depends on speed with which individuals can adapt to unfamiliar criteria and incentives. Divided élite leading the assault upon itself may be in no position to withstand the pressures of a restless population. This strategy may have the greatest potential for long-term success if the shoals can be navigated with success. But if it fails it may take the system down with it.

Prospects: Unlikely, as its implications and perils understood; and, of the four strategies, it would demand the greatest unity at the top.

3 Foundations of Power: Empire

> Whoever occupies a territory also imposes on it his own social system. Everyone imposes his own system as far as his army can reach. It cannot be otherwise.
>
> Stalin to Milovan Djilas, 1945

> Your country is in the region occupied by Soviet soldiers in the Second World War. We paid for this with great sacrifices, and we will never leave.
>
> Brezhnev to Dubček, 1968

The satirist, Saki, once observed that right and wrong, like the Russian Empire, had certain well-defined limits, albeit not always in the same place. It seems only appropriate to begin this chapter by establishing the limits of the subject, because not everyone has been in agreement as to where influence ends and control begins.

By even the most stringent criterion, any definition of the Soviet Empire would have to encompass what Saki termed the Russian Empire: the fourteen non-Russian 'Union Republics' which join with the Russian Soviet Federative Socialist Republic into an 'integral, federal, multinational state'. Constitutional provisions affirming each Union Republic to be a 'sovereign Soviet socialist state' with the rights to secede and to enter into foreign relations are honoured faintly in appearance, but by no means in substance.[1] Beyond Soviet borders, if we follow Moscow's own definitions, there are three circles of influence: at the outer rim, a variety of states enjoying relations of friendship or alliance with the USSR; then, a group of countries characterised by dependence and 'solidarity'; and, finally, an inner circle characterised by subordination. For our purposes, only the final group pass muster into the Soviet Empire, but the others are worth noting in passing.

The outermost ring, comprising 'progressive' but non-Leninist countries, is the most difficult to demarcate with precision. Four of these politically dissimilar states (Finland, India, Iraq and Syria) are party to treaties of 'Friendship and Cooperation' or 'Friendship, Cooperation and Mutual Assistance' with the USSR; a fifth, Libya, has concluded similar agreements with Bulgaria, Romania and North Korea.[2] In addition to most of the preceding, Guinea-Bissau, Mali, Nigeria, Uganda and Zambia have concluded military cooperation agreements with the USSR. Several states maintain Soviet military advisers on their soil, in Syria's case a substantial number.[3] For the most part members of the Non-Aligned Movement, many of these states maintain good relations with countries hostile to the Soviet Union.[4] The history of Soviet relations with non-Leninist friends and clients has been marked by reversals and desertions (for instance, Indonesia in 1965, Egypt in 1972, Somalia in 1978), and when trouble looms, the USSR's ability to influence events may be found wanting.

More reliable by far are the eight states ruled by parties classified by the CPSU as 'Vanguard Revolutionary Democratic': Afghanistan, Angola, Benin, Congo, Ethiopia, Kampuchea, Mozambique and Yemen (Aden). These parties are ideologically sound, all likely in Moscow's judgement to evolve into fully fledged Communist parties: no ideological hybrids here which owe more to Mussolini than to Lenin. In contrast to the first group, relations are conducted at the Party to Party as well as State to State level.[5] In at least one case, Afghanistan, the regime could be said to be fully subordinate to Moscow. These regimes, however, are recent creations, for the most part crudely and poorly grafted onto society; in some of these countries, the 'permanence' of their socialist transformations is questionable. It is, therefore, only the 15 countries ruled by fully fledged Communist Parties which are deemed to compromise the 'world system of socialism'. Each of these countries are characterised by disciplined and politically mature Communist ruling élites with a formidable apparatus of coercion behind them. However, some of the regimes (such as North Korea) are less subordinate to Moscow than countries in the preceding category; some are non-aligned (Yugoslavia), defiant (Albania) or in rivalry with the USSR (PRC). Cuba and Vietnam, for their part, are bound firmly to the USSR by a mutuality of interest and outlook, but it is questionable, despite considerable dependency on the USSR, if they could be bound against their will. Geographically, Vietnam and Cuba are remote from the Soviet Union, and their ruling élites are cohesive entities which have come to power through their own efforts. Whilst it is possible that they will remain reliable instruments for a long time to come, it is in conditions like these that Titoism spawns and prospers.

The USSR herself appears to acknowledge that Cuba and Vietnam are not bound to her by Party discipline. References to 'fraternal solidarity' abound, but one looks hard for references to 'binding internationalist obligations' or the 'permanent factors' in relations which force Warsaw Pact leaders to account to the Soviet Politburo.[6] It is hard to imagine the C.-in-C. of the Warsaw Pact addressing a Vietnamese colleague as Marshal Grechko once spoke to the Czech Defence Minister: 'When I am thinking, you be quiet.'[7] These two states are more judiciously classed within the Soviet orbit than within her empire.

In the strictest sense then, the subject of this chapter are the six Warsaw Pact members of Eastern Europe which, along with Mongolia, could alone be said to be *bound* to the 'socialist commonwealth'. Leaving Mongolia aside, the leaders of each country are the linear descendants of 'Muscovite' Communists, sheltered in the USSR during the Second World War and brought to power in the van of the Red Army: in times of friction, it takes little to remind Eastern Europe's leaders not only how their bread is buttered, but how they got into the larder in the first place.[8] To add force to their indebtedness, each satellite finds itself enmeshed in a web of controls and relationships which institutionalise Soviet involvement in their internal affairs. Far from being illicit and *sub rosa*, these practices and mechanisms are heralded as being essential to the 'norms' which make relations between socialist countries 'organic' and 'of a new type'.[9] Where even these devices prove insufficient to ensure subservience, there is ample reserve of armed force to do so, both within the satellites and in the USSR itself. Whilst a number of considerations may limit the resort to *force majeure*, there is a sufficiency of means once the will to use them is present. It is these states, bound to the Soviet Union by geography, dependency and military weakness which properly form the 'Soviet Empire', and whose contribution to Soviet power we shall now examine.

LIVING WITH STALIN'S LEGACY

For a variety of reasons Stalin rejected a 'Finnish' solution in Eastern Europe in preference to a security formula based on ideological conformity and the maintenance of control over these countries' internal as well as external policies. His decision was a fateful one.

Although Stalin's insistence on absolute control may in the fullness of time have evolved into an emphasis on ensuring *ultimate* control, Soviet leaders in the 1980s still operate within the essential security framework which Stalin bequeathed to them. Today, as in 1947, Soviet domination of Eastern Europe accomplishes five fundamental objectives:

(1) It ensures geographical security, acts as a force multiplier, and brings Soviet power into the heart of Europe. Gone are the days when a set of weak states acted as enticement to the invasion of European Russia by outside powers. Whatever dread and resentment the Soviet regime inspires amongst its own population, that regime has solved the perennial problem of Russia's vulnerability, and is seen to have done so by the common people of the land. This is a basic pillar of Communist legitimacy in the USSR, and in times of hardship may, perhaps, be the sole one.[10]

(2) It acts as a buttress to the ideological authority of Marxism–Leninism, internally and internationally, and sharply reduces the danger of contamination from without.

(3) It furnishes the Soviet Union with an economic storehouse of skills and technology not always obtainable in the USSR or available elsewhere. Despite worsening terms of trade in recent years, we will suggest that these functions are still performed to an impressive and significant degree.

(4) It provides a weighty diplomatic instrument in an overall European policy aimed at maximising influence over that part of Europe which the USSR does not control. The USSR has shown skill in orchestrating the foreign policies of the CMEA states to capitalise on the sensitivities of individual Western European countries and drive wedges in NATO's diplomatic front. In this enterprise the GDR has traditionally been cast as pawn (even bait) and Poland as stalking horse. This diplomatic leverage, particularly over a divided Germany, ensures the USSR a powerful voice in NATO counsels even when Soviet military power is perceived to be in check.

(5) Finally, dominion over Eastern Europe enthrones the USSR on the world stage as an equal of the United States: as a custodian not only of a set of national interests, but of a 'world socialist system' entitled to equal representation in world councils. Eastern Europe's opening to the Third World (along with the influence of Cuba and Vietnam) add credence to the view that diplomatic

solutions to international difficulties can have no validity without taking into account the interests of the socialist camp.[11]

Each of these assets has over the fullness of time authored its own particular problems and dilemmas.

(1) The extension of the USSR's geographical writ, with the corollary that (Brezhnev expressed it), Eastern Europe's borders are 'our borders', turns the reliability of Eastern Europe's ruling élites and their armed forces into a matter of the utmost importance. 'Security of the rear' in peace and war now embraces, in addition to the Soviet Union, a number of states which, however limited in sovereignty, are manifestly foreign. The result is a potentially unmanageable spread of vital interests in a country already lumbered with the burdens of being a multinational state.

(2) By the same token, the 'organic' linkage between Eastern Europe and the USSR increases the likelihood that the problems of the Soviet Empire may become the undoing of the Russian Empire. As one authority has concluded,

> The Soviet Union fears the short, medium and long term consequences of bordering countries which are actually sovereign nation states – that is sovereign as conceived outside Soviet ideology. As the RSFSR cannot be put at risk by being surrounded by non-obedient or independent and sovereign republics in Ukraine, Belorussia, Lithuania, Armenia, etc., so the security of the USSR as a national state cannot be put at risk by non-obedient and sovereign countries in east central Europe (and possibly elsewhere).[12]

Soviet specialists themselves have referred to this connection in the following way:

> Total Socialist integration is characterized by the increasing depth of interdependency. Such interdependency demands certain limitations in national sovereignty. In this process, the contents, forms and operations of national sovereignty should undergo necessary modifications.[13]

Any departures from the norm in Eastern Europe may pose immediate problems for the USSR. If it is in order for Dubček to grant federal autonomy to the Slovaks or Carpatho-Ukranians then what of the Soviet Ukraine? (the Politburo's worry in 1968); if genuine trades unions are to be countenanced in Poland, how can they be proscribed in the Baltic republics and Belorussia? (the Politburo's worry in 1980). The contagion which spreads from the enemy can be arrested because it is clearly subversive, but how is it treasonable to demand for one's fellow socialist citizens what is clearly permitted to others?[14] Ideologically, Soviet leaders may have discovered that they may be as much hostage to Eastern Europe's Communists as the latter are to Moscow. This is the lesson of the Khrushchev years, and this lesson is simple: if the subservience of Eastern Europe's Communist rulers is ensured by their dependence on the Soviet Union, then the Soviet Union had best be dependable. Moscow cannot repudiate the orthodoxies imposed upon its clients without repudiating its clients. In the 1950s Khrushchev's attempt to do so by de-throning Stalin and mending fences with Tito torpedoed two client regimes, Bierut's in Poland and Rákosi's in Hungary, whose authority derived as much from venerating the first as from anathematising the second.[15]

Today's Communist ruling circles may no more believe in Party infallibility than latter day absolute monarchs believed in the divine right of kings. The Holy Alliance which ties them to the USSR and to one another is the *principle* of Party infallibility, not the fact, and the certainty that the principle will be upheld – if necessary, by Soviet tanks. Once this connection is broken, Eastern Europe's élites may make other arrangements (as did Hungary's Imre Nagy in 1956) on terms consistent with their own safety rather than Moscow's. There is thus a contractual element in Moscow's authority – a state of affairs which gives Eastern Europe's conservatives a potential *veto* on reforms and experiments which the USSR might be tempted to support.[16]

(3) Although, as we shall argue, changing terms of trade are less adverse to the USSR than is supposed, the benefits which accrue through the structure of economic ties have over time become less economic and more political in substance. More to the point, the use of Eastern Europe as a crutch for the Soviet economy's deficiencies has only reduced the ability of both to compete with the outside world.[17]

(4) Diplomatically, Soviet success at exploiting Europe's division to bring about changes in Western policy has, in turn, given Western Europe inroads into the USSR's own preserve. The prerequisite to certain reductions of tensions in Europe has been *de jure* recognition by the Western powers of the territorial realities in the East. Western Europe's hope and Moscow's fear is that the process also entitles the West to stipulate what 'reduction of tensions' comprises and how it is to be judged. (Hence, the significance of the Helsinki Final Act.)

Whether the West's prerogatives are real, and whether or not they are exercised, the resolution of the territorial controversy has removed the one bone of contention which for a time made the Warsaw Pact a community of shared anxiety. Since then, Soviet dominance has appeared that much more stark and anomalous to the peoples of Eastern Europe.[18]

(5) Finally, the status and prestige derived from empire threatens to raise the stakes in any imperial difficulty beyond what a rational reading of Soviet interests might otherwise dictate. The maintenance of this imperium has become not only an essential pillar of the regime's internal legitimacy, but as essential a pillar of her external legitimacy as a Superpower. It seems likely, therefore, that the USSR will cling to the view that empire is the foundation of her strength despite the problems this may bring upon her and others.

LIMITED SOVEREIGNTY: POLITICS

The basic limitation on the sovereignty of any Warsaw Pact country is, obviously, the imposition of a regime not of its own choosing. In Soviet eyes, the continuing authenticity of such a regime is determined by a number of litmus tests, which ensure its conformity to Soviet practice. The first is that it maintain a monopoly of economic power. To a Marxist–Leninist, control of resources *is* power; the monopoly of political power follows from this rather than precedes it. In practice, historical traditions, and a degree of Soviet respect for them, qualify this requirement in particular instances (like a large measure of private land ownership in Poland). However, the *sine qua non* of any qualification to the rule is that there be no restoration of capitalism or capitalists: the state's economic power must be overwhelming compared with that of any indvidual or any foreseeable combination of them.[19]

Although the essential problem of power relations may thus be resolved, immense effort is still expended on maintaining the monopoly of political power. It is not thought enough to ban unofficial political activity, institute press censorship and monopolise the means of communication, since at most these measures serve a negative purpose. What is needed is a mechanism for ensuring that policy is carried out, rather than obstructed; and that those entrusted with promoting policy actively identify with it. This is ensured, first, by 'democratic centralism': 'the obligation of lower bodies to observe the decisions of higher ones'; secondly, by Party oversight of all State bodies; and, finally, by the system of *nomenklatura*, which reserves important appointments to the Party apparatus. In the NSWP countries, as in the USSR, control over appointment is a proven method of controlling policy.[20]

These practices do not in themselves guarantee the irreversibility of Socialism. It is hoped that they will keep the client in power, but today, as in Stalin's day, additional measures are thought necessary to guarantee that the client remains reliable himself. A prime instrument of Stalin's domination, the 'Embassy system', installed Soviet ambassadors as viceroys over their dependencies, supported by legions of Soviet 'advisers'.[21] In the post-Stalin years, the Soviet ambassador has remained a figure of enormous importance (hence the key roles assumed by Andropov in Hungary and Chervonenko in Prague in the respective crises of 1956 and 1968).[22] In contrast, very little business of substance is transacted through Moscow's resident NSWP ambassadors, whose postings are little more than sinecures.[23] A second instrument of control is the direct subordination to Moscow of the Armed Forces and security services, making it possible to bypass the national leadership. (Ladislav Bittman, a senior officer of Czech intelligence in the 1960s, has stated that day-to-day supervision by KGB liaison officers extended to departmental level).[24]

Whilst some of the more conspicuous signs of domination have diminished over the years, a more indirect but equally pervasive web of relationships has grown up. Very much at the centre of it is the CPSU CC's Department for Liaison with Communist and Workers' Parties of Socialist Countries, founded in 1957, and headed by Yuriy Andropov from that date until his appointment to head the KGB in 1967. This department, an offspring of the old CC Foreign Affairs Department, maintains direct ties to Central Committee members of each neighbouring Socialist country. (Indeed, the Soviet ambassador himself probably reports through these channels, rather than, or in addition to, the Ministry of Foreign Affairs.) It is understood that appointments to Central Committees and other key posts are to be confirmed with Moscow. Dubček's failure to do this was presented by Brezhnev as a cardinal sin:

From the outset, I wanted to help you out against Novotný, and immediately in January I asked you: Are his people threatening you? Do you want to replace them? Do you want to replace the Minister of Interior? And the Minister of National Defence? And is there anyone else you want to replace? But you said no, they're good comrades. And then suddenly I hear that you've replaced the Minister of Interior, of National Defence, and other ministers, and that you replaced secretaries of the Central Committee.[25]

This amounts to nothing less than the extension of the *nomenklatura* system to intrabloc relations. So long as other leaders do not follow Dubček's example, Moscow can be confident of dealing with known quantities in its client states and of possessing means to manipulate factional rivalries to its own advantage. By the same token, national *apparatchiki* will understand that the support of Moscow will be the deciding factor in such rivalries.

Dubček's undoing was supposing that his personal stature allowed him to adopt a creative notion of his responsibilities and depart from the orthodox notion of these things. He was a known quantity whose devotion to the Soviet Union was unquestioned; he would never countenance a multi-party system; he, unlike Nagy, had no intention of withdrawing from the WTO. All of this was clear. Dubček therefore calculated that it would be safe to whittle away the censorship of the media, break out of the *nomenklatura* network and transform the Communist Party of Czechoslovakia from a 'democratic centralist' into a democratic organisation. Since the reformist animus came from within the Party and not from anti-Socialist elements outside it, he trusted that the Soviet leaders would grasp the artfulness and wisdom of his innovations. But for the CPSU Politburo in 1968, these measures were a *casus belli*, and it is not unlikely that a future Politburo will take a similar view of such transgressions.[26] (Thus far, Hungary's cautious brand of reformism has managed to stop short of them.) One analyst of these matters has noted that 'Stalin had little reason to expect that control of Communist countries would differ markedly from control of Communist parties.'[27] Although post-Stalin leaders are more flexible about many things, that expectation survives in large measure and is to a fair degree born out by results. Many Western commentators, by focusing on what is familiar to them, namely state-to-state relations, have tended to emphasise the importance of divergence and diversity with the WTO countries. The distinguishing feature of the 'Socialist camp' is not just the obvious limitations imposed upon the state sovereignty of its members, but the centrality of relations between parties. It is this party-to-party dimension of relations, and a particularly 'centralist' and 'internationalist' notion of accountability, which keeps these diversities within limits and maintains élite solidarity in fact as well as in name. The predicament for Eastern Europe as well as the Soviet Union is that this intra-bloc cohesiveness tends to be purchased at the price of internal stability.

It is difficult to see how it could be otherwise given a political system dominated by appointment prerogatives and Moscow connections, rather than accountability to social forces with a direct stake in policy issues. In Eastern Europe, as in the Soviet Union itself, issues and interests are sacrificed in the battle for faction and patronage. Like the Vicar of Bray, political survivors in Eastern Europe know how to subordinate their policy interests to their own personal cause: venerable figures such as Novotný and Husák of Czechoslovakia, and Olszowski of Poland have migrated more than once between hardliners and soft. It is not surprising that Dubček in his ascendancy gained the support of as many 'Stalinists' as backed the 'conservative', Novotný; nor that Novotný's record was subsequently depicted as more 'Stalinist' than it was. The politics of the élite therefore proceeds very much in a world of its own. The very freedom from mass accountability which allows it to do so also makes it difficult for leaders to know what society is thinking: without mechanisms for making needs known and understood, Polish and Soviet leaders simply cannot know what the consequences of a rise in food prices or of other policy shifts will be. The noteworthy point about explosions against the system in the GDR (1953), Hungary (1956) and Poland (1956, 1970, 1976 and 1980) is not their ferocity, but their apparent suddenness.[28]

From a detached perspective, it might therefore seem that the political viability of the USSR's East European clients depends not only on greater economic and administrative competence on their part, but the opening up of communication channels between élite and mass and a narrowing of the gulf between state and society. But those who composed the Brezhnev doctrine have not been taken in by this line of thinking, at least not to date. It is this declaration which symbolises the primacy of cohesiveness over stability, and it arose, one must recall, not in response to the avowed enemies of Socialism, but to a loyal leadership which demonstrated the will and ability to deal with society on society's terms. If a loyal client has no objective need of its Soviet protectors, then how long will it remain loyal in fact or in spirit? Not surprisingly, Soviet assessments of the more recent Polish crisis are out of tune with the lessons which have generally been drawn in the West. Konstantin Rusakov, present CC Secretary for intra-bloc relations, does indeed fault the Gierek leadership for 'big mistakes and miscalculations . . . in economic and social policy', but goes on as well to indict it for 'flagrant departures from the integral regularities and principles of building socialism'. Amongst the latter, he and other figures include:

(1) 'the violation of the universal laws governing the building of socialism [which] led to incomplete socialist changes and even to retention of some elements of the transitional period' – namely, failure to fully collectivize Poland and reign-in the Church;
(2) allowing KOR, 'an avowedly counterrevolutionary grouping . . . to operate in the country essentially legally';
(3) 'anti-socialist elements . . . increasingly breaking into the mass media';
(4) an unacceptable degree of contact with the West. 'Since World War II in Poland there have been about 15 000 translations of publications by Western authors . . . about 16 000 Western-produced movies have been shown and over 3 300 productions of plays by Western authors have been staged'.[29]

At least outwardly then, Soviet authorities insist on a linkage between Socialism and stability, and deny any tension between them. But Western observers may have grounds for scepticism. It was not, as the Russians say, 'for the sake of their blue eyes' that Poland's leaders granted such concessions to their subjects. Nevertheless, there is a clear – and perhaps valid – message behind these Soviet critiques: a safer bet maintaining order through Leninist norms than putting brakes on reform once the ball is rolling. Whatever the truth of the matter, the one certainty for the future is that economic pressures will put everyone – reformers and conservatives – to the test.

LIMITED SOVEREIGNTY: ECONOMICS

As we approach the last third of the 1980s, it is an open question whether the tribulations of the CMEA economies will weaken or strengthen Soviet influence in her Empire, or for that matter erode or reinforce Europe's division.

The Council for Mutual Economic Assistance, comprising the USSR, Poland, the GDR, Hungary, Czechoslovakia, Romania and Bulgaria, was founded in 1949 as a diplomatic counterweight to the Organisation for European Economic Cooperation (OEEC) and as a multilateral forum for containing the effects of Titoism. Beyond this, it had little economic importance and did not function as a multilateral institution in any proper sense of the term. Each East European Communist Party pursued at Soviet behest an autarkic model of economic development in faithful imitation of Stalinist practice. Cooperation and coordination between the different East European economies was discouraged, whereas relations with the USSR were regulated through joint stock companies under effective Soviet control, along with bilateral treaties which imposed steep delivery requirements and unfavourable terms of trade upon Soviet clients. Stalin's frank priority was the post-war reconstruction of the USSR, not the winning over of Eastern Europe to the Soviet cause. It is estimated that the value of resources transferred by the Soviet Union out of Eastern Europe between 1945–1956 approximated the value of Marshall Plan aid transferred by the United States into Western Europe during the same period.[30] In spite of the social dislocation and consumer privations that Stalinism wrought, it must be said that the ruthless and heavy-handed mobilisation of human and economic resources did succeed in achieving impressive growth rates and in building up a solid industrial infrastructure in what, with the exceptions of Germany and Czechoslovakia, had been largely agrarian countries.[31]

But even before the uprisings of 1956, Nikita Khrushchev had come to the conclusion that such overt exploitation could no longer be justified in the interests of the USSR or the development of the region as a whole. As he put it to the 1955 Congress of the Czechoslovakian Communist Party, 'socialist ideas can only triumph when the peoples of Eastern Europe eat like the delegates at this Congress'.[32] From the mid-1950s, much of the Stalinist edifice was dismantled: in 1954 the joint stock companies were abolished; in 1958 pricing mechanisms were recast to East European advantage. The Khrushchev years also marked the beginning of a process dear to the hearts of Soviet clients: participation in the making of CMEA policy. On the other hand, these clients managed to resist a process equally dear to the hearts of Khrushchev and his successors: integration. Despite the conclusion of a Comprehensive Programme of Integration in 1971, progress on this front has been pitiful in many respects compared with that achieved within the EEC.[33]

Why this socialist commonwealth should be less integrated economically than a Europe of free capitalist states is worth pondering. As with many other puzzles, the caprices of politics have reinforced the legacy of history. The jealousies and animosities which characterised the countries of Eastern Europe before the Second World War never developed into a coherent aspiration towards supranationalism on the West European pattern. Instead, the fragmentation of the region was cleverly seized upon by Stalin, who pursued a policy of divide and rule even after the hostile nation states of Eastern Europe were transformed into People's Democracies of his own making. To this day, the sinews of this commonwealth are the transmission belts between Moscow and individual East European capitals, not multilateral institutions. Much as Moscow may, on grounds of economic sense, welcome a more integrated economic policy, she would not wish to see institutional machinery set up which compromised these discrete, private channels of manipulation and control. Much as the regimes of Eastern Europe might welcome the support of their neighbours against Moscow – and hence a strengthening of such multilateral forums – they also view their neighbours as rival claimants to Moscow's favour and are wary of giving them a greater voice in their own affairs. Each vassal is the captive of its own ambivalence: wishing to be less subordinate but also more favoured. Thus, neither Moscow nor its charges has a clear interest in multilateral institutions which truly flourish.

The real essence of integration, however, is not multilateralism, but the creation of a supranational economy. Ironically, the autarkic model foisted by Stalin on his charges in the 1940s to maintain their isolation from one another and their dependency upon him had, by the 1960s, become something of a rallying point for regimes who in no other sphere enjoyed any tangible measure of independence. In overall terms, there would be impressive savings (particularly in energy costs) if each produced only what each produced best. But in particular terms (and in terms of '*kto-kovo*'), economic rationality means that Romania must exchange its hard-earned capacity to manufacture steel or munitions for a dependence on the GDR, Czechoslovakia and the USSR which costs more in freedom and leverage than it saves in economic resources. Moreover, for a regime like Ceaucescu's economic nationalism (and the corollary of anti-minority policies at home) may constitute the only real bond between state and society.[34] To return to our comparison with the EEC, economic integration in the western half of Europe is seen as the first tentative step to a political union which many pay lip service to and few take seriously. In Eastern Europe, economic integration is the last step in a process of political extinction which all take seriously and which most dread.

By the time of Nikita Khrushchev's fall, at any event, the regimes of Eastern Europe had managed to alter the terms of trade within CMEA to their benefit. Plentiful raw materials and assured markets had improved living standards along with popular forbearance. These very palliatives, however, had also removed the stimulants to technical progress. Moreover, by the mid-1960s, many economists had identified central planning – the engine of economic construction in the 1950s – as the culprit which stood in the way of modernisation and efficiency in production. Inflexibilities in resource allocation, quality deficiencies, waste, gaps and imbalances in production were becoming both more widespread and more critical as economies diversified and grew more complex.[35] It was the identification of these problems by Czechoslovak economists as early as 1962 which launched the country onto its reformist course years before Alexander Dubček appeared on the scene.

In the context of these difficulties, the onset of East–West *détente* from 1969–70 and the provision of Western technology and credits looked like deliverance itself. For many CMEA countries, but particularly for Gierek's Poland, Western largesse became the linchpin of a strategy to refurbish the economy and reorientate production towards competitive industries capable of holding their own in world markets. By the decade's end, such expectations were exposed as pipedreams, and the strategies behind them had collapsed in ruins. The reversal of fortunes can be attributed to two factors.

The more obvious of the two was the four-fold increase in the world market price of crude oil in 1974–75 and the additional three-fold increase between 1979–1981. When added to the tapering off of Soviet oil production, the 'opportunity cost' to the USSR of energy exports to CMEA as opposed to the West has altered appreciably – all the more so once these exports became vital for financing her own grain and equipment imports from the West. In response, the USSR negotiated a new price formula for its exports to CMEA countries and imposed ceilings on deliveries. Where prices were once held constant for five year periods, from 1976 onwards they have been revised annually on the basis of a five-year moving average of world market prices. In that year the price paid by CMEA countries per tonne of Soviet oil doubled, and the price has risen substantially since. Whilst the USSR has been less successful than she had hoped in restricting export volume, CMEA countries nonetheless find themselves obliged to purchase ever larger volumes of fuel from non-CMEA countries at market clearing prices.

Secondly, the dividends realised from Western equipment imports have been disappointing. The reasons for disappointment in Eastern Europe differ little from those encountered in the Soviet Union. But the consequences have been different, because East European expectations have been higher than Soviet ones. The USSR sought growth and productivity improvements from her Western equipment programme; her East European partners have, in addition, looked to Western acquisitions to boost their own competitiveness in Western markets. For them this has been a matter of necessity. Whilst the resource-rich USSR could finance equipment imports through raw material exports, resource-poor Eastern Europe has been forced to finance her imports through Western loans, which can only be repaid out of future export performance.[36] Even had the post-1974 recession not dampened OECD demand for CMEA produce, this would have been an unusually risky strategy. Western technology has been made to assume a burden which it cannot fairly be expected to carry.

It is striking under these circumstances that no CMEA government used Western technology as a spearhead for economic reform. Rather than grasp the potential of combining the two, CMEA governments acted on the assumption that the simple purchase of advanced technologies would in itself enable them to compete with advanced economies. (The folly of the supposition is shown by the fact that, by 1980, the machinery which Poland had acquired in 1970 had become obsolete.)[37] Hungary is less the exception to this rule than is often made out. The 'New Economic Mechanism', instituted in 1968 *before* the great sea change in East–West relations, was in fact frustrated by conservative rear-guard actions between 1972–78, the years of greatest Western largesse.[38] By comparison, the GDR would seem to be the example which proves the rule: in 1972, her efficient semi-private enterprises, accounting for 12 per cent of net material product (and much of her economic vitality), were socialised.[39] Poland, whose capital equipment programme was the most ambitious in the Bloc, instituted a *re-centralising* reform in 1975.[40]

Whilst all have suffered, the variations from country to country are not insignificant. On balance, the GDR, Hungary and Bulgaria have shown themselves able to absorb Western technology and put it to effective use; but Romania and, more conspicuously, Poland, have combined high levels of dependency with ill-conceived investment decisions and the worst adaptation problems of the kind discussed in Chapter 2. Czechoslovakia – for many years the most reformist of the CMEA countries – was treated as a pariah by Western governments after the collapse of the Prague Spring and, under the watchful 'normalisation' of Gustav Husak's leadership, has preferred economic stagnation to the sort of risks and reforms which could start Western trade flowing again. By her insulation, Czechoslovakia has bought herself a safe and steady misery and avoided the worst buffetings of the decade: only 27.3 per cent of the country's trade was conducted outside the Bloc in 1978, compared with over 50 per cent in the case of Poland and Romania.[41]

The exponential growth in CMEA debt (from $6 billion in 1970 to $58.3 billion in 1981)[42] has come as a shock to borrower and lender alike. The reality we are left with today is that:

> Eastern Europe must try to maintain satisfactory levels of exports to the West in order to service its debt obligations there and satisfy domestic needs at a time when it is being pressed to greatly increase exports of manufactures to the Soviet Union to pay for increasingly costly imports.[43]

This would appear to be a herculean task for the relatively efficient and an impossible one for everyone else. If the GDR, with a 1982 debt service ratio of 63 per cent faces an uphill struggle, Poland, with a debt service ratio of 191 per cent has put herself beyond the point of return as an OECD trading partner for at least a decade.[44] The obstacles in the path of de-centralising reforms will be as difficult to negotiate in Eastern Europe as in the USSR, and in present conditions it is possible that the patient would not survive the cure. The present squeeze on resources of all kinds in CMEA economies has made them so 'taut' that the short-term consequences of market-orientated measures (inflation, unemployment) are bound to be sharp and widespread. Only Hungary – a superbly well managed economy by CMEA standards – has taken the plunge and restored direction to its flagging reform efforts (a direct consequence of which has been a 79 per cent increase in the consumer price index between 1979–1983).[45] Elsewhere, the burden of proof will be on reformists to show that their policies offer the best chance of avoiding internal instability.

For much of the Bloc, then, the solution may be to opt for the devil they know. For the time being, most have done so. Increased reliance on Moscow may now hold out much prospect of improvement in growth, productivity or living standards, but intra-bloc trade at least offers assured markets, predictable performance benchmarks, and the kind of long-term trading agreements which are the staple of central planning and of central planners.[46] Thus far, austerity measures implemented within CMEA have produced a modicum of economic restructuring away from Western-orientated production, along with fuel conservation and an improvement in economic growth (from 1.7 per cent in 1981 to 3.8 per cent in 1983).[47] The burden of debt has also declined slightly from its peak 1981 levels, but as a result of curtailed imports rather than increased hard currency earnings. It would be difficult to say at this juncture whether this upturn, achieved at considerable social cost, can be sustained.

If it cannot, there may be political as well as economic implications to reckon with. Low growth rates pose particular dangers for centrally planned economies. Given the generic distortions of output and distribution in such systems, high rates of growth are required to keep the overall machinery lubricated and in motion. (Growth rates of two per cent per annum, as experienced by Poland after 1978, do not produce EEC-style sluggishness, but breakdowns in deliveries and services and factories unable to function for want of necessary parts.) Secondly, growth in centrally planned economies has been the fruit of high levels of investment (30 per cent in some cases), which would be politically unacceptable in most liberal democracies because of effects on consumption.[48] Communist regimes, by pointing at high growth rates, could once justify this squeeze on the consumer as an investment for the future, but with low rates of growth it becomes obvious to a work force that gratification is being denied rather than simply deferred.

For the moment, the answer to the question posed at the start of this section is that economic *détente* between East and West has underscored the distinctiveness of the Eastern Bloc and, on balance, reinforced its cohesiveness. There does remain a balance to be struck. Politically orthodox Bulgaria may have more of an interest in good trading relations with the West than was once the case; but would she alter anything by way of political character, or even policy, to this end? Far more striking in the changed atmosphere of the 1980s is the case of Romania. The first country to chart an independent course in the economic sphere (and the only one to make an issue of doing so) startled all and sundry in May 1980 with calls for more effective joint planning within CMEA. Needless to say, all CMEA countries have now emerged as enthusiasts for greater integration in the realm of energy production and distribution. In sum, the results of this decade of lost hopes have been:

(1) Increased leverage for the USSR.
(2) The failure of politically motivated Western trade policies to produce their intended results. Those countries most disposed to economic cooperation with the West are those which have found trade most beneficial (Hungary, Bulgaria), not those which have been treated most generously (Romania), let alone those who have become most trade dependent (Poland). Where trade has proved damaging for whatever reason, the result has been estrangement. By the same token, politically motivated trade denials (Czechoslovakia 1968, Poland post-1981) have only provided incentives to remain in the fold. In Eastern Europe, policy has driven trade relations; trade has not been an end in itself. Moreover, the political interests of Eastern Europe's regimes have taken precedence over the economic interests of society.[49]
(3) None of this is to assert that trade cannot produce political benefit, or that policies cannot be fashioned to this end. What can be asserted is that the benefits are too marginal to warrant the attention the subject has aroused – and the undertaking too complex to be able to withstand the political controversy surrounding it in the West.

HAS EASTERN EUROPE BECOME AN ECONOMIC LIABILITY TO THE USSR?

So much for Eastern Europe's interests, but what of Soviet interests? Oil shocks, resource scarcities and the provision of raw material subsidies to CMEA countries are bound to prompt this question. Many today consider the CMEA to be a drain on the Soviet economy: to the tune of $80 billion between 1971–80 if the calculations of one recent study are to be accepted.[50] Considering that the Soviet economy is not in the pink of health in its own right, it only makes sense to ask whether the burden will remain affordable – and, indeed, whether hard economic facts will not drive the USSR to reassess the wisdom of maintaining anything so extravagant as a Socialist Commonwealth in her present circumstances.

Clear as it is that the terms of intra-bloc trade deteriorated from the USSR's point of view in the 1970s, the issue deserves to be treated with a degree of wariness. Whilst some now characterise the relationship as grossly unfavourable, others draw the line at calling it less favourable.

For at least three reasons, the controversy is unlikely to be resolved to everyone's satisfaction.

(1) *Comparing socialist caviar with capitalist strawberries*: Much of the argument turns on one's pricing assumptions. Goods imported by the USSR within CMEA are priced in soft (unconvertible) currencies, purchased through barter arrangements on negotiated terms which may be inconsistent from planning period to planning period and from one supplier to the next. Goods imported from OECD countries have an international market value; when barter arrangements are not an option, they must be purchased out of scarce hard currency earnings. In short, there is both an absence of meaningful prices within CMEA and of equivalent pricing mechanisms between one trading bloc and another. The difficulties of comparing OECD and CMEA products multiplies these confusions.

For all this, primary products exported outside the Bloc have (at least since 1974) been worth more in dollar terms than they have within it; but given the way goods are priced within it, this may mean less than meets the eye. In dollar terms Soviet oil may purchase 25 per cent more in West Germany than in Czechoslovakia, but this does not necessarily mean that it will purchase 25 per cent more railway switching gear or pipelaying equipment. Even if, as one study asserts, the USSR pays 50 per cent more for CMEA products than these products command in world markets, the question which matters to the Soviet Union is what she would have to pay for equivalent *Western* equipment (and how she would pay for it). By making some plausible alterations to pricing comparisons, one analyst, Paul Marer, found that the $80 billion in implicit subsidy contracted to a $14 billion subsidy.[51]

(2) *Intangible economic benefits*: A large proportion of CMEA imports may have no suitable or readily equivalent Western substitute: the CMEA product mix is geared to the requirements of Soviet industry which, as we have noted in Chapter 2, may differ from those in the West; and Western equipment may require complementary products or particular production methods which can be introduced into the Soviet environment only at some effort and expense. A second intangible benefit of trade with CMEA is the compatability of planning and procedures: long-term trading deals and a constant product mix.

(3) *Political benefits*: CMEA affords yet another institution for strengthening the Soviet voice in the internal policy deliberations of East Europe states. In addition to according the USSR a forceful say in the economic priorities of its trading partners, there is evidence that Soviet leverage over terms of trade has produced specific concessions in the foreign policy arena (such as material and diplomatic support for Soviet policy in South Yemen and Angola; offset costs for Soviet forces deployed in the Warsaw Pact).[52] These, to be sure, are mainly political benefits, but they accrue to the USSR by virtue of her economic relations.

If Soviet economic relations with her East European clients have become a 'net liability' to the USSR in any meaningful sense, this must mean that, on balance the USSR would be better off without them, and not simply that they involve a net expenditure. (A car represents a net expenditure, but the life it allows one to lead would be more expensive, perhaps impossible, if one did not have it). Far from encouraging a re-examination of Soviet stakes in the area, a full rendering of costs (and, most important, alternatives) is likely to confirm them: if, as one expert has calculated, the 'cost of the Soviet Empire' amounts to some 14 per cent of Soviet defence expenditure, it could be the most cost effective component of the Soviet defence effort. The most that can be said with confidence is that the relationship is a liability for the population of Eastern Europe.

LIMITED SOVEREIGNTY: DEFENCE

Of all the ways in which Eastern Europe contributes to Soviet power, its military contribution as a buffer and forward base for military deployment and intelligence gathering may be the most important to her. The Warsaw Treaty Organisation is arguable the least important. The USSR's essential military needs are met by a network of bilateral treaties entered into years before the founding of the WTO: treaties which have been supplemented by similar agreements between the individual East European countries and renewed at periodic intervals over the years. At the time of Stalin's death, some two years before the signing of the Treaty, the USSR's European clients maintained at Soviet behest over 1.5 million men under arms (half again as many as today), supervised by thousands of Soviet 'advisers' posted down to regimental level and, particularly in Hungary and Poland, by Soviet Commanders in East European uniform.

Like the CMEA, the WTO was established more in furtherance of political objectives than in its self-declared ones. Much as the CMEA emerged as a diplomatic counterweight to the Marshal Plan and OEEC, the Warsaw Pact arose principally in response to the entry of the Federal Republic of Germany into NATO. There were additional factors. Stalin's death and the first limited signs of *détente* and disengagement in Europe (notably the Austrian State Treaty of 1955) heightened the importance of national sensibilities in Eastern Europe and made it advantageous to erect a multilateral fig leaf of collective security over the USSR's continued domination of her neighbours. By 1955 it could also be seen that Stalin's direction of East Europe military policy was not only onerous, but wasteful. The increasing impact of nuclear weapons upon military planning and the perceived importance of maintaining the integrity of a future theatre of operations made it necessary to standardise doctrine and training and, hence, provide a more integrated forum for addressing joint military requirements. Out of all these considerations a Pact of Mutual Assistance and Unified Command was concluded in Warsaw on 14 May 1955.[53]

From the start, therefore, the Pact did fulfil a limited military purpose. Nonetheless, in its original form, the Pact's principal political organ, the Political Consultative Committee (PKK) and its principal military organ, the Joint High Command (OK OVS) functioned as 'dignified' rather than 'efficient' institutions. (The Joint High Command, in fact, was located in the headquarters of the Soviet General Staff, its effective operational master.) Despite a few institutional innovations in 1961 and a number of others in 1969, the WTO remains an administrative, training and (only since 1969) a consultative organisation. The Pact's supreme political organ, the PKK, although required to meet twice yearly, did not meet once during the Bloc's most crisis prone periods: 1956–58, nor between March 1968 and March 1969. The Combined Staff (OVS) of the Joint High Command, the supreme military organ, to this day appears to be without rear services (logistics) directorates, an operations department and a transport department. In peacetime, Warsaw Pact forces are responsible either to their national commanders or, in particular cases (such as Air Defence Troops) are commanded by direct command-and-control link to Moscow, by-passing national military staffs and Warsaw Pact HQ. In wartime, according to Marshal Sokolovskiy:

Operational units, including armed forces of different socialist countries, can be created to conduct joint operations in military theatres. The command of these units can be assigned to the Supreme High Command of the Soviet Armed Forces, with representation of the Supreme High Commands of the allied countries.[54]

True to this description, the Joint High Command played no part in the Hungarian intervention of 1956, commanded by Army General P. I. Batov of the Soviet Ground Forces; nor in the invasion of Czechoslavakia in 1968, which was carried out with the participation of other Pact forces. These were duly assembled, exercised and put in readiness by the Commander-in-Chief of the Combined Armed Forces, Marshal I. I. Yakubovskiy, but at the decisive moment transferred to a forward command post of the Soviet High Command in Legnica, Poland, under the C.-in-C. of the Soviet Ground Forces, Army General I. G. Pavlovskiy.[55]

Reliability and Subordination

Of 87 divisions deployed in peacetime on the territories of WTO states, only 31 are in the order of battle of the Soviet Armed Forces.[56] Given the increased emphasis in Soviet military planning upon unreinforced attack by forward deployed units, the quality and reliability of the non-Soviet military establishments is clearly of some significance. Of particular importance amongst the six non-Soviet WTO members are the three 'Northern Tier' states of the GDR, Poland and Czechoslovakia. Not only are they the most significant in terms of population, industrial capacity and military capability; it is on the reliability of these countries in war that Soviet access to NATO's vital Central Region depends. On the face of it, the greatest guarantor of the reliability of the WTO armed forces might appear to be the 550 000–600 000 Soviet forces stationed on their national territories, the overwhelming majority of which (20 divisions) are deployed in the GDR (Group Soviet Forces Germany, HQ Zossen–Wunsdorf). Additionally, two divisions are deployed in Poland (Northern Group of Forces, HQ Legnice), five in Czechoslovakia (Central Group of Forces, HQ Milovice) and four in Hungary (Southern Group of Forces, HQ Budapest). Two divisions stationed in Romania were withdrawn in 1958; no forces are stationed in Bulgaria.[57] Forces from these garrisons have been used on several occasions against recalcitrant East European governments, though with the one exception of the limited uprising in the GDR in 1953, they have always been extensively reinforced from the Western Military Districts of the USSR. (In 1956, Batov's invasion force consisted of 120 000 troops drawn from the Ukraine, as well as Romania and Hungary itself; 23 Soviet divisions along with one Polish, one East German, one Hungarian division and one Bulgarian brigade – over 400 000 men – were funnelled into Czechoslovakia on the night of 20–21 August 1968).[58] In each case, the 'temporary' augmentation of the Soviet garrison became a permanent feature of the new status quo: after 1956 the Soviet Union doubled the strength of its Hungarian garrison from two divisions to four; the Central Group of Forces owes its entire existence to the events of the Prague Spring. These examples no doubt demonstrate the ability of Soviet forces to act as the *ultima ratio* of Socialist order in Eastern Europe; their presence, however, does not guarantee that the armed forces of Eastern Europe will perform reliably or effectively. To these ends, other means have been developed over the years, most assiduously in the three Northern Tier states. They are summarised below:

(1) *Command and Advisory organs of the Warsaw Treaty Organisation*: these bodies, six in number, with joint Soviet–East European representation, provide a continual reading of the pulse and a barometer of trouble and difficulty.[59]

(2) *The Soviet 'Military Representative' and Military Mission housed each capital*: in peacetime the Military Representative is a significant participant in the making of national defence policy. In time of war, it is possible that he would become the 'representative' of *Stavka* (the Supreme High Command) and transmit orders directly from Moscow.[60]

(3) *Vetting of senior commanders*: the appointments of Defence Minister, CGS, and Head of the Chief Political Directorate are at least confirmed and may be initiated by Moscow. It is likely that some form of vetting extends to divisional (one-star) level.[61]

(4) *KGB operatives in Eastern Europe*: believed not only to monitor, but direct, the activities of East European counter-intelligence and security personnel operating within the WTO armed forces.[62]

(5) *Informal command ties*: higher military education, specialised training, exchanges and visits. A two-year course in a Soviet General Staff academy appears to be mandatory for those taking up senior appointment. Although training in the USSR is no

guarantee of greater affinity, the scope of professional ties between Soviet officers and their opposite numbers is considerable. The Soviet High Command thus possesses considerable knowledge of local conditions and personnel, as well as a further channel of influence by-passing the national command structure. It is reported that Polish commanders have lobbied directly with Moscow for higher defence spending in Poland.[63]

(6) *Operational controls*: over communications and command and control centres (an ingredient of success in Poland in 1980–81); over fuel and munitions stocks (run down before the invasions of Hungary and Czechoslovakia). In non-Soviet ground forces the largest formation is the division (13 000 men). Each in wartime would be slotted alongside Soviet divisions into Army and Frontal commands. This in itself makes independent operations most unlikely.[64]

Of equal importance are controls exercised by national Party leaderships and their respective security organs:

(1) *Politically reliable officers*: 97 per cent of whom are Party members in the GDR, 85 per cent in Poland. As their relationship to the USSR is well known, the armed forces tend to attract the more pro-Soviet elements of the population. Privileges as well as the habits of professionalism maintain distance between the officer and society.

(2) *Chief Political Directorate*: functioning like its Soviet counterpart with the status of a Central Committee Department as well as a division of the Ministry of Defence, this organisation is responsible for the political reliability of the armed forces, political education, and censorship of military publications. Its head, a Deputy Defence Minister, is directly responsible to the Politburo. Its officers, 'political deputies', posted down to battalion or company level, constitute a separate chain of command, supplying personnel evaluations on a confidential basis to their political superiors.

(3) *The unit Party organisation*: responsible for convening regular meetings of Party members and conducting 'criticism and self-criticism' of officers irrespective of military rank.

(4) *The 'security channel'*: a third chain of command. In the GDR, officers of 'Administration 2000' of the State Security Service (SSD) function as an arm of the Ministry of State Security (MfS)

in the armed forces. Its officers, often unknown to military commanders, wear the uniform of the service to which they are assigned. In Poland, the security channel functions as a distinct division within the Ministry of National Defence.[65]

It would be a bold person who claimed that these channels and mechanisms, comprehensive as they are, provide a guarantee of reliability in all contingencies. Controls are a sign of wariness, not confidence. Before concluding this discussion, it would be instructive to explore the performance of the Polish People's Army in what can only be considered a most exceptional contingency.

Poland's Army and Poland's Crisis

The move of the Polish People's Army (LWP) onto the political stage in 1981 is by Communist norms unorthodox, but by Polish norms explicable. The LWP has been the most political of the East European Warsaw Pact armies, because it is in Poland that the political authorities have been weakest. It must also be said of Poland that its society has been most resistant to Communist influence and, that of all East European countries, the gap between the state and its society has been greatest. The LWP has not gone out of its way to act as the arbiter of events; rather, it has had this role thrust upon it by Party factionalism and weakness. Throughout the post-1956 period, this most political of armies in this least reliable of countries has evolved into the greatest repository of Soviet trust. Poland has always been the first non-Soviet WTO state to receive front line equipment from the USSR. By comparison with the high levels of contacts prevailing generally between Warsaw Pact military élites, the closeness of ties between the LWP and the Soviet Armed Forces has been impressive. Finally, the Polish General Staff has not only seen itself as an avid 'consumer' of Soviet military doctrine, but a contributor as well, which has authored its own innovations with Soviet endorsement.

This paradoxical state of affairs is the result of three factors: due, first, to the large number of commanders who, like Wojciech Jaruzelski, trace their formative upbringing to the USSR and the Soviet organised First and Second Polish Armies of the Second World War; secondly, to the social ostracism suffered by officers belonging to an army which prides itself on being the guardian of Communist as well as national values. Young, professional graduates of higher educational establishments, they command high status in the state and low status in society. (A 1958 survey of secondary school leavers ranked the occupation of Army officer as 21st in desirability – behind office worker.) Finally, Poland's geographical position binds her military professionals to the USSR by a common perception of threat. As a country astride the USSR's main artery of communications, Poland risks becoming the target of nuclear attack in any conflict, and resistance to Soviet forces would turn the country into a battleground. Polish officers, therefore, have felt an instinctive affinity for Warsaw Pact 'coalition warfare' doctrine, with its emphasis on pre-emption, surprise and defeating the enemy on his own territory in the shortest possible time. The interest of some countries, notably Romania, in a doctrine of 'national defence' has not impressed Poland's military commanders any more than it has their Soviet patrons.[66]

For all the enigmas in his career, Wojciech Jaruzelski seems himself to be the prototype of what the USSR has come to trust most in the Polish military outlook. Trained in Ryazan during the wartime years, he returned to Poland to rise to divisional command (Major-General) at the age of 33. Although a regular officer, he was appointed in 1960 to head the Chief Political Directorate, a sensitive time to be moved into so critical a position. Over the next 13 years the Polish People's Army was buffeted by instability in the Party, internal divisions amongst its own commanders and unrest in society at large. Jaruzelski's rise to power seemed quite unaffected by the ebbs and flows of factional politics:

> 1960: Appointed Head of the Chief Political Directorate
> 1964: Elected to the Central Committee of the PZPR
> 1965: Appointed Chief of the General Staff
> 1968: Appointed Minister of National Defence
> 1970: Elected a candidate member of PZPR Politburo
> 1971: Elected a full member of the Politburo

From the time that General Marian Spychalski was replaced as Minister of National Defence in 1968, the Army steadily lost its appeal as a vehicle for intrigue. By 1973 Jaruzelski's men, all with similar career profiles to his own, were in place.[67] Jaruzelski's career suggests that a strong Party background is not always the surest path of Soviet favour (witness Gomulka). Trust is conferred upon known quantities with a record of loyalty to Soviet interests. In highly politicised systems, it is often the non-political professional who is the man to watch (witness Albert Speer).

By several accounts, Jaruzelski and the officer corps as a whole resented the fact that the LWP was called upon to assist the militia (police) in quelling the shipyard riots in 1970. To this day, we do not know why élite internal security units of the KBW were not used for this purpose, as they were in 1956. It is even possible that the attempt to use the LWP for internal repression played a part in Gomulka's downfall. The restrictions governing such use which were shortly to be articulated by Gierek, Gomulka's successor, provide the charter and justification for the military's conduct in 1981:

> The Party will always remember that [deployment of the PPA in civil unrest] can only result from an extraordinary situation, jeopardizing . . . the foundations of the socialist system, a situation where all the paths of political action have been exhausted, where an obvious enemy has raised his hand against the achievements of the working people.[68]

On the evidence, military intervention was perceived as a serious contingency in early 1981. The following months were characterised by intensive joint consultations, preparation and, true to Soviet traditions, an orchestrated strategy of deception and concealment. In early 1981 under the cloak of exercises, Polish military units in strategic locations were redeployed and their barracks occupied by internal security troops. In separate exercises, Polish and Soviet Signals Troops established a comprehensive communications net separate from existing military and civilian channels.[69]

Throughout these first months it appears that Jaruzelski supported First Secretary Kania's efforts to achieve a political solution. In Leninist terms, however, a political solution does not imply a compromise solution; in Kania's own words, its object was to 'kill counterrevolution in the egg'.[70] With the unsatisfactory outcome of the July Congress of the Polish United Workers' Party (PZPR) this hope was dashed. It was probably then that a military solution was firmly decided upon and additional measures taken. Whether or not, as some allege, food supplies were deliberately run down by the authorities, by autumn there was plausible reason enough to deploy troops to urban and rural areas to assist in food distribution and 'relieve bottlenecks'. In October, conscripts about to be released had their tours of duty extended: a step which, overnight, increased the size of the armed forces by 25 per cent. In the midst of these activities, Jaruzelski continued to conduct his negotiations with the representative of society, but now as part of an exercise in *maskirovka* rather than persuasion. The first hours of Martial Law themselves demonstrated that the regime had learnt the lessons of the 1970s. Whilst control over the country was transfered to the armed forces, the task of directly confronting recalcitrant elements of the population was largely entrusted to the ZOMO (motorised militia) ORMO (militia reserve) and élite security units.[71]

The dramatic and yet equivocal significance of Martial Law – restoring Socialist order whilst forestalling Soviet invasion – has allowed Jaruzelski to remain faithful, at least in appearance, to the ideal of the PPA as guardian of both national and Communist values. Throughout his career, he has been an enigma rather than a player. A Soviet product rather than Soviet puppet, it would most likely require a Soviet invasion to establish conclusively whether his loyalty to the USSR is his overriding one. For the moment, there is little reason to doubt that he regards 'internationalism' as the highest form of patriotism.

WOULD THEY FIGHT?

The armed forces of the non-Soviet Warsaw Pact countries have become professional military establishments, trained and equipped to high standards, and commanded by dedicated and reliable officers. Whilst the evident unpopularity of Soviet domination in Eastern Europe may be thought to make such forces reliable in wartime for garrison and rear duties only, the fact is that these military forces are trained and equipped for a war with NATO, according to an offensive doctrine of 'coalition warfare', designed to place them from the start of hostilities onto an 'external front'.

Any appraisal of the performance of these forces in war must be hedged by uncertainty. The proliferation of controls, for example, is bound to add to the problems of command, control and communication in wartime (as on a small scale it did in Czechoslovakia in 1968), but how much so it would be hard to say. Moreover, from the Soviet point of view, there are known deficiencies and dangers. Romania's 'military deviation' and her emphatic rejection of coalition warfare in preference to a doctrine of 'national defence' puts her reliability very much in doubt. The continued consequences of the Prague spring and its depletions of the Czech officer corps, if no threat to the reliability of the Czechoslovakian People's Army, are bound to have implications for its effectiveness. The long-term effects of martial law on the morale of the Polish People's Army remain to be seen, but the demoralisation which we now know to have followed in the wake of the 1970 disorders are an inauspicious clue to the LWP's health today. Whatever the LWP's future reliability, the weight of its contribution is bound to suffer if 'emergency' becomes a permanent state of affairs in the country. Already it is possible that the GDR's National People's Army (NVA) has displaced the LWP as the chief recipient of Soviet favour (and of advanced front-line equipment).

Against these factors, one must recall that in the Northern Tier countries (Poland, GDR, Czechoslovakia), the earmarking of the national armed forces for participation in the cutting edge of offensive war against NATO has rarely provoked dissent from their commanders. The *esprit de corps* of these forces has increased in proportion to their professionalism and the degree to which this professionalism is recognised by their Soviet patrons. Frustration where it does exist (for example, in the LWP) arises where such recognition and trust are withheld: in the fact that equipment, whilst advanced, is not of the very latest, in continued Soviet resistance to independent national frontal commands, and so on. Eastern Europe's Warsaw Pact commanders and their subordinates employ their initiative to press for more challenging roles, not less.

Professional and motivated as officers and commanders of the national armed forces might be, what of conscripts? In wartime, pitted against an enemy in front and otherwise surrounded by Soviet divisions, it is difficult to see how conscripts would have any choice other than to fight as people do when their lives are at stake. The realities of modern war do not brook much choice in the matter. Individual desertions are bound to take place, and perhaps in considerable numbers, on the rare occasion where the opportunity presents itself. But the high-tech (not to speak of nuclear) battlefield is unlikely to present this opportunity often; and it is difficult to envisage the 'opting out' of any sizeable formations in light of the integrated command structure and dependency upon Soviet communications nets. As one former NVA officer put it, 'in terms of the purely military situation, when the commander stands behind me, I have to shoot. In terms of the psychological aspect of it, the soldier on the other side is a soldier of the *Bundeswehr*. That is of no interest to me at all'.

It must also be understood that the national armed forces have not been designed with civil unrest in mind, and that their employment in civil disturbance has been exceptional. In the GDR, the

Wachsregimente of the Ministry of State Security (MfS) and the *Bereitschaftspolizei* of the Ministry of the Interior have more than sufficed for this purpose, enabling the NVA to keep its hands clean and its morale high. In Czechoslovakia, the People's Militia perform a similar role. In the NSWP countries as a whole, there are over 150 000 border troops and other specialist units under Ministry of Interior or Ministry of Security control, not to speak of designated Soviet formations, which can be expected to provide security of the rear areas if war breaks out.

On reflection, it would seem that garrison and police duties amongst the civil population would be the worst role possible for NSWP armies in time of war. Not only would such tasks be unsuited to their skills, but any involvement in public order functions under wartime conditions would be most likely to magnify whatever conflicts of loyalty exist and bring out discontent. The Soviets are unlikely to depend upon NSWP formations to ensure the safety of their own rear and lines of communications.

These realities, pressures and residual doubts probably add rather than detract from Soviet incentives to favour a pre-emptive, lightning offensive, carried out with a minimum of warning and consultation. Given the horrific effects which are bound to be visited upon the countries of Eastern Europe in the event of a prolonged conflict, the Warsaw Pact's non-Soviet members may be disinclined to resist the logic of Soviet strategy.

4 Army and Party, War and Politics

> Russian monarchs traditionally considered the military, that is, the army, the closest to their heart among all branches of the administration. It is precisely there that they considered themselves the most competent and consequently interfered in all spheres of its life.
>
> P. A. Zayonchkovskiy

> Socialism is against violence being used on nations. That is indisputable. But socialism is in general against violence being used on people. However, no one except a Christian anarchist or a Tolstoyan has ever deduced from this that socialism is against *revolutionary* violence.
>
> V. I. Lenin

When Sir Winston Churchill characterised the Soviet Union as 'a mystery wrapped inside a riddle inside an enigma', he might have added, 'and so she would wish to appear'. No past rival of Western democracies, not even Hitler's Germany, has presented to the outside world a more opaque image of policy-making than has the USSR, and in no sphere does this arouse greater confusion and concern than defence policy. Soviet success in turning secrecy into a prime purpose of government is likely for the foreseeable future to deprive the West of any definitive understanding of these matters, and leave even knowledgeable *émigrés* in dispute about them.

Western students divide roughly into those who find continuing enlightenment in the concept of 'totalitarianism' and an increasing number for whom the 'ideological and organisational unity' and 'monolithic cohesion' of the CPSU rule book is, if not Potemkin facade, of declining utility to the real stuff of policy-making. The substance of much present-day Western analysis consists of frictions between contending interests and élites, accommodations, bargains and rear guard actions: a political set-up in which the Armed Forces

General Staff, with its prestige and professional competence, is seen to have acquired a firm foothold. Many Western scholars have thus been prepared to speculate that the military programmes of the 1970s represented Brezhnev's way of 'buying off' the Armed Forces establishment for supporting East–West *détente*. On the morrow of Marshal Ogarkov's removal as Chief of the General Staff, Western press comment included speculation that his policy stance had come to obstruct the reassessment of arms control and East–West policy sought by the leadership; according to one respected newspaper, senior Western military attachés in Moscow were tipped by Soviet army officers that the Kremlin blamed Ogarkov for the disasters of the SS-20 deployment and the shooting down of the Korean airliner off Sakhalin Island.[1] One former American Secretary of State has gone so far as to characterise the Armed Forces as an institution 'operating entirely outside Party control'. If, as one *émigré* scholar has put it, it is 'inexcusable' to think in this way – to suppose that in the USSR the General Staff has autonomy over major weapons programmes, generals have 'policies' or obstruct them, and that the Armed Forces must be 'bought off' by Parties leaders – then, the 'inexcusable' has become commonplace.[2]

Formally, there is little ambiguity about the mechanism of policy and the place of the Armed Forces in it. The Party leads; it is not led. Like full-time Party officials, military officers with Party membership are bound by the norms of 'democratic centralism': freedom of discussion until decision is taken, accountability of lower organs to higher, 'strict Party discipline and subordination of the minority to the majority'. Moreover, '[a]ll manifestations of factionalism and group activity are incompatible with Marxist–Leninist Party principles, and with Party membership.[3] These norms are rendered specific to the military sphere. As stated in the Soviet Officers Handbook, 'present-day military doctrine is the political policy of the Party and Soviet government in the military field'.[4] The General Staff is, in the words of one expert, 'a highly centralised and powerful organisation with immense prestige'; but it is not a law unto itself.[5] This understanding of Party–military relations is stated in all authoritative military publications, such as the *Soviet Military Encyclopedia*, and reiterated in every military establishment in the USSR.

Thus at least it is written. Nevertheless, many wonder whether any administratively sophisticated society can be run on this basis. Two criticisms of this orthodoxy have emerged. One spotlights the increasing scope and sophistication of the General Staff and its proliferation of Directorates beyond the strict confines of military–technical policy. Now 14 in number, these include External Relations, Main Foreign Military Assistance, International Negotiations, and Main Directorate for Warsaw Pact Affairs. The Party, whilst retaining its formal prerogatives in the military–security field is in fact alleged to be increasingly hostage to the technical competence of what Frunze once called the 'brain of the Army': an organisation with the expertise as well as the staff support to determine the framework within which issues are discussed and decisions taken.[6] The second critique is more authentically pluralistic. Even the General Staff is but one actor in an increasingly complex policy process. The formulation of defence policy cannot be divorced from economic and foreign policy issues of concern to a wide assortment of bureaucratic interests: Ministry of Foreign Affairs, KGB, Council of Ministers – not to speak of a variety of State Committees, Institutes of the Academy of Sciences, *Gosplan* and the Military–Industrial Commission. In this reading of things, each bureaucracy has become adept at marking out turf and advancing its own interests, whilst the Party–State leadership finds itself in the position of 'broker' between contending interests and 'constituencies'.[7]

There is, perhaps, useful corrective in this perspective to the polemical overkill which characterises the 'totalitarian' school at its most unyielding. Yet there is a distinctly Western flavour to many of these arguments, along with their implication that de-centralised decision-making on the Western (or at least American) pattern corresponds with the requirements of modern society. Perhaps we had best ask ourselves why our political institutions function as they do. Is it because of 'administrative rationality' or for more noble and more cynical reasons? The noble reason is that 'the defence of democracy is democracy', not efficiency or competence. We adhere to our procedures to ensure liberty and representation: if these procedures produce good policy as well, that is a bonus. The cynical reason is self-interest. Given the constitutional separation of powers in the American system, for example, 'adversary politics' is a matter of survival for politicians. It is 'rational' because of the incentives and penalties of a particular system of government. But it has been deleterious to good decision-making on more than one occasion. It is not insignificant that private economic institutions rarely take Western political institutions as their model for decision-making.[8]

The ethos which has shaped the Soviet system, and the self-interest which sustains it, could not be more different. It is a system with sights set on a preordained 'historical' task, to be realised by 'scientific' means. In T. H. Rigby's distinction, government in the USSR is a 'task achieving' organisation, not a 'rule enforcing' organisation. As in any military enterprise, the goal is 'victory', to be pursued through proven and tested principles. The task of leaders is not representation, but command; their requirements are coordination, discipline and action on the basis of timely and accurate advice. Society, as Frunze put it, is to be 'militarised', as is the vocabulary of life.[9] The defence of any practice is its ability to promote the end; all means are instrumental. Criticism and discussion must, therefore, be solicited and encouraged, but never for its own sake, and only up to the point that decision is taken. Discussion, too, must be organised, not spontaneous.

These are not empty words and phrases, but principles given powerful institutional sanction. Accountability of lower organs to higher is enforced by appointment and disciplinary prerogatives vested in higher Party organs (the system of *nomenklatura*), with power of reprimand and removal. The Secretariat of the Central Committee is given the teeth to do what it is meant to do: appoint, control access to decision-makers and supervise the policy which the Politburo formulates. This state of affairs neither eliminates bureaucratic in-fighting nor does it rid the system of mid-ranking officials attached to interests and issues and skilled at maintaining their prerogatives. But the ethos of the system and the reality of democratic centralism lend to its political machinations a different flavour and bias from that found in any system plausibly termed pluralistic. In any system, 'constituencies' are those one speaks for and accounts to. In the USSR accountability flows upwards, not to bureaucratic colleagues, let alone to those below. Khrushchev in removing Marshal Zhukov did not have to confront 'the military interest': by manipulating Zhukov's own subordinates, Marshals Malinovskiy and Golikov, into position, he was able to turn Zhukov's bureaucratic *confrères* into his own allies.[10] Power to appoint is power to divide and rule. Those who fight rear guard actions in the USSR do so in the calculation and gamble that they are useful enough to higher-ups to be screened and protected. But the USSR is without outside élites and pressure groups, let alone an electorate, to rescue the careers of those who push their luck too far. It is a society with few sanctuaries when protectors turn upon you.

THE ARMY AND THE PARTY

The paradox at the heart of Party–military relations is that the Soviet Armed Forces are simultaneously the most privileged organisation in society and the most assiduously controlled. 'Probably no other organisation in the Soviet Union is as watched and courted by the Party leadership as the Soviet Armed Forces'.[11] The Party has gone out of its way to foster the image of the Armed Forces as guardian of the motherland, school of patriotism and the expression of those qualities that the Party seeks to promote in *homo Sovieticus*. As the demographic balance shifts against the Russian population, the Armed Forces have also become a critical instrument of what Westerners often term 'national integration', but what the Soviet authorities, with their characteristic mixture of Socialist and Great Russian chauvinism, prefer to term 'the elimination of national conceit'.

Much of this is part and parcel of the regime's religion of struggle. It is also the complement to the extraordinary cult of the Great Patriotic War, whose presence in Soviet society it is impossible to escape: in the Ural Military District, where no German soldier set foot, there are 675 monuments to war dead.[12]

The militarisation of the Soviet economy, baffling to an outsider, is complemented by a militarisation in the sphere of education. The 1967 law of military service, which reduced the term of conscription from three years to two (and from four years to three in the Navy and Air Forces) at the same time set in motion the expansion of an already considerable effort at pre-conscription and para-military training: between 1967–1972 the budget of the para-military training organisation, DOSAAF (Voluntary Society for Assistance to the Army, Air Force and Navy) underwent a threefold increase. Officer education itself is presently carried on by about 140 officer commissioning middle and higher military schools, offering four to five year courses and conferring higher education degrees: fully 13 per cent of all higher education in the USSR is now carried out in the military sector. In addition, 23 military academies and institutes offering three-year courses at staff college level and above, are entitled to confer the highest academic degrees in the USSR. Migration of Generals and Admirals in and out of the civilian sector (such as defence industry, universities and institutes of the Academy of Sciences) is a routine practice.[13]

Thus, it is not a question *either* of military concerns *or* of civilian control. The military priority makes itself felt throughout society, but 'military goals and values are important because of the values of civilians'.[14] The inordinately elaborate system of controls visited upon the Armed Forces is designed to produce a fusion of military professionalism and Party mindedness.

Nevertheless, these controls also betray a mistrust of the military's potential. Paradoxically, the help rendered to the Party by the Armed Forces during political crises has reminded the party of this potential and invariably produced a redoubled effort to ensure military dependence upon Party and State. Following Stalin's death in 1953, a divided Party leadership had reason to feel apprehensive as well as grateful for military support in the struggle against Beria and the MVD–MGB apparatus. By Khrushchev's own account, Beria was arrested on the instruction of the Politburo by Marshal Zhukov and Colonel-General Moskalenko, Commander of the Moscow Air Defence District.[15] Marshal Konev is believed to have presided at his trial.[16] Shortly thereafter, the Party took the unusual step of assembling the Armed Forces heads and demanding their collective endorsement of Beria's arrest – a step which might not have been judged necessary by a leadership firmly in the saddle and truly confident of its prerogatives.[17] Four years later, Khrushchev again enlisted the support of Marshal Zhukov (now Defence Minister) in his struggle against the Stalinist rear guard (the so-called 'anti-Party group'), which had produced a Politburo majority in favour of his resignation. Thanks to Zhukov, critical Khrushchev supporters were brought to Moscow in time for the Central Committee meeting which then overturned the Politburo's verdict.[18] Thus, whilst in 1953 Armed Forces support was invoked by the Party, in 1957 it might be said that it had been enlisted by a faction, albeit the First Secretary's own. Nevertheless, Zhukov's intervention had been solicited by the highest authority; by Party norms no impropriety had been committed (as would have been so had Khrushchev's colleagues been acting in accordance with Central Committee sentiment). And yet for a moment Zhukov was thrust into the position of kingmaker. The precedent was not a comfortable one, not even for Khrushchev himself, and three months later, Zhukov was dismissed by the man he had saved. There was doubtless a second reason for his dismissal. As Minister of Defence between 1955 and 1957, Zhukov had vigorously pressed for a less onerous regime of Party supervision and for greater General Staff autonomy in military–technical matters.[19] Then as now, such aspirations were unacceptable to the Party leadership. Zhukov's display of loyalty did not soften Party thinking on the subject, and the Chief Political Directorate (the political arm of the Armed Forces) stood its ground with greater determination after Zhukov's intervention than it had before.

Finally, we turn to the hostility of the Armed Forces to Khrushchev in his final years, and the question of his downfall in October 1964. Khrushchev's remodelling of the Armed Forces – his restructuring of individual services, reductions in the size of the Ground Forces, and the enforced retirement of field grade officers – provoked controversy throughout the services and a considerable degree of resentment.[20] The more significant fact, however, is the Khrushchev's Politburo colleagues took issue with the ham-fisted and idiosyncratic character of these measures – and, in addition, faulted Khrushchev for similar methods in agriculture and in the restructuring of the Party–State bureaucracies. It is these colleagues who deposed Khrushchev, not the Armed Forces. Had they stood behind him, the General Staff would have suppressed the dissension within its own ranks.[21] In view of the consternation which Khrushchev's policies aroused in the Party itself, his eventual deposition is less striking than the degree to which he succeeded in imposing his will on a reluctant leadership. Finally, it is worth recalling that the remodelling of the Armed Forces continued after Khrushchev's demise (though on a less frenzied and 'hare-brained' basis).[22]

What is one to make of Party–military relations in this period, and what do they imply for the present? In the very special circumstances of the 1950s and early 1960s, with leadership in transition, de-Stalinisation in motion, and the 'Revolution in Military Affairs' under way, it was only natural that Army–Party relations showed signs of buffeting and stress. To be sure, similar fault lines were present between the Party and State bureaucracies and at the top of the Party pyramid itself.[23] But at no point in these years did the Armed Forces take the initiative in resolving political disputes and at no stage was it brought into intrigue by discontented Party factions (exempting, of course, the First Secretary himself). Whilst line officers pressed for greater autonomy on their own operational turf, these years actually witnessed a strengthening of the prerogatives of political officers, not their diminution. Party etiquette, then as now, excludes the Armed Forces from the Party's internal squabbles. Prudence, *amour propre* and 'reason of state' give the Party an interest in maintaining its pre-eminence in both the military–technical and military–political realms. Even – perhaps especially – in times of intra-Party strife, attempts by the General Staff to widen its prerogatives produce a closing of Party ranks. The will to enforce its *diktat* is present. Four mechanisms of control – little changed in their essentials since the founding of the Red Army – provide the means.

These mechanisms comprise:

(1) The Communist Party organisations at unit and subunit level, and their standing committees and bureaux. Through regular meetings, they institute the practice of 'criticism and self-criticism' and enforce Party discipline, irrespective of military rank.[24]

(2) The system of Military Councils, extending from the Chief Military Council of the Ministry of Defence to the Military Councils at Military District level and below. Composed of military commanders, political officers and Party officials, their concerns range over the entire panoply of administrative and disciplinary functions, as well as troop control and civil–military relations in the USSR's 16 Military Districts. Through these bodies regional and local Party Secretaries are afforded direct input into military policy and confront military commanders as equals.[25]

(3) The Third Chief Directorate of the Committee for State Security (KGB). These officers, who wear the uniform of the service to which they are assigned and are not accountable to the Ministry of Defence, are often unknown to their nominal military superiors. Responsible for security functions in the Armed Forces, they provide an independent check on the loyalty of officers and, like their parent organisation, act as 'eyes of the Party'. (They are not to be confused with the GRU, whose function is military intelligence.)[26]

(4) Most important is GlavPU, the Chief Political Directorate of the Soviet Army and Navy, at one and the same time an organ of the Ministry of Defence and of the Central Committee, where it has departmental status. Its head since 1962, Army General A. A. Yepishev*, a former KGB officer, has direct access to the General Secretary of the CPSU and probably works closely with Central Committee Secretaries responsible for ideology and cadres. The 'political officer' (*zampolit*), posted down to company level, is the linchpin of political control, charged with overseeing military–political training and the enforcement of Party policy. Despite the principle of 'unity of command', the recommendations submitted by the political officer on fitness and promotion through the

---

* Since July 1985, Colonel-General Aleksey Lizichev.

Directorate's confidential channels provide him with real prerogatives over the 'real' officers who surround him. The military–technical qualifications of GlavPU officers has vastly improved since the 1950s. The Chief Political Directorate also possesses its own military academy (the Lenin Military–Political Academy) and journal (*Communist of the Armed Forces*).[27] According to John Dziak, a specialist in the US Department of Defense,

An examination of the general tone of [military–political publications] reveals that these political officers are among the most vocal proponents of the so-called hawkish positions that mistakenly are atributed to professional line officers by many Western observers. Such interpretations tend to infer that the military are pushing assertive and dangerous arms policies on a somewhat hesitant Party leadership. Yet . . . such concepts as 'quantitative and qualitative superiority', 'nuclear war as a continuation of politics' and 'victory in a nuclear war' are as much a feature, if not more so, of the political–military literature of the [Chief Political Directorate] as they are of the journals and books which are more clearly military. In fact, it is difficult simply to categorize works as either 'political' or 'military' since they are frequently authored by 'collectives' of writers from both sides of the house.[28]

One of the most crucial prerogatives of the Directorate is the control of *all* military publications and the articles which appear in them. On some testimony drafts must also be submitted to the KGB and the Central Committee's Propaganda Department as well.[29]

INSTITUTIONS AND POLICY-MAKING

A more structured, rationalised and institutional approach to policy making has become the hallmark of the Soviet political system since Khrushchev's enforced retirement. This institutional development has strengthened those features of the system which foster a community of political–military interest at policy-making levels. Over the years, the expansion in the size and competence of the Party's control apparatus has more than kept pace with the growth of the General Staff, and the proliferation of in-house staff supporting Politburo and Secretariat members has been a noteworthy aspect of the process. In the military sphere, the most impressive innovation has been the Council of

Defence (*Sovyet Oborony*), the supreme policy-making organ in security policy, but for the Politburo itself. The linear descendant of the wartime State Defence Committee (GKO) – and, indeed, of Lenin's Council of Workers and Peasants' Defence – it seems to be a much revamped and strengthened version of its immediate predecessor of the Khrushchev years, the Supreme Military Council (not to be confused with the Chief Military Council of the MoD, whose task is the narrower one of leadership of the Armed Forces. In wartime it would become the *Stavka*, HQ of the Supreme High Command, whereas the Defence Council would be transformed into the GKO). Writing as late as 1971, John Erickson could still pinpoint a widespread frustration with the absence of a clear C.-in-C. of the Armed Forces and with military policy imposed by *ad hoc* command changes rather than clear and systematic institutional mechanisms and procedures.[30] These have now been put in place, whilst in July 1976 Brezhnev was publicly identified as Chairman of this body as well as C.-in-C. The Defence Council is therefore the body which joins together the top political and military leadership. Its existence is one factor obviating Party–military showdowns of the kind which characterised the Khrushchev era, and the formulation and supervision of security policy is therefore placed on a more structured and continuous basis.[31]

The main task of the Defence Council is to formulate an annual, as well as a five-year, 'plan of military construction' (*Plan Voennogo Stroitel'stva*) in accordance with the Party's reading of political and strategic interests. Because Soviet military doctrine regards strategy, deployments, force structures and defence production as integrated and interdependent activities, the Defence Council is concerned not only with a finite number of economic tasks, but with the scrutiny and elaboration of all aspects of defence policy. Formulation of the plan seems to be the result of a complex but highly structured process of consultations and meetings carried out over a six month period, and culminating in the ratification of the plan by the full Politburo. Drafting of the plan begins long before the completion of the stipulated planning period and is brought into balance with the socio-economic plan for the country as a whole. The point of the exercise is to ensure: (1) that all actors properly concerned with defence participate in the process, and that views and considerations bearing upon defence are ventilated; and (2) that a unified, coherent plan emerges on the basis of Soviet military doctrine.[32]

But for confirming the General Secretary's position as Chairman, the full membership of the Defence Council has never been identified in open Soviet sources. Not surprisingly, Western sources are far from unanimous about its composition, its staffing arrangements and its procedures. By all accounts, the Defence Council is dominated by civilians. Apart from the General Secretary, all authorities known to the author count amongst its permanent members the Minister of Defence (Marshal Sergey Sokolov) and the Chairman of the Council of Ministers (Nikolay Ryzhkov). The CGS (Marshal S. F. Akhromeyev) is thought to head the Council's Secretariat (and by most, but not all accounts, has the status of a permanent member). Whether or not the Chairman of the KGB (Victor Chebrikov), the Minister of Foreign Affairs (Eduard Shevardnadze) and the senior Party Secretary for defence production (until July 1985 Grigori Romanov),* have the formal status of permanent members, it is clear that they are in regular attendance, as very likely are the Chairman of the MVD (Vitaliy Fedorchuk) and the Chairman of the Military–Industrial Commission (Leonid Smirnov). Others from the Party and ministerial apparatus are brought in as needed.[33]

Opinion divides further over staffing arrangements: in the opinion of most authorities a function performed almost exclusively by the General Staff. However, Sergei Freidzon, a former Soviet planner, identifies two additional standing bodies: an Institution of Permanent Advisers (19 civilians, as well as the CGS and two First Deputy Defence Ministers) and a larger Institution of Permanent Consultants (50 per cent military, 50 per cent civilian), both of which are in harness to the Council for much of the year. Freidzon also attributes impressive functions of analysis and arbitration to the personal chancellories of Politburo members, which are thought to comprise individuals who are highly expert in their particular fields. (By way of contrast, the Social Science institutes of the USSR Academy of Sciences, such as IMEMO and Arbatov's Institute of the USA and Canada, are thought to have a minor input into the policy-making process). If for all this, the General Staff still performs the lion's share of staff work, this is hardly evidence that the military lead the Party by the nose in defence matters, either over details or essentials. If the Politburo were unhappy with these arrangements, it would change them.[34]

In sum, there are seven conclusions to be drawn from this survey:

(1) The Party is arbiter, not broker. Differing tendencies are brought within the Party fold and taken up by the leadership; otherwise, they perish.

* Now Lev Zaykov.

(2) Democratic centralism concentrates power in a few hands and at the end of the day produces decision rather than fudging. Defence policy is *policy*, not what participants in pluralist systems term 'policy outcome' (a compromise between different policies). The 'scientific' ethos of the Party and the 'unity, integrity and coordination' of military doctrine reinforce this imperative. Military build-up must therefore be understood as a component of the policy of East–West *détente*, not a concession to those who opposed it.

(3) The USSR is not so monolithic as to be devoid of élite politics. Differing views have an opportunity to arise and make themselves felt – but there the similarity with Western politics end. Party discipline has bite. In the struggle to advance, outmanoeuvre rivals and be heard by superiors, factional loyalty (loyalty to one's patron) may take precedence over policy interest. There are many exceptions to this rule, but the exceptions usually apply to those who fail and the rule to those who succeed.

(4) If Ogarkov's demotion in September 1984 revealed anything beyond a straight-forward preference to utilise his skills more effectively, then punishment came not from losing an argument, but from breaking the rules – for carrying on arguments after being overruled and pressing for prerogatives in the military–technical and military–political areas which were not rightfully his.

(5) Policy in the USSR is not lightly changed by the top, not because of powerful 'interests' below, but because the scope of issues absorbed and integrated into defence planning and the exhaustiveness of the process militate against doing so. The strong silence which greeted Cyrus Vance on presenting Carter's arms proposals to the Politburo in 1977 reflected not only their radical nature, but their unfavourable content. If Vance had been able to convince 17 Politburo members that a far-reaching restructuring of strategic forces was in the Soviet interest, this would have become Soviet policy.

(6) In fact, and not just to all appearance, the Politburo was embarrassed by the KAL affair. There is no reason to suppose it or even the General Staff authorized the downing of flight 007: in all likelihood a routine decision of regional Air Defence command charged with prompt action in defence of Soviet frontiers. But there is no basis for deducing a calculated *attempt* to embarrass the leadership. Party controls would make this almost inconceivable in theory and extremely foolhardy in practice – with

certain disgrace, imprisonment, or even execution, of those officers involved. Punishment, by several indications swift and far-reaching, has been meted out for incompetence, not insubordination.

(7) For all the travails of the Soviet economic system, the policy-making structure is not in crisis. Democratic centralism is alive and well. As a principle aiming to combine hierarchy with participation, it may be cumbersome, but it is neither unworkable nor irrational. Whereas Americans have grown accustomed to participation at the cost of policy coherence, and Europeans to a more professional and collegial structure which risks shackling politicians to the imperatives of officials, the Soviet system at its best avoids both of these pitfalls. Typically it hinders 'real' participation: opinion, even where solicited, invariably has 'career implications'. In this process, 'society' seems neither to be represented nor consulted; in the military sphere, as in most others, the élite consults itself.

WAR: THE WHYS AND THE WHEREFORES

Any honest attempt to unfathom the Soviet view of war runs into a set of paradoxes. The USSR's commitment to Communism's expansion and triumph seems to co-exist with a psychology of threat and a view of herself as victim. The USSR's legacy of vulnerability has left an indelible mark; even in the new found era of military boldness and 'operational confidence', adversaries are always on the verge of undoing previous gains, military planners face 'harrowing choices and uncertainties'. Security means defence against all comers and contingencies; as such, it can only materialise when the world is purged of uncertainty. It is never achieved; it is never enough: military power is to be developed not just for security of the homeland, but for restraining Imperialism throughout the world. This too is security. Soviet military power is a vital factor in the 'world correlation of forces': as the Soviet Union grows stronger, progressive mankind benefits; as 'progress' advances, the Soviet Union becomes safer. This dualism, neither 'mere rhetoric' nor 'disinformation' is real enough and, as we have seen, the product of a coherent but dialectical system of thought. Amongst other things, it provides surprisingly clear answers to the questions: 'What role is war to play in policy? What is to be the peacetime function of the Soviet Armed Forces? How are the Armed Forces to perform their purpose in war?'

In one sense, war is alien to Marxist–Leninist thinking. War is the product of capitalism, its exploitive nature, its rivalries and its economic contradictions. Socialism, on the other hand, is not born out of armed conquest and aggrandisement, but economic development and the class consciousness it creates. Once this process is firmly under way, war becomes the Imperialist's way, and eventually their only way, of frustrating it.[35] Blinkered and self-serving as this picture may appear (it entirely ignores the gains which the USSR has achieved through war), it will be clear on reflection that what is meant by 'peace' is conflict without war: or, to invert these terms, 'a form of warfare which permits the settlement of unavoidable clashes between Socialism and Capitalism without having recourse to *general armed conflict*'[36] (author's italics). In *Pravda*'s words, 'the Marxist–Leninist concept of peaceful coexistence does in no way contain the pacifist-like promotion of peace'.[37]

In the nuclear age the maintenance of this threshold between conflict and war is a basic objective of Soviet policy. In the Third World in particular, but also in Europe, enormous attention is devoted to the socio-economic 'substructure' of society, and relations are cultivated with political actors across the whole spectrum of discontent. Even as the 'external functions' of the Soviet Armed Forces acquire real importance, the principal means upon which the USSR relies to influence change are what Westerners are accustomed to call 'other means': moral, political and material support furnished below the legal threshold of intervention, designed to encourage and revolutionise or at least influence and infiltrate. This contrasts with the tendency of the United States to pin its hopes on one faction, invariably the one in power, and put faith in military and economic aid to maintain stability. In time of crisis, the United States has more than once confronted the 'all or nothing' choice of military intervention or abandoning its client.[38]

The Soviet Union also considers the might of her Armed Forces (and in particular her nuclear arsenal) instrumental in this endeavour to make the world safe for ideological struggle. To both Western and Soviet thinkers, the advent of nuclear weapons represented a profound secular development in international relations and military science. To Leninists, however, it has been a development with profoundly asymmetrical effects. Far from foreshadowing greater moderation and comity in international relations, the 'revolution in military affairs' has had revolutionary implications in politics, because without war, imperialism cannot defend itself from history. As Khrushchev expressed it, 'We consider, proceeding from a Marxist–Leninist analysis of the present situation, that war is not inevitable today. And not because the imperialists have become wiser and kinder, but because they have become weaker, because the camp of peace is now strong as never before.'[39] With the creation of a formidable nuclear force, the Soviet homeland can no longer be held to ransom against Socialism's expansion; as the West's capacity for direct intervention is blunted by 'the growing might of the Socialist camp', the ideological struggle is not only safer, but free to intensify. As the Director of the CC International Department, Boris Ponomarev, has stated. 'The policy of peaceful coexistence . . . does not only hold back the revolutionary struggle, but promotes its upsurge. . . . the might of the Soviet Union serves as a decisive obstacle in the way of imperialist plans for unleashing a new world war.' In short, as nuclear capabilities have developed and conventional forces become more global in their reach, it becomes possible to extend the canopy protecting the forces of progress from the United States and others who would arrest natural and necessary changes. The outposts of Imperialism in the Third World are to be denied the support of Imperialist powers. This is what Dr Trofimenko calls 'the wider social logic of *détente*'.[40]

In 1974 Marshal A. A. Grechko, member of the Politburo and Minister of Defence, identified several 'external functions' for the Soviet Armed Forces in an important revision of Soviet military doctrine:

> At the present state the historic function of the Soviet Armed Forces is not restricted to their function in defending our Motherland and the other socialist countries. In its foreign policy activity the Soviet state purposefully opposes the export of counter-revolution and the policy of oppression, supports the national liberation struggle, and resolutely resists imperialists' aggression in whatever distant region of our planet it may appear.

This statement is a tribute not simply to new power projection capabilities, but to the nuclear build-up which preceded their appearance. The clear inference is that the nuclear threshold is becoming robust enough to withstand even fairly overt military challenges. 'At the present stage', even the projection of conventional military power 'in distant regions' may fall below the threshold of war. The direct intervention of Soviet and allied forces, as in Angola (within a year of Grechko's pronouncement) and, subsequently, in Ethiopia and Afghanistan, are not departures from the norms of peaceful coexistence. They are now considered to lie within them.

A third mechanism for maintaining the threshold between conflict and war is what is generally termed 'presence'. 'War', as Clausewitz said and as Lenin restated, 'is a tool of policy'. If diplomacy is to function in war, then the Armed Forces must also serve as a tool of policy in time and peace. A prime purpose of the Soviet Armed Forces is to move Soviet diplomacy along: to act as its complement or counterpoint, to intimidate, encourage and impress. In an exhaustive study the Brookings Institution identified 190 incidents between 1944 and 1979 where the armed forces of the USSR have been used as a political instrument in peacetime. Plentiful and noteworthy examples can be found in Europe itself, despite the absence of armed hostilities between East and West. Mobilisations, deployments and manoeuvres have been carried out over the years to discourage resistance to Communist takeover (Czechoslovakia 1948), to block undesired contacts with West Berlin (19 separate occasions, including two seizures of West Berlin territory), to apply pressure in negotiations (Norway and the Barents Sea), and to mask intentions in crisis (Czechoslovakia 1968 and Poland 1981). In all, 91 examples of this sort can be cited.[41]

Not insignificant in this respect has been the upsurge of Soviet submarine activity in Swedish and Norwegian waters from the time a Whisky class submarine ran aground in October 1981; in August 1984, these incursions were given a new twist by a Sukhoi fighter bomber's six minute escort of a Swedish airliner into Swedish airspace. There is no self-evident motivation for these intrusions, but three hypotheses present themselves:

(1) they reflect the growing military importance of the Nordic area to the Soviet Northern and Baltic fleets, just as the Northern Flank has attracted more attention in NATO defence planning;

(2) that, with inverted logic and subtlety, they are meant to reinforce the Soviet peace offensive in Europe by underscoring the controversial character of NATO modernisation programmes;

(3) that they are meant to demonstrate a new correlation of forces in the Nordic region, the obsolescence of traditional policies and the dangers to the Nordic states of clinging to them: in short, to distance Norway from her NATO allies and produce a pattern of Swedish alignment more attuned to Soviet requirements.

All three factors may be at work. Curiously, the Sukhoi intruded over an area of Swedish airspace recently stripped of its air defence cover, owing to defence cutbacks.[42] What better way of showing that in today's climes Sweden can no longer look after herself? Whatever the explanation, episodes of this nature make it plain that in peacetime the purpose of Soviet forces is not just to 'be there' but to be used.

In sum, the 'peaceful' purpose of the Soviet Armed Forces, as of Soviet policy, is to move history along in that part of the world where Socialism has not yet triumphed – by casting a shadow and making its presence felt, by posing as an 'obstacle' against Imperialism's interference with the 'revolutionary struggle'; by erecting a protecting canopy over change. One might be forgiven for saying that the purpose of all this power, conventional and nuclear, is deterrence: Soviet might is not to be used to strike the enemy but hold him back. But a curious deterrence this, which aims to restrain states only to unleash peoples, to intensify rather than mitigate conflict and make the world safe for revolution rather than order. The Soviet formulation is more exact: 'the active defence of peace', by which we can infer 'victory without war'.

On the other hand the USSR has been steeped in war, and so is Marxist–Leninist ideology. Engels may well rank as the nineteenth century's most significant military thinker after Clausewitz. By comparison with the intellectual patriarchs of Anglo-Saxon democracy, it is astounding to what degree the patron saints of Soviet Communism, Marx and Engels, made war – interstate and civil – an object of study and the raw materials for their theories and insights.[43] This only stands to reason. Socio-economic conditions may focus the mind, mobilise the troops and prime the mechanism of revolution, but revolution itself is an act of violence. As it is necessary for a Marxist to make a science of society, so too must he make a science of violence.

'Great questions in the life of a people', said Lenin, 'are decided only by force.' The Great Patriotic War is testimony enough to this, but the Soviet regime was conceived in war: an interstate war turned by pressure of events and conscious strategy into civil war.[44] In three years the newly formed Red Army not only managed to defeat three White armies and detachments of their foreign allies, but helped to impose Soviet control over the Muslim and Far Eastern borderlands, and Soviet dependencies in Tannu–Tuva, Outer Mongolia and Northern Iran. In 1920 it routed a Polish army to the suburbs of Warsaw and at the end of the following year launched an invasion of the Menshevik Republic of Georgia after its government had quelled an internal Bolshevik uprising.[45] Soviet arms were despatched to Communists in Finland, Bavaria, Berlin and northern Germany, and only a White offensive in 1919 prevented the despatch of troops to assist the fledgling Bolshevik regime of Béla Kun in Hungary.[46] With the conclusion of the Russian civil war, as prospects of revolution faded in Europe, Soviet arms were enlisted to deepen Imperialism's crisis on its own flanks. Material sufficient for three divisions was despatched to the nationalist regime of Mustafa Kemal Pasha in aid of his war against Greece, and the honeymoon period with Sun Yat-Sen and Chiang Kai-Shek (1922–27) saw the granting of more than $2 million in military aid to the Kuomintang: whilst Soviet advisers set up the Whampoa military academy and trained soldiers of the National Revolutionary Army in the field, Soviet troops performed limited combat missions, including aerial bombardment and reconnaissance. In the autumn of 1929 the USSR became the first state to break the illusions created by the Kellogg–Briand pact by unleashing its Special Far Eastern Army upon the Manchurian nationalists, who rashly thought they could put an end to Soviet control of the Chinese Eastern Railway.[47] By any reckoning, this represents an impressive decade of military adventure and achievement for a country recovering from war and famine and for a government which 'needed peace'.

Today's Soviet leaders are the products of a long-standing tradition of thinking about war and the use of force. For over two decades, the distinctiveness and integrity of this tradition have been obscured by the West's superior military power. But as nuclear parity becomes the first order of the day and conventional power projection capabilities expand, Soviet departures from Western attitudes in the realm of war become more visible and telling.[48]

To the Soviet mind, the 'bourgeois' view of war as a breakdown of normality, and peace as a time of cooperation and goodwill, is quixotic. War may not be an overall preference (Lenin was particularly fond of Clausewitz's remark that the aggressor would prefer to walk in and occupy a foreign territory peacefully rather than fight for it); but if it is the most effective way of achieving an aim, it is necessary to pursue it.[49] Lenin tirelessly reiterated Clausewitz's dictum, 'war is a tool of policy', not only to establish the subordination of generals to politicians, but to legitimise war and divest it of taboos. Even in the nuclear age, war must be approached as a purposeful political act. Today, Soviet strategists think not only about how to deter war, but about how war might occur: how to prepare, how to prevail, how to survive. The corollary to this perception of war is a distinctive attitude toward peace. When Clausewitz described war as 'the continuation of policy by other means', Lenin also understood this to mean that peace was the continuation of war by other means. Negotiation, is a form of struggle. As Lenin expressed it, 'concessions are a continuation of the war, but in a different sphere'.[50]

War is also understood to be a product of class society and of class antagonisms. In specific terms, we can take this to mean: that war remains a political act; that war must also be understood to be a revolutionising act; and, finally, that it thereby acquires the potential to become 'absolute war' – whose corollary is total victory and absolute peace. Let us take each of these points in turn.

In the first instance, Soviet military thinkers are not so ready as their modern Western counterparts to adopt the view that military imbalance is the primary cause of war. Nor are they convinced that 'equilibrium' or 'strategic stability' is a guarantee of peace. All things being equal, a favourable balance makes war less likely, but other things are not always equal, and they may be hard to ignore. War is the product of real antagonisms and a calculus of *political* opportunities and threats, not (to use John Erickson's term) 'military metaphysics'.[51] It is for this reason that Khrushchev's Cuba missile gamble was so outrageous. To be sure, Khrushchev committed the obvious folly of challenging his rival from a position of weakness; but the greater folly consisted of challenging the rival's vital interests from weakness. For the USSR in October 1962, retreat meant loss of face, for the United States, loss of primacy. It is obvious how this affair had to end: the political logic of the contest would have made the gamble 'adventurist' even if the military logic had not. Gambles of any kind are 'adventurist' to the Kremlin's way of thinking, and the episode only goes to show what a maverick figure Khrushchev was. The Brezhnev leadership, like Stalin's, showed a proper regard for the political stakes in interstate rivalry. It grasped – as one hopes its successors have – that the pressure to bring military potential to bear may be more important than military potential itself.[52] From this standpoint, Soviet intervention in Angola (1975–76) and the Horn of Africa (1978) was not 'adventurist': the United States was under strong political pressure *not* to bring its military potential to bear. Had it been otherwise, the USSR would not have acted.[53] But this political calculus will not always be a moderating influence. To be sure, the USSR will not initiate a war it knows it will lose, but as the political stakes mount, so will the risks she is prepared to take. One may dismiss too lightly Brezhnev's insistence to Dubček that he would have invaded

Czechoslovakia even at the cost of World War III.[54] War is a flesh and blood thing; even in Europe 'the military balance' does not purge it of its political character.

Even when not launched for a revolutionary purpose, war according to Marx has a revolutionary effect. 'War puts nations to the test; and just as Egyptian mummies crumbled into dust when exposed to the shock of air, war spells the sentence of death upon any social institution which has become calcified'.[55] This effect is doubtless less for victor than for vanquished, but the victor will not be spared it. In spite of victory, Britain's participation in two world wars accelerated social changes, altering both social attitudes and power relations. By 'militarising' their society in peacetime, the Soviet authorities aim to spare their society similar effects, ensure that the nation stands the test and that the Party will not be pronounced 'calcified' at the moment of truth. But, as a multinational state with restless minorities and a multinational empire with resentful subjects, the CPSU has reason to confront the prospect of major war with apprehension and a long war with dread.

But if war *should* occur, it will be war not only between states but between exploiter and exploited; there is thus real potential for war to turn into what Clausewitz called 'war of hatred'. It is noteworthy that Lenin – perhaps a more serious student of Clausewitz than any political leader produced by the West – chose to emphasise that aspect of his teaching which his 'bourgeois' disciples often ignore: *absolute* war and the tendency of violence to progress to extremes. 'We must hate – hatred is the basis of Communism' wrote Lenin in his pamphlet, 'Defeat of One's Own Government in Imperialist War'.[56] Today's Chief Political Directorate stresses in *interstate* war the need to 'strengthen the indoctrination of Soviet soldiers in a spirit of high vigilance and class hate for the Imperialist aggressors'.[57] In Sokolovskiy's seminal treaties, *Military Strategy*, a Third World War is classified as a 'revolutionary war' in which opposing classes as well as opposing states risk annihilation.[58]

If war is to be understood in these terms, any victory worthy of the name must produce the defeat of the opposing class as well as its state. Lenin was very conscious of Marx's warning that each war contains within it the seeds of a fresh war, an observation amply born out by the conflicts between France and Prussia–Germany in Marx's lifetime and in Lenin's time by the First World War. Victory, therefore, solves nothing unless it eliminates the source of the antagonism which produced war in the first place. Measured against this standard, the punitive sanctions imposed in 1919 by the Allied Powers against Imperial Germany, considered draconian by liberal opinion at the time, were superficial and lenient. Neither the exactions of the Versailles Treaty nor the creation of a republican form of government rooted out the nationalist old guard or revolutionised the German social structure; within 15 years, Germany was set on a course of *revanche*. These 'shackles of Versailles' are notably in contrast with the treatment meted out by the USSR to Poland and the three Baltic republics in 1939–40. According to Order No. 0054 of the Sovietised Lithuanian Ministry of the Interior, 14 categories of citizens were earmarked for 'elimination'. These included members of non-Communist political parties and students belonging to non-Communist student organisations; Mensheviks, Trotskyists and persons 'removed from the Communist Party'; military judges, state police, *gendarmerie* and prison staff; aristocrats, bankers, merchants, industrialists, hotel and restaurant proprietors; clergymen and persons active in parishes; persons who had travelled abroad; even Esperantists and philatelists. In all, some 700 000 out of a population of three million were thus eliminated.[59]

In Soviet eyes, these Leninist–Clauswitzian percepts have been born out by experience. In a very rich catalogue of experience, the Great Patriotic War may be worth the balance of the collection. From its outset, Operation Barbarossa assumed a class character, and it quickly escalated into a 'war of hatred'. The initial débâcle was as much a comment on the inability of society – as of the Red Army – to withstand the blow directed against it. Any explanation of what occurred in the war's opening stages in incomplete unless it includes the traumas of collectivisation, the purges, the antagonism of the peasantry and the strength of national sentiment in recently annexed regions – and any accounting for Vlasov's 'Russian Liberation Army' is impossible. The residues of this débâcle survive today in the regime's mistrust of its people, its dread of weakness, and its determination that an alternative ideology be given no chance to emerge in the country.

But recovery also brought its lessons, and these have not been lost on posterity either. In the broadest sense, the Soviet triumph was a confirmation of the strength of Socialist society: a triumph which would have proved impossible but for mass mobilisation, centralised control and the military–industrial recovery which they produced; but this triumph also required a regime capable of decisive action against its internal opponents. Western scholars may never discover how many Soviet citizens perished at the hands of Beria's NKVD troops (or

Abakhumov's SMERSH, operating in the enemy rear), but the scale and significance of their operations is well understood by those who command today's KGB Border Guards and MVD Internal Troops, along with the 'special detachments' of the KGB and Armed Forces.[60] Secondly, the fruits of this victory testify to war's revolutionising effects and its profound social repercussions. The establishment of the 'People's Democracies' not only changed the social map of Europe but promoted Socialism's prospects elsewhere. Victory advanced history, not just the security of the state. Thirdly in the eyes of the regime, victory demonstrates the superiority of Marxist ethics over the bourgeois variety. Measures and sacrifices which the bourgeois–liberal mind contemplates with horror are vindicated by the country's transformed position in the world and the protection afforded future generations against similar tragedies: in the scheme of history, timely, resolute action has been the greatest kindness.

There are also three lessons of particular import for the West. Thanks to the war, the USSR maintains an abiding respect for the traditional instruments of military power. Whether this perspective represents wisdom or only a curious anachronism today, it commands the scrutiny of a post-war generation in the West brought up to respect the limits of military power more than its utility. The messianic streak in the Communist and Great Russian makeup has also been reinforced by the USSR's ordeal and its triumph. Perhaps no society which had surmounted such a trial could consider itself as simply one power amongst many. The war confirmed the country's uniqueness: the USSR does not intend to be, in Trotsky's phrase, 'a country like any other'; nor, perhaps, could she be. Finally, the war accounts for the strategic orientation which we discuss in the following chapter. Not only does the USSR understand the reality of modern war; she has been given – perhaps uniquely – a glimpse into war as it might occur in future. Robert McNamara's measure for 'assured destruction' – 20 to 33 per cent loss of population, 50 to 70 per cent loss of industry – stand in some contrast to the USSR's wartime losses – 12 to 15 per cent loss of population and 50 per cent loss of production – particularly when we consider the time over which these losses took place.[61] But the difference is not stark enough to warrant definitive assertions that there would be 'no winners' in a nuclear war. If there is a standard of comparison for the USSR's wartime losses, it lies in McNamara's statistics, rather than in the experience of the Second World War. Perhaps most significantly of all, the Great Patriotic War demonstrates that society can endure the unspeakable and recover. The USSR need not, in that cavalier phrase, believe she could 'fight and win' a nuclear war to retain the orientation she has acquired: nuclear war is 'thinkable'; it is, in principle, survivable; and it must be conducted as *war* – which is to say, as a continuation of policy.[62]

To conclude, how warlike is the USSR today? To some appearances, unusually so. The USSR is by most standards a highly militarised society; in common with militarist movements of previous eras, the CPSU considers war to be the ultimate test for society and regards peace as a pre-war period. Thanks to the Clausewitzian unity of war and peace, a warlike spirit is infused into the most 'peace-loving' enterprises. No taboo or sentiment is allowed to enter into the question, 'when to choose peace, when to choose war?' For a state which defines 'security' as favourable *movement* in the 'world correlation of forces', peace is no more than war by other (conventional, non-violent) means.

But in another sense, the USSR is profoundly anti-militarist in character. War is to be respected, not romanticised. It is subordinate to policy, as generals are subordinate to those who make it. The Armed Forces have immense prestige, but no mystique; generals are masters of a trade, the Party has a monopoly on insight. In all of its dealings, the USSR adopts a strictly utilitarian approach: which tool of policy will be the most effective? Which will achieve the aim at the least risk and cost? Very often, war is a distinctly inappropriate tool for changing the correlation of forces. As Engels said, 'the victorious proletariat cannot impose its blessings upon a subject population by bayonets'. This admonition dampened Soviet enthusiasm for invading Poland in 1980–81 and inspired the search for other means. (But if the other means failed, then the military blow would have needed to be that much more massive).

'Everything', as Stalin said, 'should be determined by the correlation of forces'. This dictum should inspire comfort in the West. Even when the military balance is in her favour, the Soviet Union will maintain a healthy regard for the political stakes in East–West rivalry, as well as its social undercurrents; she will be aware that the ability to act effectively depends not only upon military trumps, but the psychological and moral intangibles of world politics. The long, drawn out battle between capitalism and Socialism is in the short and medium term a battle for influence and opinion. The USSR will not lightly seize a military opportunity that discredits her overall strategy. As events in Angola, Ethiopia and Grenada show, she will contrive, and indeed she will always prefer, to remain inside the conventions of international

law and put the onus on others for transgressing them. The invasion
of Afghanistan may be less an exception to this rule than many think.
Given the triumph of fundamentalist Islam in Iran and the strength of
similar forces in Afghanistan, many who saw no justification for Soviet
intervention in law in 1979 could see one on grounds of 'national
security': much as such justifications were offered for the flagrantly
illegal annexations of western Poland, the Baltic republics,
Bessarabia, northern Bukovina and parts of Finnish territory in
1939–40. Under different, 'unthreatening' conditions, these actions
would have sounded the alarm, and only the most incurable apologists
would have apologised for them. The perceptions of outsiders
therefore matter to the USSR. One should not expect her to resort to
military force 'whenever she can get away with it': if nothing else, she
needs to keep the world's 'useful idiots' in business.

But must we go so far as to say that the USSR will not resort to force
unless she *is* certain to get away with it? Much will depend on whether
she seeks to snatch a prize or forestall a threat. If the former, she would
wish to be very certain of the value of the prize and fully confident that
war will secure it. The revolutionising effects of war have been very
pronounced in Russian history; the USSR will not lightly embark on
war, because she knows that a setback to the state could present a peril
to the regime. However, states are often under pressure to act because
they fear history will turn against them if they do not. This was the case
with Imperial Germany in 1914. In the USSR's case, this pressure
would be especially great, as the regime's legitimacy demands that
history move in its favour. In conditions of threat, the question is not,
'are we certain to win?' but, 'which poses the greater risk, war or
peace'? It is not inconceivable that the USSR would exchange the
known perils of peace for the uncertainties of war if the perils of peace
were serious enough. This should worry the West. Military attack to
rescue political defeat is, by the Leninist calculus of reasoning,
eminently justifiable. Moreover, is the tables are to be turned, the
USSR will do so at a time of her choosing, rather than wait for the hour
of maximum danger to herself. To date, the USSR has never attacked
a stronger opponent, but it is not out of character for her to steal a
march on her equals when their guard is down.

Curiously, like Imperial Germany, the USSR confronts adversaries
on two fronts; like Germany's ally, Austria–Hungary, she possesses a
multi-national empire, sullen and subdued for the moment, but
periodically explosive. Empire may strengthen the hand of prudence,
because international humiliations tempt subjects to believe that their

Emperor has no clothes. Perhaps, then, adventure is best avoided. On the other hand, there is attraction for the USSR in removing problems at their source. The greatest stimulant to 'false hopes' in the Warsaw Pact countries is not NATO's hostility, but its existence; the permanence of Socialism in Eastern Europe may never be assured whilst the pre-eminence of the Soviet Union in all of Europe is in dispute. A *fuite en avant* might be tempting if it became feasible. On her other flank, would the USSR ever say of China what Germany once said of Russia: today I can afford to go to war, tomorrow I may not have that luxury? It may well be that she considers China to be as much of a long-term complication for the West as for herself: too capricious to make a dependable ally for NATO, too ambitious to fit into America's design for the Pacific, too shrewd to challenge vital Soviet interests. But if she faced a China intractably hostile, staunchly pro-American and modernising with a vengeance, would the USSR become more amenable or would she look for a means of escape? I do not pretend to answer the question by having posed it. There is nonetheless in this mixture of internal and external anxieties something which may bode trouble. The historian, Geoffrey Hudson, once wrote that 'no factor leads to war more ineluctably than the steady decline of relative power'. This may be especially true where the 'absurdity' of distinguishing foreign from internal policy is well understood, and where the movement of history is assigned such importance. The greatest danger to the West may be a USSR militarily strong and politically on the defensive: 'politics', as Lenin said, 'is the reason, war only the tool'. In time of crisis, the West will have reason to be grateful for its defences. But crisis – particularly one which puts the USSR's world position at risk – is something that the West should wish to avoid in the first place.

Finally, should war in fact come, there should be no illusion as to what sort of enemy one would face. War between East and West would not only be a contest between states and power blocs, but ways of life ('classes'): more likely to be 'a struggle for the very existence of the two opposing world-wide systems' than a limited engagement. Confronting equal or superior power, the USSR may be cautious, moderate, even conciliatory. But unchecked, she seeks total victory and final solutions. Magnanimity is not in the Leninist vocabulary.

5 The Changing Scope of Military Strategy

World war has ceased to be an inevitability. But this does not mean that nuclear war has ceased to be an instrument of politics, as is claimed by the overwhelming majority of representatives of pacifist, anti-war movements in the bourgeois world. This is a subjective judgement. . . . It . . . gives rise to illusions about the 'automatic destruction', the 'self-negation' of nuclear war, and dulls the vigilance of peoples.

> Major General A. S. Milovidov,
> Colonel V. G. Kozlov, ed.
> *The Philosophical Heritage of V. I. Lenin and Problems
> of Contemporary War* (1972)

When it comes to confronting the Soviet military challenge, strategic provincialism and its companion, strategic introversion, may prove more damaging to the West than Soviet power itself. 'The threat' has become, in Soviet parlance, 'well known', and well stereotyped: on their side, an economy locked into a scale and tempo of war production which we may lack the will or wherewithal to match; on our side, a technological edge eroding under pressure of rising capital costs and determined Soviet effort; and finally, the forfeiture of strategic and nuclear superiorities which historically have served as NATO's trumps against traditional Soviet strengths. Without doubt, the latter development represents a secular change in the strategic environment of profound importance. It would be both remarkable and alarming if that change alone did not bring greater scrutiny to bear on the perennial dilemmas of NATO strategy and of roles and responsibilities in the Alliance. Deterrence, being a political as well as a military enterprise, cannot profit if those who deter are in disarray. Nonetheless, the object of deterrence is to impress an opponent, not to make ourselves comfortable. It would be welcome indeed if security improved as consensus were widened and as the 'stresses and strains' of the Alliance diminished, but if 'deterrence' and 'reassurance' are related undertakings, it is worth reminding ourselves that they are also separate ones.[1]

Deterrence, to be precise, demands that we impress a *particular* opponent. The prevention of war will not depend on what 'any rational man' would do today, but on the judgements and predilections of a particular set of men at the point where they see war as the solution to their problems. This point is occasionally lost sight of in a strategic culture which has made a theology of deterrence – in the process investing it with a metaphysic distinct from, and perhaps at variance with, the business of conducting war itself. Ours is also a culture which favours models and concepts to the mundane and particular, and which is absorbed in technologies and capabilities – in what can be counted and quantified – over the wherefores and the how. We are less interested in the art of war than with its tools and paraphernalia.[2] The point made by Harriet and William Scott is well taken:

> In the nuclear age, some see the art of war and its study as irrelevant. Sophisticated weapons systems created by electronics, computers and high technology often are thought to be the sole means by which wars will be won or lost. . . . But as past wars show, advanced weapons and numbers of men are not the only criteria for success in a battle or a war. Victory may go to the side whose commanders have the better grasp of the art of war and skill in its application.[3]

To be sure, many in NATO defence establishments understand the art of war itself and address it with great expertise. This issue is what influence these considerations have on overall policy and whether hardware, deployment, strategy and training come together at the end of the day to produce cacophony or something more harmonious. Many who are not mesmerised by numbers consider other variables of warfare to be self-evidently in our favour – morale, motivation, training, initiative, leadership – but the critical variable may be coherence. Its realisation is bound to be an uphill struggle in a coalition of democracies, where force structures and deployments must reflect compromises between differing national perceptions and competing domestic requirements. The issue is not 'deterrence' *versus* 'defence' or 'war' *versus* 'policy' (two false distinctions); the issue is whether policy can triumph over politics. For all their liabilities, our opponents do not face this dilemma. The 'unified military doctrine' of the Warsaw Pact is purposeful activity writ large. Our opponents have put great effort into devising a type of war in which our skills would be irrelevant and our weaknesses decisive. In war as in diplomacy, the USSR is the disciple of Sun Tzu, who said: 'what is of supreme importance is to attack the enemy's strategy'. In war, the Warsaw Pact would exploit our lack of strategy.

Finally, the greatest handicap to preserving the peace may be the conviction that war is impossible. It would be highly undesirable in present conditions – but that is not the same thing. Soviet defence policy, like our own, aims to ensure that war does not occur. But it might, and the *first* purpose of the USSR's defence policy is to ensure that her armies will be victorious if it does. Indeed, the Soviets would say of war what Bismarck said of revolution: 'if there is to be a war, we would rather make it than suffer it'. At the critical point, the political decision to go to war will be influenced by military advice. Our deterrent will then need to persuade the opponent of the folly of the war *he* would fight. It is for this reason that an understanding of the Soviet art of war is of such importance.

THE PITFALLS OF 'THREAT ASSESSMENT'

'Threat' is a function of strategy and intention as much as it is of numbers and hardware. 'Capabilities', crudely understood as so many aircraft, so many tanks, do not reveal their own purpose or potential: there is room for argument in the most expert circles as to what an opponent might achieve with his forces and why they have arisen in the shape they have. Capabilities and 'military art' must therefore be looked at as a piece. The task of doing so is bedevilled by three factors:

(1) *Lead times*: in the USSR as elsewhere, it can take 10 to 15 years between the time a requirement is conceived and the time a system becomes operational. Where the unexpected truimphs over expectations, weapons may suffer mid-course 'kinks' in development, or end up being pressed into roles which no one had originally envisaged for them. When it comes to major systems designed for a long service life, redundant and exotic capabilities may work themselves in as insurance against an uncertain future. (The provision by Britain of Trident D5 illustrates the point well enough).[4] For reasons such as these, the threat one perceives may be more than the threat intended. And yet, it is also true (as the Falklands conflict demonstrated) that purpose-built systems can be turned to very different pursuits when the need presents itself.

Also, if capabilities can be stretched, given a surplus of capability, intentions can expand.

(2) *Doctrine*. Soviet military writings must be classed as an asset in the enterprise of threat assessment, not a hindrance. For all the complexities of the procurement process, weapons are built for a purpose, particularly in the USSR. Unfortunately, however, many are inclined to write off as rhetoric, service infighting and disinformation Soviet doctrinal statements. To be sure, these writings present traps for the unwary (and a larger dose of disinformation has crept into them in recent years, as Western analysts have come to pay more attention to them).[5] 'Reading the tea leaves' is not for everybody. The voluminous Soviet military press is a forum for controlled debates with their own coded meanings and subterranean rules; in retrospect, it may be clear what was only advocacy or trial balloon, but not necessarily on the day an assessment is sought. But retreat from these complexities into the home ground of capabilities and force balances enhances the likelihood of imposing our own assumptions upon Soviet policy and planning. The nuclear age has bred its own orthodoxies and conventions: safety through 'strategic stability', 'mutual assured destruction', and the assumptions that some weapons are only for 'deterrence' and that not all means of force are military usable. It is not sufficient to ask whether such assumptions 'are still valid' or what 'any rational person' would do faced with NATO's defences but to come to grips with a strategic culture whose salient themes are usable superiorities, counterforce, damage limitation and the maintainance of war waging capabilities under all conditions.[6] The peril of ignoring such things is brought out by the fact that (as Harriet and William Scott have noted), the three editions of Marshal Sokolovskiy's *Military Strategy* (1962, 1963, 1968), offered a far better guide to Soviet military trends than official United States defence posture statements throughout that decade.[7]

(3) *Geo-strategic asymmetries* whilst we have dwelt, sometimes remorselessly, on Marxist–Leninist ideology as a key to Soviet perceptions, the geo-political position of the Soviet Union is equally unique. In any explanation of Soviet military power and its application, geopolitics may come up trumps. The following characteristics amongst others have helped to shape a distinctive view of the objectives, techniques and material paraphernalia of war:

(a) the country's expanse; Moscow is as far from Vladivostok as it is from New York;

(b) a common frontier with 13 countries, unprotected for the most part by natural barriers;

(c) few outlets to the sea, and fewer which are secure;

(d) vast interior space, much of it flat and featureless;

(e) wide dispersal of resources, industry, population and administrative centres.[8]

It is these asymmetries to which we shall turn first.

THE USSR'S STRATEGIC PREDICAMENT AND OURS

This peculiar geographical situation – peculiar, that is, by European standards – has furnished the USSR with a set of security interests and 'needs' out of scale with those of most other countries. To many readers of this volume, Europe is a middle kingdom; to the USSR it is a flank. As Marshal Rotmistrov once put it, '[t]he Soviet Union is a continental power; it must maintain control of the European continent'.[9] Ideology articulates and magnifies what geography renders inescapable: a global perspective and a sense of the interconnectedness of events. When events of world importance take place, they are felt on Soviet borders. Thus the Soviet defence perimeter is always in other countries. The CMEA countries of Eastern Europe, Afghanistan, Mongolia, North Korea, and (formerly) China count as protective *glacis*; today, Scandinavia, Western Europe, the Middle East, the Gulf and Japan are earmarked as strategic space: areas whose quiescence is impeded by the existence of hostile military blocs, but in particular by the instrusion of American power. Whilst Soviet expansion since 1945 has in one sense been the tale of growing capabilities and ambitions, it has also been a story of how this defence perimeter has been gradually drawn out in response to the greater reach of the opponent's armed forces and their weapons systems.[10]

In this quest for physical invulnerability, geography conspires to cast the United States in the role of spoiler and turns her into the object of a good many phobias and fixations.[11] The United States is the one power which can put pressure on the USSR from all sides, and, but for Soviet intercontinental missiles, she is virtually immune to military pressure from the Soviet Union. (Before the 'Revolution in Military Affairs' brought ICBMs into the equation, she seemed invulnerable altogether.) With few means of egress into open ocean, the Soviet Navy has operated against a 'stacked deck'; heavily dependent, even in its modern, ocean-going form, on land-based air power to accomplish its minimal tasks against US carrier battle groups in peripheral seas.[12] Regional nuclear forces are, of necessity in Soviet eyes, 'strategic' forces: her own as well as those classed in the taxonomies of NATO as 'long range theatre' or 'intermediate' forces.[13] 'Flexible response' was for years seen as little more than a face lift of the doctrine of 'massive retaliation' it replaced: designed like the former to ensure that the American continent would be kept at arms length from a nuclear conflict and that 'punishment' would be confined to the territory of the Soviet Union and its allies.[14]

If the geography of Superpowers puts the USSR at a disadvantage with respect to her rival, the geography of alliances turns these asymmetries to better account. The United States is separated from her European allies by 3000 miles of ocean, and much further from the Gulf and Far East. The USSR is adjacent to her allies and enjoys relatively short lines of communication with those of her opponent and, indeed, to most of the strategic centres of the world. If 'encirclement' makes the 'decoupling' of America from her allies necessary, proximity makes it possible. Even at a time of acute military inferiority, the USSR possessed the ability to put pressure on American allies which the US could not easily counter; in conditions of global nuclear parity, her ability to do so may be especially problematic, even where vital interests are at stake. The implication of most Soviet military writings is an all too clear endorsement of what is often portrayed as an extreme view in the United States: that the credibility of American guarantees to NATO Europe hinges on military superiority and nothing less.[15] It is tempting to fantasise about how much simpler world politics would be if the USSR and the countries of North America swapped places.

What bedevils security confounds arms control asymmetries in geography, doctrine and weapons acquisition make it all too possible for one party's solution to become his opponent's next problem. The SS-20 missile, presently replacing IRBM and MRBM deployed some 25 years ago, is a case in point. The MIRVed configuration, mobility, range, accuracy and prompt launch characteristics of the systsm present NATO with a more serious array of threats than SS-4/5 represented when first deployed. 'Replacement' system it is, 'substitute' it is not. By the late 1970s NATO for the first time had to face the possibility of a counterforce strike against which there would be little warning, no defence and no plausible counter: European-based aircraft would have the greatest difficulty reaching even westernmost SS-20 bases and could not do so promptly; Poseidon C3 could not do so promplty or accurately; and Pershing IA, with its 740 km range, could not do so at all. Many would argue that NATO's paucity of counterforce systems diminishes pressure for a Soviet pre-emptive strike and contributes to its own safety. Fewer, however, would argue that NATO can afford to dispense with a survivable deterrent. On military and not 'merely' on political grounds, there was little likelihood that SS-20 would be ignored.[16]

In NATO's view, GLCM and Pershing II deployments could not generate equivalent anxieties for the Soviet Union. To be sure, they are relatively survivable and they diminish the SS-20 threat; they also provide a modest counterforce capability. But thanks to various limitations – speed (in the case of GLCM), range (40 per cent of SS-20s), number deployed (in the case of Pershing), and the absence of MIRVed warheads – there was no potential, in NATO's view, for deployment to 'ratchet up' the arms race. Indeed, NATO was shopping for a minimal solution.[17] Nevertheless, thanks to geography, the Soviets insist – and may well perceive – that it is GLCM and Pershing II which introduce a new element into the equation: in their eyes, a more devastating forward element of US strategic forces which enable the Soviet homeland to be attacked without adequate warning. 'Strategic' for the USSR is what can attack them. Pershing II may have no first strike potential in itself, but as the first wave in an all out US attack, it acquires a different significance. SS-20, which from its easternmost bases near Mongolia can strike even Israel, does not pose an analogous threat because it cannot strike the territory of the other Superpower.[18] However, the Soviet proposal to eliminate NATO INF and bring SS-20 into balance with British and French sea-based deterrents failed to note that sauce for the goose would be sauce for the gander. If Polaris/Trident and the French MSBS have, along with GLCM and P-II, a strategic significance for the USSR, how much more menacing the picture must appear to NATO Europe, confronted not only with the SS-20 but SLBM in the Baltic (uncounted in SALT) and various operational and 'operational–tactical' systems like the SS-22. Moreover, Andropov's proposal rode roughshod over the more obvious political asymmetries between the two alliances – and the folly, from the British and French point of view, of trading their 'strategic reserve' (Trident) against a secondary component of the

USSR's forces. In fair measure, therefore, the INF negotiations of 1981–83 foundered on an inability to agree appropriate comparisons and geographic terms of reference – but also on the basic truth that threat assessment is not a simple numbers game. But if explanation is needed as to why the USSR opted for a maximal rather than minimal solution to its problems in the first place, it is doctrine and strategy, not geography, which will provide the answer.

A UNIFIED MILITARY DOCTRINE

The first point to note about military doctrine is that the Soviets possess one. This fact alone, in their eyes, may be the deciding factor in war with NATO. The USSR sets great store by the fact that the Warsaw Pact as a whole operates in accordance with a unified, authoritative doctrine, integrating matters as far afield as strategy, weapons design, procurement policy, the training of troops, the roles of the five armed services, arms control policy, and the preparation of society for war. As stated in 1982 by Marshal N. V. Ogarkov (then CGS), military doctrine (*voyennaya doktrina*) is:

> a system of *views* adopted by a given state at a given (certain) time on the goals and nature of a possible future war and the preparation of the armed forces and the country for it, and also the methods of waging it. [author's emphasis][19]

As such, there is no readily equivalent term in NATO. 'Doctrine' in Western parlance comes closest to what the Soviets call 'tactics'; the closest approximation to Soviet military doctrine is the American term 'national security policy', which still falls short of Soviet doctrine's rigour and inclusiveness.

Many Western observers wonder how, in a fluid and unpredictable world, such an all embracing formula can be anything but a corset. Apart from political imperatives (which are dominant) and economic and technical possibilities, the principal influence on doctrine is 'military science' (*voyennaya nauka*), the 'unified system of *knowledge* about preparation for and waging of war' (author's emphasis). Even after the broad outlines of doctrine (policy) are established, investigation in the realm of military science (knowledge) continues. Thus, the components of military science (e.g. tactics) will change in the light of experience, though usually with reference to a more slowly changing body of principles; occasionally, it is the principles which are transformed – as in the 'revolution in military affairs' – and the implications gradually filter down. Thanks to this dependence on military science, doctrine is not a form of dogma, beyond the reach of practice, but a coherent set of views which are modified in response to fresh lessons and challenges. It aims to be both forward and backward looking; it has moved in revolutionary directions, but its overall thrust is evolutionary and cumulative.[20] Failure (such as the Russo-Finnish War of 1939–40 or the opening stages of Operation Barbarossa) is mined for lessons as much as success. For many Americans, Vietnam was a military disaster, and memories cannot be discarded quickly enough. Some hope, similarly, that Afghanistan will teach the USSR something of 'the limits of military power' – which it may – but the likelihood is that, next time, she will be better equipped to accomplish her tasks: much as the débâcle of Finland became the terrain of study for the successful Manchurian campaign of 1945.[21]

A second source of scepticism in the West is the fact that Soviet doctrinal 'claims' are often at variance with capabilities: hence, the suspicion that doctrine is mere disinformation. But the purpose of doctrine is to map out priorities and an agenda of challenges to be met. It reveals the potential of new technologies and techniques; it does not limit itself to the question of how existing capabilities are to be utilised. Over the fullness of time, military advance has in fact been remarkably faithful to doctrinal precept. Whereas deficiencies in mechanisation and firepower during the early stages of the Great Patriotic War precluded mounting the 'deep operations' which doctrine called for, by 1944–45 offensive operations were proceeding much along the lines mapped out in the 1920s and early 1930s.[22] Similarly, the expansion in the 1960s and 1970s of the Strategic Rocket Forces was entirely in keeping with the challenges established by the 'Revolution in Military Affairs' and the new doctrine articulated by Nikita Khrushchev in 1960. It would be incautious to say the least if present discussion of 'Operational Manoeuvre Groups' were made light of as some earlier ideas have been.

Military science is extremely comprehensive, embracing questions as diverse as military structuring, training, logistics, and reserve organisation. Its principal component, and our chief interest here, is 'military art': that body of theory and knowledge concerned with 'actual methods and forms of armed combat'. Whereas in Western armies, the performance of combat tasks is customarily divided into strategy and tactics, in the Soviet Armed Forces, there is a third category, 'operational art', which connects the two.

While strategy encompasses questions dealing with the preparation and use of the Armed Forces in war, operational art involves resolution of problems of preparing for and waging joint and independent operations and combat actions by operational formations and Services of the Armed Forces in individual theatres of military operations.[23]

In more concrete terms, tactical formations range in size from a section (or battery) to a division (13 000 men); operational art concerns itself with 'armies' (roughly 85 000 men) and 'fronts' (or army groups) whilst the concerns of strategy are a Theatre of Military Operations (TVD) or the overall Theatre of War (TV).[24] Of the three levels, strategy plays the predominant role; that is to say, 'operations' are subordinate to the requirements of strategy, whereas the conduct of 'engagements' (tactics) is subordinate to the 'operations' of which they form part. As set out in the *Soviet Officer's Handbook*, 'Strategy, operational art, and tactics are interrelated, interdependent, and supplement each other'.[25]

Whilst this would in principle be applicable to all armies, in the Soviet Armed Forces, these principles are carried out with a rigour not found in NATO formations. When in difficulty, commanders of tactical formations do not expect to receive support from the armies or fronts of which they form part. The operational commander is expected to use his resources to reinforce operational success, irrespective of the tactical consequences; he will therefore throw his fire support and operational reserves behind the one division making headway, leaving those in parlous circumstances to fend for themselves.[26] This principle applies at all levels, from regiment to frong. Any other course of action dissipates effort and diminishes the likelihood of accomplishing the overall objective. This principle is but the analogue in the military sphere to the 'subordination of lower organs to higher' found in the CPSU.

This principle of interdependency produces a strict demarcation between administrative and operational commands and between peacetime and wartime organisation. The Commander-in-Chiefs of armed services are administrative heads, without operational responsibility. In wartime each formation, be it Air Army, Tank Army or Fleet, is fully subordinated to the commander of the operational or strategic entity of which it forms part. On reflection, this arrangement can be seen to be in everybody's interest. No frontal commander, merely because he is a Colonel-General of the Ground Forces, will slight the needs of the Air Army for which he is responsible, because his success depends upon the latter's optimal performance.[27] The consequence of these arrangements will be obvious: 'Strategy is common to and unified for all branches of the country's services, since war is waged, not by any one Service or branch of the Armed Forces, but by their combined efforts'.[28] What invariably proves to be most problematic for Western forces, combined operations, is thus built into the very fabric of Soviet military organisation. What Peter Vigor states, regarding the 1945 Manchuria operation, could be repeated for the 1968 invasion of Czechoslovakia, the 1979 invasion of Afghanistan, and would also hold good for a future war against NATO:

> All three Soviet fighting services participated in the campaign, and the efforts of all were coordinated for the purpose of winning victory speedily. There was thus no plan of naval operations that had a strategic purpose different from that of the ground forces, unlike the situation obtaining in the British Armed Forces in 1914 or the Imperial German Forces in the same year.[29]

By the same logic, the 16 Military Districts, the geographical and administrative linchpins of the military system, do not concern themselves with operations, nor do District commanders have operational responsibilities. Should the USSR be invaded, as in 1941, districts would transform themselves into 'fronts' as the enemy appeared, abandoning their territorial character and proceeding as battle required (thus, Berlin was stormed by the First Ukrainian Front). In event of war fought outside Soviet territory, commanders of Soviet military districts would bring cadre divisions up to strength and transfer them to frontal commanders in the relevant TVD. Indeed, some of today's district commanders may be camouflaged frontal commanders who would transfer to forward command points in war, leaving their deputies behind to run their districts. Today's Groups of Forces in Eastern Europe are, in effect, military districts on a war-time footing; even so, we cannot be certain from their peacetime organisation how wartime commands would be allocated.[30]

MILITARY ART: ENDURING PRINCIPLES

The prototype for the strategy, operational art and tactics of today's Soviet Armed Forces is the concept of operations formulated in the late 1920s and early 1930s known as 'Deep Operations' (V. K. Triandafilov, 1929). Under the influence of M. N. Tuckhachevskiy and A. I. Yegorov and other officers of the General Staff, Operations in Depth became official doctrine in 1933 and, though marred by Stalin's purges, was put to effective use in the latter half of the Great Patriotic War. Inspired by German experiments in Russia in the 1920s, it is in many respects the Russian equivalent of *Blitzkrieg*, enriched with numerous home-grown concepts. Like *Blitzkrieg*, it is a doctrine for offensive war. Its emphasis on shock, mass and mobility is well in keeping with the Marxist–Leninist view of war as a revolutionary and revolutionising act.

Deep Operations calls for the seizure of the strategic initiative: in short, the achievement of surprise as to time, place and method of combat; the concentration of overwhelming force along narrow breakthrough sectors, the launching of deep armoured thrusts into enemy rear and the maintenance of high tempos of advance. A war of this kind aims to deliver the maximum shock to an enemy in its opening stages, ideally in the 'initial period' before he has properly mobilised; it also seeks to transfer combat operations as quickly as possible into the enemy's rear areas, thereby shattering the enemy's Armed Forces as well as the fabric of his society.[31] In the Second World War these manoeuvre and strike formations were of necessity confined to aircraft and forward detachments of tank troops, but today will be supported additionally by rockets, airborne forces and 'diversionary' troops.[32] Three *leitmotifs* of such operations are:

(1) *Mobility and firepower*: mobility (*mobilnost'*) is the first principle of operational art and tactics, but in the Soviet Army's formative years, the relative absence of mechanised formations was the chief impediment to implementing official doctrine. Perhaps the greatest contrast between the latter part of the Great Patriotic War and the present is the astounding mobility and firepower of today's 'motor rifle' formations. With half the numerical strength of a NATO brigade, a modern motor-rifle regiment is at least the latter's equivalent in firepower. Most impressive within the past 15 years is the extent to which fire resources have been made organic to subunits.[33]

(2) *Combined Arms*: the 'all arms' approach is as conspicuous within individual services as it is between them. One of four regiments in today's motor rifle division is a tank regiment (similarly, one battalion in a motor rifle regiment is always a tank battalion). An impressive effort is made to ensure that the panoply of functions performed by an Army are as in a Matrushka doll reproduced in subordinate formations in simplified and scaled down form: thus, the motor-rifle regiment comprises fire support (howitzers, mobile rocket launchers, self-propelled mortar, heavy assault guns), a reconnaissance company and a signals company, and its own distinct engineer, chemical defence, maintenance and motor transport companies.[34]

(3) *Intelligence and reconnaisance*: these have a more aggressive connotation than in NATO. These tasks are accorded the highest importance in tactical, operational and strategic success. Sabotage as well as observation fall within the meaning of these terms; a function which today includes 'diversionary' troops (*Spetsnaz*) and a prodigious investment in 'radar and electronic struggle'. Reconnaisance formations can be found down to battalion level and will normally absorb the best troops in each unit and sub-unit. The intelligence resources of today's Soviet Armed Forces have been estimated as equal in strength to the entire *Bundeswehr*.[35]

(4) *Surprise and deception*: The word *maskirovka* embraces a variety of practices, from political and psychological deception and disinformation to camouflage, feigning actions, 'radar struggle' and physical sabotage. Surprise is essential to the object of winning quickly. In today's conditions, anything other than speedy victory may be a pyrrhic victory.[36]

(5) *Operational Flexibility*: the second meaning of *mobilnost'* is 'flexibility'. In NATO, great store is set by tactical flexibility – the ability to make assessments on the spot, improvise and respond – qualities which play a large part in the tactical competence of NATO forces. In Soviet thinking, tactical competence lies in the mastery of *drill* – for fording a river, carrying out raids, destroying a command post, laying siege to a built up area, and so on. Many such drills demand proficiency and tight coordination, but not the lower level 'initiative' which we prize so highly. The Soviets are well aware of their deficiencies in this regard. Their emphasis on performance by rote is a natural response to the constraints of a multinational conscript force of uneven and occasionally deficient standard.

In the Soviet Armed Forces, great store is set by *operational* flexibility: the ability to assemble, manoeuvre and direct large bodies of men, to concentrate commanders in the ideal place, to commit reserves at the ideal moment and, in short, concentrate force and effort at the decisive point. These qualities are in large part the fruit of combined arms organisation and of a simple, unencumbered command structure. In NATO, latitude is given to subordinates, but command arrangements are cumbersome. In the Warsaw Pact, subordination is strict, and command is flexible: the Supreme High Command (VGK) can exercise direct control over forces and fleets; it can designate an intermediate organ of command (GK); or despatch a representative to the TVD with unlimited powers. As Victor Suvorov notes, the fixed system of command and control in NATO can result in a good general being in a quiet place at the decisive moment. His observations are worth quoting at length.

> Hitler . . . had some outstanding field marshals, but they were scattered over vast territories. Stalin, on the other hand, gathered his most talented Marshals . . . around him and created the *Stavka VGK* (HQ of the Supreme High Command). At decisive moments of the war Stalin would send a top-ranking representative to the decisive place with unlimited powers. . . . In this way the experience and detailed knowledge of the local commander was reinforced by the wider overall view and full powers of the Supreme Command. In critical moments the local commander did not have to waste time on telephone conversations, decoding telegrams, compiling reports, etc., and the *Stavka VGK* representative was able to call in any forces necessary for the local crisis. Whereas the German local commander, such as Field-Marshal Paulus [*sic*] at Stalingrad, concentrated local forces and *asked* his supreme command for help from his neighbours, a Soviet commander such as General Rokossovskii, in a similar situation, concentrated local forces, while Marshal Zhukov, operating from the same command, *ordered* help from his neighbours and co-ordinated their actions himself. [emphasis in original][37]

The various qualities of tactical virtuosity which NATO possesses could, if incorporated into the Soviet Armed Forces, play havoc with the kind of war the USSR conducts with proficiency. As Christopher Donnelly has observed, for operational success to be achieved, 'a cog must remain a cog'. This strategic and operational orientation comes naturally to a military establishment which conceives of war on an immense scale (immense enough to turn divisions into tactical formations). The ability to understand the whole as more than the sum of its parts – and to master warfare at the operational level – is seen as the key to defeating NATO. Tactically, the Russians scored poorly against the Germans even in their finest moments, but the Great Patriotic War demonstrates that flawed operational performance cannot be rescued by tactical success.[38]

Our reliance upon the Ground Forces in these illustrations reflects the extent to which this service has influenced the development of military art as a whole. But the basic principles of military art are universal ones. The Strategic Rocket Forces (RVSN), which subdivide into armies, divisions, regiments and batteries, derives much of its operational philosophy from the artillery. The Soviet Navy (VMF), which groups ships into brigades and divisions, displays the tendency of Ground Forces formations to pack a quart of firepower into a pint pot (thus the Kresta II concentrates the firepower of a large capital ship into a hull little larger than a destroyer); it also places emphasis on 'the combined and systematic employment of all existing forces and means' (i.e. combat and patrol aircraft, helicopters, attack submarines and surface ships). There is a distinctly Soviet, rather than maritime, ring to Milan Vego's description of how enemy submarines must be attacked:

> as soon as the contact has been classified, that is from the maximum effective range of the shipboard sonar, simultaneously, from different directions, and by combined use of all the weapons available. The object is to overwhelm the target's defences, to prevent it avoiding attack, and to maximise damage on the target. The Soviets emphasise greatly the need to obtain a hit with the first salvo.[39]

As Peter Vigor has observed:

> [The] Soviet Union believes it highly desirable to deliver as weighty a blow as possible on each and every occasion, and against any and every enemy. In Soviet thinking the concept of economy of effort

has little place. Whereas to an Englishman the taking of a sledgehammer to crack a nut is a wrong decision and a sign of mental immaturity, to a Russian the opposite is the case. In Russian eyes the cracking of nuts is what sledgehammers are clearly designed for.[40]

This is an appropriate point of departure for assessing the 'revolutionary' impact which nuclear weapons wrought in Soviet thinking.

THE REVOLUTION IN MILITARY AFFAIRS

The story of how Soviet strategy evolved from Stalin's death to the present day forms a chronicle of how the nuclear weapons and guided missiles threatened at first to overturn most of these principles of military art, only in the end to be 'synthesised' with them in good, Marxist, dialectical fashion. It also serves to remind us that whilst the USSR reacts to its opponents, it does not 'mirror' or mimic the other side's strategic behaviour. Soviet authorities assert that a 'revolution in military affairs' occurred between 1953–59, an 'objective' phenomenon which has affected all major military powers, and one that is still unfolding.[41]

In the USSR, the revolution was slow in coming. Under Stalin, the USSR had pursued a vigorous nuclear weapons programme, in the late 1940s detonating an atomic device and testing guided missiles, and by 1950 establishing design plans for missiles of medium and intermediate range. But the realm of strategy was still dominated by Stalin's five 'permanent operating factors'. Voices in the West which suggested that war would never be the same after Hiroshima and Nagasaki were not echoed in the USSR during these years, even (to the best of our knowledge) in restricted military writings. This is the better known part of the story. But whilst the Great Patriotic War was portrayed as a treasure of knowledge for all future contingencies, Stalin's *amour prôpre* also prevented any proper discussion of that war: notably of Germany's *Blitzkrieg* and, by extension, the principles which had shaped Soviet military thinking in the past. Doctrine was put on ice: it was neither possible to look forward nor back.[42]

But in 1954–55, at the Party's initiative, an outspoken debate unfolded in the military press on all aspects of military science: after a dearth of discussion on the subject, some 50 articles on nuclear weapons appeared in *Krasnaya Zvezda* (Red Star) alone.[43] To be sure, there were now any number of incentives to examine Stalin's orthodoxies. But the deployment of tactical nuclear systems by the United States in Europe from 1953 and her adoption of a nuclear strategy in the following year made such an examination essential. In 1954 the Soviet Union conducted its first large-scale troop exercise under nuclear conditions, during which a live bomb was detonated.[44]

Given the immense limitations in offensive Soviet nuclear capability at this time, attention understandably focused on how a largely conventional army could conduct operations on the nuclear battlefield. How should forces be deployed so as to exploit the results of friendly nuclear strikes (then vested entirely in high-level bombers)? What principles of troop control (concentration, mobility, dispersal) were required to frustrate enemy targetting and facilitate escape? Far reaching as many tactical and operational revisions were, they did not in their ensemble amount to a new view of warfare. The pre-eminence of the Ground Forces, as well as their principal missions, remained unchallenged. Nuclear weapons had not altered the nature of war. General Olisov's summation in 1954 probably expressed the view of a fair proportion of the military establishment even two years later:

> Strategic atomic bombs, which are a source of great danger to cities and civilian populations, have little effect on the battlefield. Strategic bombing will not decide the outcome of war, but soldiers on the battlefield.[45]

It was the matching of the nuclear weapon to the guided missile which transformed warfare and ushered in a 'revolution in military affairs'.[46] In 1957 an MRBM was successfully tested and, in August, an ICBM.[47] That year also witnessed the first Soviet missile deployment (the SCUD operational–tactical missile), followed in 1958 by the FROG tactical rocket. Of far greater importance was the deployment of the SS-4 strategic MRBM in 1958 and the SS-6 ICBM in 1959.[48] These developments signalled the conclusion of a long and by no means satisfactory dependence on the medium-range bomber as a counter to NATO's sea and land based nuclear capable aircraft and the 'forward deployment' of US strategic bombers in Europe.[49] But the implications were far more profound than this. Three properties of the nuclear guided missile made it necessary to re-examine every principle of military science: the ability to deliver a payload within moments of committal, the ability to deliver a devastating blow to the homeland of the opponent, and their invulnerability to weather and enemy air defence.[50] The exploration of these implications under General Staff auspices in 1957–59 led to the creation in December 1959 of a new armed service, the Strategic Rocket Forces, and in January 1960 to the promulgation of a new military doctrine by Nikita Khrushchev and his Minister of Defence, Marshal Rodion Malinovskiy.

This doctrine enshrined the nuclear guided missile as the decisive weapon of conflict. A world war would 'inevitably take the form of a nuclear rocket war, that is, such a war where the main means of striking will be the nuclear weapon and the basic means of delivering it to the target will be the rocket'.[51] Victory would go to the side which was most advanced in the techniques of 'nuclear rocket warfare' and the means of waging it; as well as the side which was best prepared from a socio-economic point of view. Massive nuclear attack would also be the means of initiation such a conflict. The range and speed of nuclear missiles, and the danger of surprise attack, ruled out any possibility of sanctuaries, limitations or delay. In the words of Marshal V. D. Sokolovskiy (CGS between 1952 and April 1960):

> Decisive importance for the outcome of the entire war will be given to its initial period and also to methods of frustrating the aggressive designs of the enemy by the timely infliction of a shattering attack upon him . . . [M]assed nuclear rocket attacks [will be] inflicted for the purpose of destroying the aggressor's means of nuclear attack and for the simultaneous mass destruction and devastation of the vitally important objectives comprising the enemy's military, political and economic might, for crushing his will to resist, and for achieving victory within the shortest period of time.[52]

In the unlikely event of a conventional opening to the conflict, escalation to nuclear combat would be quick and 'inevitable'.[53] Finally, the doctrine called for a remodelling of the entire Armed Forces. No longer would battlefield nuclear missiles support the traditional missions of the Ground Forces. The nuclear weapon was to be Queen of the battlefield; the RVSN would be the 'primary service', and the Ground Forces would henceforth be restricted to 'supplementing' and 'completing' the 'decisive' missions which they performed. The Ground Forces Artillery Troops were duly transformed into the Rocket and Artillery Troops; mobility was to be improved, and manpower drastically reduced. However, the remodelling was not to be confined to one particular service: production of manned bombers was to be cut back, and surface ships were pronounced to be weapons of the past.[54]

The new doctrine's emphasis on counter-force and the pre-empting ('frustrating') of enemy nuclear strikes could not have been further removed from NATO's conception of nuclear weapons as tools of deterrence and punishment. This did not mean that the authors of the new doctrine had taken leave of their senses. Much as superiority had accustomed one side to believe that nuclear weapons prevented war, it had long accustomed the other side to regard such a war as a real possibility. The Soviet military establishment was responding rationally to its perception of military threat. It was not the place of doctrine to chart the war one would like to fight, but to address the challenges which would actually arise. The missiles of the Strategic Rocket Forces offered a possibility of escape from the American nuclear corset. Even though the opponent would acquire such a force himself, the nuclear missile represented a net gain to the USSR. It handed her a convincing means of attacking the 'main enemy' directly. It allowed her to break out of her encirclement and regain the initiative. As Sokolovskiy portrayed it:

> The centre of gravity of the entire armed combat under these conditions [will be] transferred from the zone of contact between the adversaries, as was the case in past wars, into the depth of the enemy's location, including the most remote regions. As a result, the war will require an unprecedented spatial scope.[55]

Radical as these changes doubtless were, they also restored continuity with an older tradition whose *motifs* were shock, decisiveness, and the penetration of the depths of an enemy at the opening stages of war. To the Soviet military mind, the new course had definite attractions; indeed, given the country's geographical dilemmas, it seemed irresistible. The new doctrine was therefore embraced with enthusiasm, not despair.[56]

Military strategists must worry about countering military threats. But Khrushchev's first concern was to thwart political intimidation. This concern provided the political rationale for the Strategic Rocket Forces. Already at the Twentieth Party Congress of 1956, Khrushchev declared that war between capitalism and socialism was no longer inevitable. Now it was hoped that the Soviet answer to the American nuclear challenge would neutralise it altogether. The USSR's hands could then be untied for anti-Imperialist struggle overseas, and the traditional course of advance could be resumed in Europe. In an interview given to the *New York Times* in 1960, Khrushchev made these points very explicitly:

> Khrushchev believes absolutely that when it comes to a showdown, Britain France and Italy would refuse to join the United States in a war over Berlin for fear of their absolute destruction. Quite blandly he asserts that these countries are, figuratively speaking, hostages to the USSR and a guarantee against war.[57]

The new doctrine was therefore something more than a response to the US ICBM programme. It offered solutions to geostrategic and geopolitical concerns of long standing. Its political and its military justification each complemented the other: the nuclear guided missile – the decisive weapon of war – would restore the initiative to other means of struggle in time of peace.

Once the broad essentials of the doctrine were formulated, important disagreements arose between Khrushchev and the military establishment. This is not because the broad essentials were themselves in dispute, rather because the issues left unresolved were naturally contentious. The terrain of argument was more limited than is often assumed. Would the decisiveness of nuclear missiles enable them to achieve victory on their own? (Hence, would there not still be a need for balanced forces?) Would the present defence programme and the military–industrial base of the country be sufficient to bring capabilities to the level required? (Hence, was it not premature to cut conventional strengths whilst missile deployment lagged?)[58] Already by the 22nd Party Congress of 1961 Malinovskiy was retreating from the doctrine's more extreme implications: 'although the nuclear weapon will be the defensive factor, victory can be achieved only with the joint actions of all the services'.[59] This revised standard version was repeated in Sokolovskiy's seminal and authoritative work, *Military Strategy*, published in 1962. But the real issue of capabilities and force levels could not be resolved through a new form of words. Khrushchev's nuclear sufficiency was a hope for the future (compared with 63 ICBM's and 96 SLBM's deployed by the United States in 1961, the USSR possessed between four and 50 ICBMs and had no SLBMs to speak of); however, his conventional force reductions were already underway.[60] Having already reduced the Armed Forces by 2.14

million between 1955–58, he called for a further reduction of 1.2 million men in 1960.

The political and military concerns which produced agreement on first principles, therefore, pulled in different directions when it came to practicalities. The establishment of the RVSN gave Khrushchev the excuse to shift resources into the area he considered decisive in peacetime rivalry with the capitalist world: economic competition. The military's natural and proper concern was with what would be decisive in war. It mistrusted Khrushchev's whittling away of the Ground Forces (actually abolished as a separate command in August 1964) and his jettisoning of the all-arms approach which lay at the root of the Soviet military tradition. Most of all, it considered his minimal deterrent insufficient even for minimal defence needs, not to speak of the forward policy which he was wont to pursue. Shortly before his sacking as CGS, Sokolovskiy was reported to have told Khrushchev: 'Just look at the military forces which are needed, and the money allocated for them. Under these conditions I cannot provide adequate defence for the country'.[61] The Cuba 'missile crisis' resolved the argument conclusively, although the battle itself dragged on for a further two years. Ironically, Khrushchev's attempt to install IRBM in Cuba may have been prompted by the wish to satisfy his critics whilst proving his point: 'look at the dividends which Socialism's peaceful expansion offers us!' he seemed to be saying. 'In today's conditions a militarised economy is a foolish anachronism.' Instead, the affair drove home the folly of seeking political primacy on the cheap. Military power, to be sure, was only one element in the correlation of forces, but that did not mean that one could simply substitute other things for it – least of all when an opponent offered a military challenge. When Khrushchev's hopes for the Soviet economy finally fell to the ground, then so did his entire case.

RETREAT FROM ONE VARIANT WARFARE

'Too much venture, too little capital' might be one epitaph for Khrushchev's policies. Brezhnev and Kosygin were sober men, untempted by adventure, with a more orthodox Leninist calculus of means and ends. The objective demand was retrenchment and a regrouping of forces. Henceforth, progress in advancing the gains of Socialism would proceed from capability; bids for influence would be supported by tangible strengths. Soviet quiescence in Berlin and elsewhere (interrupted briefly by the 1967 Middle East War) was therefore the logical accompaniment to what ten years later would be termed 'the Soviet buildup', not an acceptance of the West's self-styled 'lessons of the missile crisis'. The Soviet Union had decidedly *not* learnt the folly of confrontation in the nuclear age, let alone the lesson that, from this point on, Superpowers would have to solve their differences more 'rationally'. Rather, weakness had brought home the real possibility of defeat in such an 'unthinkable' war and the urgency of acquiring the full panoply of capabilities to defend the country's interests. The changes instituted after Khrushchev's deposition were not in the nature of a reversal, but what John Erickson terms a 'continuation' and 'revision'. They are best discussed under two headings.[62]

Doctrine

Whilst the achievement of nuclear sufficiency had to be considered the first order of business after the Cuban disaster, the gap between aspiration and reality concentrated minds on what would be sufficient and what could be achieved. By this time, the writings of American civilian nuclear strategists (some published in greater quantity in the USSR than in the United States)[63] had been absorbed, but mainly to be argued against. The philosophy of deterrence known as 'mutual assured destruction' (MAD) established 'strategic stability' as the overall goal of nuclear force planning. It also conveyed the distinctly Newtonian message that such stability was part of the natural order of things: counterforce was destabilising and hence harmful, defence and damage limitation were fruitless, superiority was meaningless. In principle, the Soviets took issue with a doctrine which equated safety with mutual vulnerability rather than with usable power. In practice, the rationality of MAD seemed artificial and contrived: a world removed from the behaviour of rivals in conditions of threat and uncertainty. It seemed, in short, to deny the possibility of war. How could one entrust one's own safety to the 'moderation' and 'rationality' of a sworn enemy? How would an opponent be deterred by a force posture which made one's own victory impossible? Surely, one hoped one's forces would not be used, but how could one justify investment in forces which could not be used? How could the objectives of policy be achieved by renouncing one's freedom of action in advance? How could the missions of the Armed Forces be articulated or justified in these circumstances, and what could they possibly be? Even if a 'mutual hostage' relationship did deter, such deterrence could always fail and then one would need to be defended; indeed, it seemed that deterrence could more likely fail in the ideal world of the American strategists than in conditions where the superiority of one side was clear to its opponent. Had this not been so during the missile crisis? Would the United States find 'mutual vulnerability' so comforting when her superiority had disappeared? But what did nuclear superiority actually mean?

[T]he earlier discussions (such as those promoted by Marshal Sokolovskiy and Major General Cherednichenko) of 'superiority' tended to the view that it was largely a matter of *relative* strength and its essence consisted of being able to maximize damage on an opponent while minimizing that inflicted on the Soviet Union, whereas a subsequent version (first made explicit by Colonel Bondarenko) used 'superiority' to mean a peacetime build up of weapons sufficient in 'quantity and quality' to make 'winning' a significant term.[64]

The consensus which emerged emphasised the importance of a favourable margin of usuable offensive capability, along with defensive capabilities, active and passive. The years which witnessed the buildup of the Soviet offensive arsenal therefore also saw the upgrading of the Air Defence Forces, the beginnings of an anti-satellite programme and the integration of Civil Defence into the Ministry of Defence (in 1960) and the centralisation of its many functions (under Marshal Chuykov in 1965).[65] Where a clear and absolute superiority was out of reach, the best 'second best' was to 'tie off' enough of a margin so as to be cushioned against the unexpected: the issue, as one General put it, was not only what an enemy possessed, but what he might possess.[66] A third point was 'fitness': the readiness of systems and troops for nuclear combat and, particularly, for timely pre-emption, along lines of the Second World War artillery *kontrpodgotovka*, used to 'break up' an impending attack. 'Superiority' in the final analysis emerged out of the mix and fit of troops, systems and techniques, not by numbers alone.[67]

It was also a function of one's overall force structure and the geostrategic position of the country. In the years after 1964 the conventional forces savaged by Khrushchev were put back into the main stream of military strategy. The arguments in favour of doing so were strengthened by NATO's new policy of 'Flexible Response' (which the USSR dates from its initial formulation in 1961, not its formal endorsement in 1967).[68] Dismissed in political terms as a gimmick, in military terms the new policy focused attention on the possibility of a conventional phase of war, (not that it required any impetus from NATO to rehabilitate the combined arms approach). This return to a balanced force structure was not allowed to become a stampede, and the military–political leadership was careful to ensure that it did not overturn the military doctrine of 1960. Conventional force expansion was presented as a retreat from that doctrine's 'oversimplifications' and 'exaggerations' – no more than that. This formula was designed to synthesise revolutionary change with the best of tradition; it had the advantage of promoting debate *and* consensus. Whereas the revised standard version of the Khrushchev doctrine acknowledged that 'final victory' required 'the combined efforts of all services', there was sufficient continuity in the post-Khrushchev changes for the Minister of Defence, Marshal Grechko, to say as late as 1970: 'The main and decisive means of waging the conflict will be the nuclear rocket weapon. In it, 'classic' types of armaments will also find use. In certain circumstances, the possibilty is admitted of conducting combat actions with conventional weapons.'[69] In the words of General Lomov, escalation to global nuclear conflict was 'always great and . . . under some circumstances . . . inevitable'.[70] In short, what was formerly discussed as inevitable was now discussed as probable. Despite that change, the effort put into traditional arms after 1964 was designed in the main to achieve what was stipulated but in fact highly questionable before 1964: the support of the operations of the Strategic Rocket Forces, and the exploitation of missile strikes of the Rocket and Artillery Troops. Thus, Soviet conventional force modernisation had a very different meaning from the conventional improvements sought by NATO as part of its strategy of Flexible Response. Whilst a conventional phase of war was now acknowledged to be possible, the purpose of conventional arms was not to fight 'conventional war', nor was the purpose of nuclear forces to step in when 'nuclear war' could no longer be deferred. From the start, there would be only one war, and nuclear and conventional forces would be structured for an integrated battle.

Nuclear strikes do not represent some kind of isolated act, but a component of combat. The operations of tank and motorized rifle formations are closely coordinated with them. Nuclear strikes and troop operations represent a uniform and inseparable process, joined by a common concept.[71]

This was 'combined arms' at its purest.

Capabilities

The post-Khrushchev years therefore witnessed a refurbishment of the forces at all levels. Conventionally, the emphasis lay on mobility, fire power and protection, with implications not to be grasped in the West until the mid-1970s. The provision of self-propelled artillery, SAM, AFV; the streamlining of logistics; and the increase in organic firepower of units and subunits would make it possible for conventional as well as nuclear forces to conduct war on a broad scale and at 'furious tempos'; these improvements would also reduce the time needed for mobilisation and, hence, warning time to the opponents. True to the requirements of nuclear battle, new AFV and tanks (such as the T-62) incorporated filtration systems and pressurised cabins for NBC conditions. Perhaps overshadowing all else was the quantitative buildup, symbolised by the addition of five divisions to the Central Region in 1968.[72]

In the 1970s, however, it was the Soviet nuclear programme which focused minds in the West. At the time of the 1962 Cuban Missile Crisis the USSR possessed only a 'shop window' ICBM force. Three years later, little had changed but for the size of the window display. Although more reliable than the SS-6, the second generation SS-7 and SS-8 (deployed in 1962 and 1963 respectively) were greatly constrained in their ability to perform their missions in wartime conditions. The idiosyncracies of propellants and missile guidance components affected the ease with which they could be placed or held on alert. Exposed basing left them vulnerable to attack, and their radio command guidance systems were notoriously unreliable at great distances from the USSR. The technical complexity of ICBM also taxed manufacturing capacity. Numbers rose considerably after 1962, but relative disparities actually increased: compared with a US production rate of one missile per day, the USSR produced one per week.[73]

When it came to regional strategic forces, the picture was brighter, but not radiant. Even before Khrushchev's departure, IRBM, MRBM and bombers provided a convincing riposte to American 'forward based systems' and NATO's long-range theatre nuclear forces. By 1965 the RVSN's regional strike force could boast over 1300 on-line and reload missiles, supplemented by 170 Tu-22 Blinders of Long-Range Aviation.[74] But for how long would these forces be adequate? French and British deterrents were moving beyond the rudimentary stage, and the capability of America's forward based systems was improving. In as much as the SS-4 and SS-5 were plagued by many of the same deficiencies which beset early ICBM, survivability was becoming an honest worry. When one then recalls the reasons which traditionally have pitched regional requirements higher than intercontinental ones, the SS-20 and Backfire decisions appear to have been a foregone conclusion. At the intercontinental level, superiorities were considered desirable; on 'her' continent, the USSR viewed them as a right and a necessity.[75]

What followed was a steady effort to expand regional capabilities and overcome the hurdles in the path of a reliable intercontinental force. The fatalist's recounting of this enterprise would chronicle the tenacity of many technological problems, the scrambling for 'quick fixes' in the face of fresh ones, and the nimbleness of the United States at 'changing the rules' at the point that solutions were found. Thus, the first reliable, mass produced ICBM, the SS-11 (a weapon of Minuteman proportions and of modest accuracy) was degraded by the hardening of US silos and of Minuteman launch centres; the assignment of the SS-9, a heavy missile with substantial throw-weight, to target the launch centres was undermined by the creation of airborne control centres; a 'fractional orbital bombardment system', able to creep under early warning radars was rendered irrelevant by the establishment of satellite early warning in 1968.[76] Such obstacles, however, pale in comparison to the magnitude of the accomplishment. Between October 1966 and October 1967, the USSR more than doubled her force to 720 ICBM. By 1970 the total exceeded 1200. This 'active struggle for the creation of definite capabilities for achieving victory' produced a more limited triumph: catching up. This in itself amounted to a revolution in the correlation forces, and once it had been achieved, the USSR signalled her readiness to enter into bi-lateral arms negotiations with the United States.

'Strategic parity' was far from being a first choice. Indeed, its acceptance seemed at variance with doctrine and tradition. Was it? There were sound reasons for the course adopted, and perhaps some traditional ones as well.

(1) The trophy was worth collecting. America's formal ratification of Soviet military parity was transformed by the USSR into a political act: a *de jure* recognition of the political equality she had long sought and a confirmation of the right to be heard wherever Superpowers were consulted.

(2) Genius meant knowing where to stop (a point Brezhnev's 'adventurist' predecessor had not understood). With the Minuteman and Polaris force in place, the United States had become a restrained and tolerant competitor. Even so, she had proved herself a wily opponent with a facility for pulling rabbits out of hats. What would happen in an all-out contest? Not by accident, Gromyko's first approaches followed four days upon America's initiation of an ABM programme.

(3) Parity was in the eye of the beholder. In the wake of SALT, 'superiority' became a term of moral opprobrium, like original sin. But in hard and fast military terms, parity could be manipulated because nobody could be certain what it really meant. SALT and *détente* signified the triumph of the indirect approach, not an end to the contest. Arms control had thus become the new terrain of struggle: the challenge would be to transform parity into what Americans later called 'clinging parity'.

(4) Strategic parity gave a new significance to margins of advantage at other levels. The point was not lost on America's allies. The USSR may have interpreted the withdrawal of US IRBM from Europe in 1963 as an acknowledgement of her 'right' to a monopoly of Euro-strategic missiles. But NATO Europe could no longer take this view (if she ever held it), now that US inter-continental superiorities had been neutralised. Although 'modernisation' was a genuine basis for the SS-20 decision, that decision must also be viewed in the context of the Euro-strategic war waging strategy devised in those years.

Parity and SALT I therefore intensified the search for a war waging potential below the threshold of strategic intercontinental exchange.[77] This search, however, did not signify acceptance of the 'limited nuclear war' discussed by certain American strategists. Such a 'limited war' postulated rules, 'signals' and conventions tacitly agreed with an adversary. Considering that the USSR had already rejected the 'mutual hostage' principle as a basis for deterrence in time of peace, it stood to reason that she would dismiss its applicability to war itself. 'Limited war' also implied that limitation was to be the object of war –

a rational enough view if one presumed the irrationality of war, but this was not a perspective which the USSR shared. In war the challenge was to limit the options of the opponent, not tie one's hands to his. Where, after all these developments, did doctrine stand at the close of the Brezhnev era? Slow as the pace of evolution had been, by many appearances doctrine in 1980 seemed to have come full circle from the axioms set down 20 years before. The postulated 'inevitability' of all out nuclear rocket war had given way to the exploration of variants more limited in means and scope. The overriding concern was no longer with a decisive attack in an initial period against the homeland of the rival Superpower, but a rapid victory on the European continent, conclusive enough to persuade the United States to call it quits. Finally, conventional forces – sidetracked by Khrushchev into a 'mopping up' role – were now to be prepared for a number of all arms contingencies, including prolonged conventional conflict. But from the authoritative perspective, these modifications were an elaboration and refinement of doctrine, not a refutation or reversal.[78] The nuclear missile would remain not only the decisive factor, but the defining attribute distinguishing future war from wars of the past. The proliferation of nuclear means and the perfection of nuclear capabilities provided the new options which promised to make victory a more meaningful term. Still, there was no guarantee – perhaps little likelihood – that war would not escalate into what Americans called 'central war'. Therefore, as much as in the past, the armed forces needed to be prepared for all-out war and trained to take the initiative if it occurred.

In its political aspect, doctrine showed the same mixture of revision and continuity. Khrushchev had banked on a minimum deterrent to make US military superiority irrelevant and allow the correlation of forces to be adjusted by other means. These other means received increased attention under Khrushchev's successors. Nonetheless, by the mid–1970s, military power had become the principal, perhaps the preferred, tool for moving history forward, because the United States had effectively turned its natural economic strength to its advantage. This military buildup was dedicated to Khrushchev's proclaimed objectives: the decoupling of the United States from Europe and the advance of the national liberation struggle overseas. Everything had therefore changed in order that everything might remain the same. In diplomacy and strategy, Brezhnev was as much concerned as Khrushchev to manoeuvre the struggle onto ground of greatest advantage to the USSR. Any 'revolutionary turn' in military science is likely to be harnessed to the same objective by Brezhnev's successors.

A REVOLUTIONARY TURN?

In a major work published in 1982, Marshal N. V. Ogarkov (then CGS) declared:

> a profound, and in the full sense, revolutionary, turn is taking place in the military affairs in our time in connection with the development of . . . non-nuclear weapons, rapid advances in electronics, development of weapons based on new principles of physics, as well as in connection with extensive qualitative improvement of conventional weapons.[79]

Lest the reader be tempted to conclude that the incremental changes of the post-Khrushchev period have finally been pronounced revolutionary in character, he should scrutinise Ogarkov's words. In military as in political matters, the term 'revolution' is not employed lightly. Whilst the High Command have yet to state that a new revolution in military affairs is upon us, Ogarkov and other spokesmen maintain that a 'revolutionary turn' is the product of technologies only now coming into their own, just as the Revolution in Military Affairs in its time was built on new principles rather than the perfection of what had existed previously. Before deciding how revolutionary a 'revolutionary turn' might be, let us consider those factors that influence Soviet doctrine.

Doctrine fuses politics with the gun. In 1960 the Soviet military establishment postulated the inevitability of escalation to all-out nuclear war for one obvious political reason – NATO's policy of 'Massive Retaliation' – but also because of a strategic environment which made sanctuaries impractical and delay imprudent. Not only were administrative and economic assets vulnerable to attack, but so were military forces: exposed basing, limited warning, and vulnerable communications were but three of many factors which made it imperative to get one's blow in first and ensure that it would be as overwhelming as possible. With forces brought up to the appropriate strength and readiness; with society fortified to withstand the opponent's counterblow, victory could be made a meaningful term.

The 'revisions' of the post-Khrushchev years were, likewise, the product of politics – NATO's policy of 'Flexible Response' – and of a more complex military–technical environment. Writing in the late 1960s, Colonel V. M. Bondarenko cited the proliferation of nuclear systems as the chief factor making a conventional phase of war possible:[80] along with improvements in survivability, warning, command-control-and-communications (C^3), there would now be less incentive and, by the same token, less urgency to launch a strike at the outset of war because of the diminished chances of achieving total success. Doctrine, however, resisted the conclusion that conflict would remain conventional over the entire course of a war because of the likelihood that the losing side would resort to nuclear use to stave off defeat. As before, it would be necessary to beat one's opponent to the punch; as before, a decisive advantage would accrue to the side striking first, but there would now be less reason to strike at once. A second, if complicating, military–technical factor was the dramatic improvement in the accuracy of weapons guidance. High accuracy, to be sure, eroded many of the improvements which Bondarenko had discerned, adding yet again to the advantage of striking first. But accuracy also brought operational flexibility – targeting and safety to friendly troops – and it is this which made integrated nuclear–conventional battle feasible. Accuracy, therefore, strengthened the chances of achieving strategic results at an intermediate threshold. This threshold could also be strengthened by a second political factor, arms control, which could be used to deprive the opponent of any strategic margin for escalation.

Today's 'revolutionary turn' in thinking is, from one standpoint, merely the continuation of this evolutionary trend: conventional war, not merely a conventional phase, has become today's topic for discussion; escalation to the Euro-strategic nuclear level is to be prevented, not deferred; escalation to the intercontinental level is to be made that much more futile. The new focus owes its appearance to a nuclear 'balance' which makes it of questionable interest to NATO to initiate a nuclear strike at any stage, as much as to a political climate which hampers NATO's ability to alter that balance.[81] Ten years ago the challenge was to manoeuvre the opponent into a nuclear decision at a moment of least advantage to him; today's challenge is to deprive him of any possibility of striking early and of any perceived advantage in doing so at all. One can see that INF deployment, and Pershing II in particular, will make this more of a challenge – but the nuclear balance is only part of the story.

The 'revolution' is to be found in technologies and techniques which may allow conventional forces to win early and not just conclusively. Much as the Revolution in Military Affairs was the product of nuclear weapons, guided missiles and electronics, the 'revolutionary turn' is made possible by micro-circuitry and directed energy systems: technologies with revolutionary application to the fields of target acquisition, weapons guidance and fire control, communications and overall 'battle management'. As *Krasnaya Zvezda* (*Red Star*) summarised these developments in 1980:

> conventional weapons are becoming more and more, in a manner of speaking, unconventional, approaching in many of their combat characteristics weapons of mass destruction.[82]

As a result, not only may conventional forces be sufficient to destroy the conventional forces of the other side (which perhaps is nothing new), but NATO's nuclear assets – and in an initial period before nuclear release can be authorised and NATO forces fully deployed.

These new technologies are transforming the means by which the Soviet Armed Forces have traditionally sought shock, surprise and a speedy victory:

(1) *Mobility*: as incremental improvements in mechanisation continue and new weapon platforms (self-propelled artillery, MLRS, helicopters, long-range all weather attack aircraft) are introduced, more revolutionary technologies make their appearance in precision-guided munitions, hand-held anti-tank and AA weapons, and automated fire-control systems. Units and subunits are not only becoming more potent but more tightly packaged: less dependent on extensive logistic support or prior reinforcement. Attack 'from a standing start' – far removed from today's capabilities – is clearly an objective for the future.[83]

(2) *Firepower*: new technologies may also transform the ability to acquire and reassign targets, and combine arms with devastating effect. 'Integrated fire destruction' (air + artillery + missile) promises 'to be able to routinely bring all components of fire support together against the enemy in selected sectors with such intensity and simultaneity that the effect on the enemy would differ little from that of a nuclear strike'.[84]

New means and techniques must be welded into a strategy of surprise attack of war is to be won in its initial period. Three characteristics which distinguish NATO from the Warsaw Pact make such a strategy attractive to Soviet planners.[85]

(1) *Political de-centralisation*: political fragmentation can be a serious liability in peacetime, but in a crisis period it may be fatal. It is not the Supreme Allied Commander who determines when to transfer forces from national to NATO command, but the national command authority of each sovereign NATO country. In aspiration, this is a collective decision; in practice, and in terms of treaty obligation, an individual one. All may agree on what constitutes a *casus belli*; all may recognise an attack for what it is. But there is far less certainty that governments will jointly recognise the *imminence* of attack or agree on the point at which mobilisation should commence. The arbiter of such matters will be human judgement. Technology makes assessment possible, but a human being must decide against a rich background of data what is pertinent and what is in store; sophisticated technologies and more information may complicate the task. As disastrous as preconceptions may be to intelligence assessment, discrimination is essential to good intelligence, and deliberation is a natural part of the process. In NATO, consultation is very thorough, but the actual work of collection and assessment is to a large degree performed by national (and primarily American) institutions. This may not produce unity at the critical moment. A prime objective of Soviet planning is to frustrate attempts to discern the pattern of events.

(2) *The absence of a unified doctrine*: in crisis, an encumbrance to mobilisation and deployment; in battle, an impediment to coordination at the vital 'operational' level. NATO's eggs are placed very largely in the baskets of strategic and tactical success.

(3) *Geographical handicaps*: the Central Region possesses limited operational depth; thanks to the Austrian State Treaty, AFCENT and AFSOUTH have, since 1955, lacked a land bridge between them. NATO must also cope with the possibility of conducting nuclear operations on its own territory against an enemy who will try to shelter near built up areas. But by far the greatest liability in today's conditions may be the deployment of NATO forces at locations far from designated wartime operating areas. A strategy of Flexible Response demands *strategic* warning: warning sufficient to allow redeployment to take place. Strategic surprise, therefore, does not depend upon total surprise: the hour of attack may be known, but strategic surprise will still be achieved if it is not known early enough. Western Europe's natural and man-made obstacles offer immense assistance to a defender in place, but if he

is not, they can become anvils against which he can be pinned by his opponent. Given these constraints, Moltke's warning has a pertinent ring: 'he who is wrongly deployed at the start of a war never recovers'.

Strategic surprise and its ally, strategic deception, are therefore essential to exploiting NATO's weaknesses and winning speedily by conventional means. Strategic surprise demands trade-offs in operational effectiveness – attack below one's full strength and before most forces are mobilised but these sacrifices are considered to be tolerable risks if surprise can be achieved.[86] In times past, it was enough to deceive an adversary at the moment operations began; at present, he must be deceived in time of pre-war crisis, if not long before, if strategic surprise is to be achieved. Deception at the crisis stage demands that military and political measures be orchestrated to complicate the task of distinguishing 'signals' from 'background noise'. The Czechoslovakian crisis of 1968 and the Polish crisis of 1980–81 demonstrate that peaks and lulls of tension can be contrived so as to manipulate an opponent's perceptions contrary to his interests. The invasion of Czechoslovakia by Warsaw Pact forces followed seven days after the Bratislava summit, whose communiqué was described by *The Times* in the headline, 'Bratislava powers agree on the right to be different'.[87] General Jaruzelski maintained the façade of negotiations with Lech Walesa and Archbishop Glemp in November 1981, though it now appears that a military solution was decided upon in July. Deployments and manoeuvres, which may be thought to constitute the surest sign of trouble, can also be staged to deceive. In early 1981 the redeployment of LWP troops in strategic locations disguised the redeployment of Internal Security Forces to the barracks they vacated. In April 1981, under the cloak of a training exercise, Polish and Soviet forces erected a separate military communications net which facilitated planning, surprise, and command and control. In the summer, the annual return of Soviet troops from the GSFG to help with the harvest was delayed – justifiably increasing alarm – and then took place, unjustifiably allaying it. In October–November, LWP troops deployed to their operational locations without arousing suspicion, on the pretext of alleviating food bottlenecks.[88] A third technique of deception is the use of repetitive mobilisations and manoeuvres to de-sensitize an opponent (as in Korea in 1950, Czechoslovakia in 1968 and Israel in 1973). A variant is Peter Vigor's 'dead volcano': troops kept long enough on a war footing to lose their novelty: attack, when it comes, seems to arrive out of the blue (France 1940).[89] In the Polish crisis, every move was detected accurately by the other side and yet misinterpreted. As Christopher Donnelly noted after the imposition of Martial Law: 'This is the third time in three decades that Warsaw Pact forces have launched a major military operation in Europe, each time in the glare of publicity attending a crisis, and each time they have obtained complete surprise'.[90] The meaning of such indicators may be clear to individual intelligence officers, but the question is whether they will be clear enough to produce consensus amongst the professionals and persuade politicians, who alone have authority to act.

No matter how proficient Soviet techniques of deception might become, the odds of success will diminish if the targets of deception are predisposed to view Soviet activity in an unfavourable light. In 1948, at a time of great anxiety, Western commanders may have read more into the Berlin blockade than was intended. Today the greater danger is that we would convince ourselves that war is impossible at the point when it is imminent. The prime focus of strategic deception is the manipulation of perceptions in time of peace, long before crisis occurs. This enterprise is properly the concern of the following chapter. But we can safely say for the moment that success will depend less on the activities of 'Fifth Columnists' than upon the perceptions of NATO's loyalists. If a respectable proportion of Western political élites believe on the day that the USSR has nothing to gain from war, that she is defensively-minded (or, indeed, that the United States is trigger-happy), odds are that in the frenzied atmosphere of crisis some governments will consider mobilisation a provocative rather than a prudent step. Again, not everyone need be deceived for deception to produce its intended effects of discord and delay.

Achieving strategic surprise with large conventional forces depends upon detailed and prolonged planning: an undertaking very different in kind from pre-empting a nuclear strike. It is a workable strategy for those who have the luxury of going to war at the time of their choosing – far less so for those who fear that war will be thrust upon them. Its application to war with NATO testifies not only to new technologies, but to a new correlation of forces. This is not to suggest that crisis is in future more likely to lead to war than in times past, only that if there *is* to be a war, the USSR sees herself as its initiator and is likely to use crisis to cloak her final preparations for it. The new strategy is also tribute to innovations in the realm of political–military coordination through the mechanism of the Defence Council; it testifies to the interpenetration of peacetime and wartime concerns: deception in time of peace is a task assigned to the General Staff and its Main Intelligence Directorate (GRU) as much as to the Ministry of Foreign Affairs and Committee for State Security (KGB). Finally, the strategy is tribute to a command structure which concentrates power of decision into very few hands and compartmentalises knowledge effectively. The reflections of Zdeněk Mlynář, a former member of the Secretariat of the Czechoslovakian Communist Party, about the Soviet invading forces in 1968 could be extended to higher echelons:

> [The troops] had no idea why they were in Czechoslovakia, and often didn't even know that that was where they were. There are known cases of ordinary soldiers who thought they were in West Germany or even Israel. But in the end, does it really matter what such soldiers think? Their personal opinion does not in any way change the fact that their commanders and government can treat them like a mindless herd, nor the fact that they will shoot and kill whomever their commanders point to.[91]

Officers, in contrast, will know where they are and whom they are fighting. But by British, American or German standards, commanders of Soviet divisions were treated as a 'mindless herd' by the Supreme High Command in the Great Patriotic War, and today's commanders of Armies and Fronts will probably be less knowledgeable about plans and policies than their opposite numbers in NATO. For the purposes of achieving strategic surprise, this may be essential. In 1941 the German High Command produced 30 copies of its directive for strategic concentration and deployment pertaining to Operation Barbarossa.[92] Soviet authorities consider this number far too high if surprise is not to be compromised.

Once hostilities commence, then it is surprise at the operational level which may hold the key to the war's outcome. The re-emergence of the Second World War Mobile Groups in the form of Operational Manoeuvre Groups, analysed by Christopher Donnelly, may become the key to this enterprise. Of divisional size or greater, OMG's will be combined arms, but essentially tank, formations which will seek to create a zone of operations deep in the enemy's rear in the opening stages of war – ideally within the first 24 hours. Committal will be a combined arms operation, demanding the coordination of air, rocket, artillery (and possibly naval) fires to create a breach, and involving support from the *desants* of airborne forces and the operations of

Spetsnaz (diversionary) troops. As stated in the Polish journal, *Air Force and Air Defence Review* (February 1982):

> The aim of deploying an army's Operational Manoeuvre Group (OMG) is to switch the focus of the fighting into the depths or rear of the enemy formation, to destroy important objectives which cannot be destroyed by other means, to achieve chaos and disorganization, and to limit the freedom of manoeuvre and the effectiveness of the enemy action.[93]

Destruction of nuclear systems and supporting infrastructure will be the most pressing task of an OMG and its raiding detachments; havoc is to be played with deployment to deny NATO the separation between friendly and enemy forces and the stable battlefield required to launch nuclear strikes. In short, the gunfighter is to find his enemy on top of him before he can grab his gun. HQs, radars, command-control-and-communication facilities will also be high priority targets. The intent of the OMG is not so much to deprive the opponent of life and limb, as to blind, deafen, gag and render him helpless. To vary the metaphor yet again, if the enemy is distracted and exhausted by brushfires behind him, he will succumb more speedily to the blaze ahead of him.[94]

Exploration of the OMG concept demonstrates the proficiency of the Soviet Armed Forces at a level of operations (operational art) which finds no clear counterpart in NATO. But it is also making demands at the tactical level which will be difficult for the Soviet Armed Forces to fulfill given its command structure, training, traditions and biases. Considerable strides have been made in the direction of tactical flexibility and in the develoving of decision-making to lower level commanders, but these are chronic deficiencies and known to be such. In part for these reasons, whilst the OMG, in Donnelly's words,

> is clearly completely accepted in principle in its modern form by Soviet operational planners, and is indeed clearly in an advanced state of development, the details of the concept are by no means fully resolved . . . and there is clearly doubt in some areas that the principles established can actually be implemented.[95]

Does the shift to a strategy of surprise conventional attack suggest that NATO will be marking time if it continues to rely so extensively on nuclear weapons to deter war? This might well be so. The exploration of a conventional war-fighting strategy by the USSR is the product of two shifts in the correlation of forces: a nuclear balance which deprives NATO of a decisive counterforce margin and new technologies which hold out promise of neutralising NATO's nuclear assets by conventional means before authorisation for nuclear release can be secured. Many will therefore conclude that conventional military power will be the only usable military power for the future and that NATO needs a conventional war-fighting strategy to counter the threats emerging against it.

On the other hand, the USSR's shift from a pre-emptive nuclear strategy can be justly regarded as a tribute to NATO's nuclear capabilities and as recognition that the proliferation of nuclear systems makes a disarming first strike a very chancy undertaking. Far from being irrelevant to warfare, the very urgency attached by the Soviets to destroying NATO's nuclear assets suggests that even in today's climes NATO's nuclear capability is what the Warsaw Pact most respects and fears. If so, the Soviet campaign against NATO's programme of theatre nuclear modernisation stems from real worries and not just mischief making: with an abundance of mobile, survivable nuclear forces in a variety of basing modes and environments, NATO can target Soviet forces with devastating effect, and a strategy of lightning conventional war will fail. To be sure, in today's environment, the USSR will also be able to retaliate, but mutual destruction has never been a Soviet war aim. It is the USSR, after all, which must take the decision to go to war, and we may safely assume that unless she is confident of her ability to disarm NATO, she will not cross that threshold. In contrast, each NATO nuclear system retired without replacement is one raiding party or forward detachment less that the Soviets must train, equip and fret about. Carried on far enough, neglect of the nuclear component of NATO's forces could restore a nuclear impetus to Soviet war planning. This would be particularly the case if nuclear neglect were coupled with improvements to NATO's conventional force posture. What David Isby stated in 1980 would be as valid for the future: the Soviets would be likely to 'use nuclear weapons to restore mobile warfare if they have been halted or fear a battle of attrition'. What matters to the USSR is winning, not the mode of fighting; theirs has never been the strategy of 'tit for tat', but the exploitation of vulnerabilities, the search for the weakest link and the choice of the path of least resistance. NATO may paint itself into a corner if it takes the view that today's choice is *either* conventional *or* nuclear modernisation. The irony is that nuclear modernisation strengthens the chances of confining war to conventional combat, conventional improvements buy more time for the nuclear response which may prove necessary despite our efforts to avoid it. Pursued in tandem, nuclear and conventional force improvements raise the threshold of war – provided that 'improvement' comes in the form of real capabilities and fighting qualities and not the simple accretion of hardware.

Extensively as doctrine has evolved since 1960, the continuities are still strong. Even if the Soviet Armed Forces make speedy progress with their latest agenda of challenges, war in future will still be fought under the shadow of nuclear weapons. This in itself suggests that the Revolution in Military Affairs, begun in 1953, will continue to make itself felt: if war is no longer certain to be dominated by nuclear weapons, it will continue to be dominated by the threat of their use at any time. As much as 25 years ago, troops today must be prepared for nuclear combat. As much as 15 years ago, Soviet commanders recognise that the ability to switch from one form of combat to another at the most favourable – the most decisive – moment is probably the most critical skill to possess.

NATO's greatest challenge for the future may be the foiling of strategic surprise: an enterprise not only demanding survivable weapons and capable technologies, but institutional reform and contingency planning which takes account of the Soviet view of 'crisis management'. A unified intelligence capability would seem to be of the essence. Should the threshold of war ever be crossed and strategic surprise be achieved, one of three possibilities may lie in store:

(1) The Warsaw Pact will succeed in its aim of disarming NATO conventionally;
(2) It will succeed only in accelerating NATO preparations for a nuclear strike, in which case pressures will mount for a pre-emptive strike along *kontrpodgotovka* lines;
(3) It will succeed in depleting NATO's nuclear assets to the point that a disarming nuclear strike becomes the most attractive option to the Supreme High Command.

No doubt, variations on the theme can be composed. But the notion that this opponent will allow us to dictate the rules of engagement to him is the stuff of which dreams are made and kingdoms lost.

6 The Invisibles of Power

It is impossible to obtain possession of a great country with European civilisation otherwise than by aid of internal division.

Karl von Clausewitz

Look where your vulnerabilities are, and there you will find the KGB.

Stanislaw Levchenko
(former official, KGB First Chief Directorate)

A Russian saying has it that Russia will never start a war, but will wage peace so vigorously that no stone will be left standing upon another. Her method and style of 'waging peace' bear more than a passing resemblance to her manner of waging war: a strategy which aims to exploit weakness rather than match strength, a premium placed on intelligence and on the centralised control of one's forces, the transfer of the locus of fighting to the enemy rear, and the 'combined and systematic utilisation of all means available'. The answer to Lenin's question, 'when to choose peace, when to choose war?' hinges upon which is more vulnerable, the opponent's society or his armed forces. In Afghanistan society is a bed of nails; in Europe, the United States and much of the developing world it is a soft target.

If one difference stands out between the Soviet approach to peace and to war, it is the urgency perceived that war in its modern form be short. In contrast, the struggle to adjust the correlation of forces by peaceful means is perceived by necessity, but also by strategic choice, to be a long-term affair, intense and sustained though it must be as well. The USSR well appreciates the force of what might be called the Falklands or Pearl Harbor effect in 'bourgeois democracies': when challenges are clear, offensive, and direct, public opinion and even 'inveterate peace mongers' move to the right of governments themselves perceived to be of the right (a phenomenon which certainly could be observed in the United States when KAL flight 007 was shot down and the Reagan Administration suddenly found itself to the left of public opinion). But the long-term and indirect approach does not arouse the collective indignation of Western society; rather, it brings out other characteristics nurtured by our culture, our civic tolerance, and our democratic institutions: a short attention span, impatience for result and for 'progress', and various morally loaded values associated with the idea of 'peace': its association with cooperation rather than struggle, and with private virtues and comforts rather than with vigilance, duty and sacrifice. Understanding is seen as tantamount to agreement. Negotiation between Superpowers is thought of as a form of therapy – a slow incubation of moderation, goodwill and trust – between parties who have become unnecessarily and dangerously estranged. We need hardly reiterate that the CPSU do not see it in this way.

The professional foreign policy establishments of Europe and North America do not see it in this way either. But the professionals are, for professional reasons, often inclined to deprecate the less conventional side of Soviet activity and equate Soviet foreign policy with Soviet diplomacy.

In the old school diplomatic world, 'pragmatism' is widely taken to be the measure of seriousness. Self-proclaimed ideologies are frequently treated as smokescreens for 'national interests' or as the nostrums of those who have not matured fully. There is the hope that responsibility civilises, and that if 'legitimate demands' are met, radicals will become reluctant conservatives. Like corporate oligopolists, much of the foreign policy establishment conceives of diplomacy as a means of 'adjusting interests', not as a method of struggle: we all want to 'maximise our influence', but in the end we all settle for what we can get. The professionals no more yearn for a diplomacy 'beyond power politics' any more than corporate obligarchs expect their labours to produce a market without competition. They are tough bargainers; they know the value of things; they will not give away solid assets for gestures of goodwill. But 'pragmatism' tends to be the *Realpolitik* of the short term, the code of practice of the conservative in a world of clubbable rivals. It frequently produces a willingness to deal with issues 'on their merits': however, in diplomacy as in battle, one can win every tactical engagement and lose the war.[1]

The business of diplomacy is communication between states. It is natural for diplomats to equate international relations with interstate relations, or at least assume that non-state relations are private in character or of secondary importance. The orthodox diplomatic order, and the legal order underpinning it, draws a strict demarcation line between internal and international politics. The Soviet regime, as we have seen, compartmentalises international politics into a 'social' and an 'inter-state' dimension; it represents Party as well as State; its conduct of 'relations between peoples' is an organised and sophisticated activity, brought fully into harness with state policy. These relations – intensive and continuous – usually fall below the legal threshold of intervention and affect world order in ways that are not always appreciated. In the West, the Soviet Ministry of Foreign Affairs is accorded an attention out of proportion to its importance; comparatively little attention is paid to the activities of the Central Committee's International Department.

The 'social' and 'ideological' dimension of Soviet policy, even when grasped for what it is, is not seen to be the foreign policy establishment's *métier*, since any consideration of such matters is bound to involve it in the *internal* politics of countries, including their own. The *esprit de corps* of a Foreign Ministry consists in being 'above party'. Pluralism, disagreement and dissent are the defining *attributes* of Western democracy, and it is difficult to counter Soviet activity in this area without treating them as weaknesses. That, after all, is *their* system and their game.

Finally, many in the First World have come to the conclusion that the 'Soviet model' has nothing to offer the Third World. This is an eminently reasonable position to take if we proceed from the assumption that the creation of individual freedom and economic prosperity are the first order of business for any society. But as Samuel Huntingdon noted some years ago, priorities in the Third World are apt to be different.

> The primary problem of politics is the lag in the development of political institutions behind social and economic change. . . . Authority has to exist before it can be limited, and it is authority that is in scarce supply in those modernizing countries where government is at the mercy of alienated intellectuals, rambunctious colonels and rioting students. . . . History shows conclusively that communist governments are not better than free governments in alleviating famine, improving health, expanding national product, creating industry, and maximising welfare. But the one thing communist governments can do is govern.[2]

Leninism is a theology of gaining power and keeping it. Non-Leninist governments betray socio-economic expectations, brutalise their opponents and fall from power. Leninist governments achieve precisely the same and strengthen their hold on society. Soviet assistance to the national liberation struggle helps to consolidate, not just to create, revolutions: the consultant's advice is respected and his tuition is appreciated. Often, the tutor exceeds his brief, and even where he has not he has discovered that his charges can be impertinent and ungrateful. But the support furnished to aspiring élites is an asset, not a liability to the USSR; a means of influence, not a weakness. In this sphere as in others, the USSR is eager to learn from her mistakes: today she is a more discrete patron. If the Soviet Union took the national liberation struggle less seriously, her position in the world would be much diminished.

E. H. Carr has stated that 'the initiative in introducing propaganda as a regular instrument of international relations must be credited to the Soviet government.'[3] The same must be said for the whole trove of techniques and practices which the Soviets term 'active measures' (*aktivnye meropriatia*): espionage, propaganda and disinformation, infiltration, sabotage, terrorism and para-military operations. In their study, *Dezinformatsia*, Richard Shultz and Roy Godson define active measures as practices which:

> may entail influencing the policies of another government, undermining confidence in its leaders and institutions, disrupting relations between other nations, and discrediting and weakening governmental and non-governmental opponents. This frequently involves attempts to deceive the target (foreign governmental and non-governmental élites or mass audiences), and to distort the target's perceptions of reality.[4]

As with military strategy, it is the Soviet Union's own history which has provided the storehouse of wisdom in these pursuits, as well as testimony to their importance. Clandestine operations, the recruiting of agents, and the creation of front organisations were staple to Bolshevik practice long before 1917.[5] The deposition of the Provisional Government was not the work of a band of armed men, but of a sustained active measures campaign: the band of armed men merely performed the *coup de grâce*. The destruction of the Mensheviks, of left and right 'deviationists', and the discrediting of Trotsky, provided the paradigms for the 'salami' tactics which emerged in Eastern Europe in the 1940s and for the post-colonial transformation of 'broad popular coalitions' into Leninist dictatorships. A November 1983 speech by a member of the ruling Sandinista Front in Nicaragua is indication enough that the strategy of 'splitting' 'zig-zag' and 'displaying the utmost flexibility in tactics' is far from moribund:

> Bourgeois democracy contains an element which we can manage and obtain positive elements for the construction of socialism in Nicaragua. . . . The most important . . . is the elaboration of a new constitution because . . . it will allow us to shape juridical and political principles for the construction of socialism. . . . This new juridical framework will let us adopt a new rhythm, more dynamic. That is what we will obtain from the electoral process.
>
> So in this context . . . we ask what role will our allied forces play? We have not declared ourselves in a public and official way as Marxist–Leninists. Isn't it time to make a single party? Why are we communists putting on different shirts? Well, after the elections, we are going to drop the fiction that there is a Socialist party which is Marxist–Leninist and there are those of the Sandist Front who still have not taken off their shirt.
>
> We still have not started to move the crowds – because the moment has not yet arrived.
>
> This is going to be the first experience in the construction of socialism with the dollars of capitalism.[6]

(It would have been more accurate to have said 'not the first'.)

Active measures draw in part upon the USSR's impressive pedigree in para-military expertise. Whilst special categories of troops not responsible to the Ministry of Defence were created from the start of the Bolshevik revolution to perform sensitive tasks for the Party leadership, it was the experience of the Great Patriotic War in the operation of 'special detachments' and partisan units which have had the greatest effect on their subsequent development. In the 1940s the MGB (the KGB's immediate precursor) drew on the talents of this network to build up an underground infrastructure against American bases on the Soviet periphery, an infrastructure which has evolved into the *Spetsnaz* forces of the present day as well as the network of agents in every NATO, neutral non-aligned European country. The extensive undertakings of the GPU and GRU on behalf of revolutionary forces in the British Empire, China and elsewhere in the 1920s and 1930s have also provided the prototype for the far-flung and specialised GRU–KGB infrastructure which schools and trains many Third World revolutionary élites, their national liberation armies, and their praetorian guards.[7]

Any mention of the unconventional means deployed by the USSR invites attention to the covert means possessed by all powers of substance and is enough to remind one that in these matters no one's hands are idle or clean. The purpose of such activity, however, is worth a moment's scrutiny. Intelligence, political and military, serves as the eyes and ears of any state; it is indispensable to the effort of distinguishing appearance from reality, and therefore helps to ensure that politics remains the art of the possible. Of those factors which aid peace and those which aid war, the maintenance of strong intelligence capabilities on all sides ought to be considered a positive, if not altogether benign, influence. It could even be argued that covert operations, being one of very few intermediate options between diplomacy and overt conflict, produce a similar effect. If the less savoury side of intelligence were made impossible, the world might become a more lawful place, but states might turn to war more frequently. This point of view, which many in the West consider cynical, questionable or beside the point, would not seem controversial to the CPSU. Active measures are seen as a component of 'peaceful coexistence', helping to maintain the threshold between conflict and war. Like war, intelligence is but a tool of policy. In the West the legitimacy of this tool is often in dispute, and the subject of intelligence is approached with greater ambivalence. Even should the Reagan Administration succeed in undoing the restrictions placed on the American intelligence services by Congress and by its predecessor, the United States intelligence effort will, for reasons of politics and tradition, retain its bias in favour of analysis, rather than operations. This is one contrast between Soviet intelligence activity and that of its principal rival.[8]

A second contrast, which we need not labour, is the proportion of intelligence effort devoted to internal security in the Warsaw Pact: the budget for jamming foreign radio broadcasts in the USSR has been estimated to exceed the budget of the BBC External Services. But a third and more relevant contrast is that of scope and resources. The coverage of the FRG by five Soviet agent networks makes the point in itself. Two of these are part of the Committee for State Security (KGB): the counter-intelligence network operating within the Armed Forces (the KGB's Third Directorate, or 'Special Department'), and the agents recruited by KGB residencies (which are subordinated to the First Chief Directorate). Three networks are part of military intelligence: saboteurs and other 'Fifth Columnists' tied to the 'diversionary' troops (*Spatsnaz*), agents run by the Armed Forces' four frontal commands, and agents recruited by the Chief Intelligence Directorate of the General Staff (GRU), reporting to GRU operatives in embassies and residencies on West German soil.[9] Non-Soviet Warsaw Pact activity, organised on roughly similar lines, are formidable in themselves. According to former members of the KGB and the International Department, expense is not a seriously limiting factor in intelligence activity. Operations proposed by field officers are vetoed by the Centre if judged imprudent or at variance with policy; reservations on grounds of cost are unusual. This loose financial leash is a world removed from the day-to-day constraints known to all Western intelligence operatives.[10]

Life peaceful coexistence itself, active measures are a method for carrying on the 'inevitable struggle' between social systems, whilst insulating them from the disputes of states. A prime aim of Warsaw Pact intelligence is:

> to penetrate the HQ of international Capitalist organisations, with the aim of aggravating contradictions and difficulties occurring in their activities. (Statute of the Committee of State Security.)[11]

Penetration for purposes of 'aggravating contradictions', as opposed to intelligence gathering, is an activity almost unknown to NATO intelligence services. In the Warsaw Pact, this effort – which is continuous as well as extensive – is considered to be of major assistance to state policy.

In the 1920s and 1930s, penetration, propaganda and other active measures compensated for economic and military weakness; yet as the Soviet Union has acquired the traditional attributes of power, these activities have increased in scale. Increased attention to active measures can also be associated with periods of East–West *détente*. In the wake of Khrushchev's policy of 'peaceful coexistence', the Soviet propaganda offensive increased and institutions dedicated to active measures were enlarged and upgraded in importance. A similar expansion of effort initiated in the early 1970s. At the outset of Soviet *détente* with the FRG, and over the course of its development, KGB Chairman Andropov is known to have issued at least two directives (no. 0039 on 28 April 1970 and no. 0042 of 8 May 1973) calling for a more sustained recruitment drive and greater efforts to penetrate the FRG's media and foreign policy establishments. Throughout this period, the KGB, the Ministry of State Security of the GDR (MfS) and other Warsaw Pact security organs came under increased pressure to penetrate, compromise and recruit. *Détente*, far from moderating such conduct, as expected in the West, became the grounds for intensifying it.[12]

Within the Warsaw Pact the conduct of active measures extends across a wide number of Party and State bodies. These activities are highly centralised and are coordinated with policy-making at the highest level. The principal clearing house of these activities is the International Department of the Party's Central Committee.

THE INTERNATIONAL DEPARTMENT OF THE CC CPSU

The International Department of the Central Committee (ID) is one of those institutional novelties of a society which divides foreign relations into 'relations between states' and 'relations between peoples'. Whereas the province of the Ministry of Foreign Affairs (MFA) is state-to-state relations, one will be told on enquiring of Soviet spokesmen that the ID, a Party organisation, exists to develop relations with non-ruling CPs abroad. Brief reflection and the most casual glance of the Soviet media's reporting of the comings and goings of key ID personnel is enough to establish that the Department has a brief to conduct relations with a variety of non-state movements and actors: 'national liberation movements', 'revolutionary democratic' and 'bourgeois nationalist' parties in the Third World, as well as 'progressive' forces in Europe and elsewhere.

The ID is one of three linear descendents of the Third International, or Comintern, and by far and away the principal one. Despite the Comintern's dissolution in 1943 (at Roosevelt's and Churchill's insistence), the USSR has never accepted that it should confine its activities to the state-to-state sphere. Within months a Foreign Affairs Department emerged in the CPSU Central Committee; and with the onset of cold war, its activities were supplemented by the Cominform. In 1957, the year of the Cominform's dissolution, the infrastructure for 'relations between peoples' was enlarged and rationalised. The Foreign Affairs Department was divided into three: the Department for Liaison with Communist and Workers Parties of Socialist Countries (the so-called 'Socialist Countries Department', first headed by Yuriy Andropov), the International Department (headed then as now by Boris Ponomarev) and the Department for Cadres Abroad, closely linked to the KGB and responsible for supervising Party cells in Soviet establishments abroad.[13]

Whilst a great deal is done to conceal the workings of the ID, the late

Professor Leonard Schapiro concluded that it is probably the decisive influence on foreign policy as a whole, and not just of its social and ideological dimension.[14] This conclusion has since been reinforced by Stanislaw Levchenko, a former ID and KGB official, who defected in 1979. *Prima facie*, this would be a difficult case to disprove, considering the pre-eminence of Party over State in other spheres of Soviet life and the instrumental role performed by Central Committee departments in the day-to-day supervision of State organisations.[15]

Before his retirement as Minister of Foreign Affairs in June 1985, Andrey Gromyko had achieved considerable public prominence. The Chairman of the International Department, Boris Ponomarev, is an interesting contrast. Although only a Candidate (non-voting) member of the Politburo (since 1972), he is one of that key circle who combine Politburo membership with membership of the CC Secretariat, to which he was elected as long ago as 1961. Gromyko was not a member of the Party's Secretariat, nor could he easily have been, since the Ministry of Foreign Affairs (MFA) is not a Party organisation. Whilst the Politburo is the supreme organ of policy-making in the USSR, the Secretariat is the apex of the hierarchy concerned with policy implementation. It is also the key influence on the agenda of Politburo meetings. Gromyko's long professional experience is matched by that of his counterpart who, nearly 50 years ago at the age of 32, was appointed to the Executive Committee of the Comintern.[16] In addition to the scrutiny it receives from the Central Committee through the International Department, the Ministry of Foreign Affairs is also circumscribed by the Socialist Countries Department (another Central Committee department), which acts as the major instrumentality in intra-Bloc relations. Yuriy Andropov, whilst Ambassador in Hungary in the 1950s was probably associated with the CC Foreign Affairs Department (precursor to the Socialist Countries Department) and not the MFA.[17] This arrangement, by which Soviet ambassadors report to the Central Committee, is typical of intra-bloc practice. Perhaps Gromyko's replacement by Eduard Shevardnadze – a career Party official – rather than the logical professional choice, First Deputy Foreign Minister Georgiy Kornieyenko, puts the institutional standing of the MFA in its proper perspective. When all is said, Soviet foreign policy is not Gromyko's policy, Shevardnadze's policy or Ponomarev's policy, but Party and State policy as defined by the Politburo. The fixation with the MFA, and with the figure of Gromyko in particular, is as great an example of 'mirror imaging' as anything to be found in the military sphere.

Apart from these essentials, uncertainty exists regarding the nature and intensity of supervision exercised by the ID over the Ministry of Foreign Affairs. The Politburo has not only tolerated, but fostered institutional rivalries in order to strengthen its hold on policy. According to some sources, however, the tenor of ID–MFA relations is professional and collegial; on balance evidence suggests that the ID functions more as an umbrella organisation rather than a rival which duplicates the Ministry's functions. It coordinates the activities of the various institutions concerned with foreign policy: KGB, Ministry of Foreign Trade, USSR Academy of Sciences and other bodies, not only the Ministry of Foreign Affairs.[18] Whilst potential for friction is bound to exist in such an arrangement, each of these institutions needs the cooperation of the other, given the sweep and complexity of Soviet foreign policy. Even in the area of arms control, where the MFA acts, along with the General Staff, as front runner, ID as well as KGB advice is essential to a reading of the pulse within NATO countries, an evaluation of the correlation of forces, and a proper appraisal of negotiating tactics. Institutional links are thought to exist between the ID and the General Staff, which includes an External Relations Directorate, a Chief Foreign Military Assistance Directorate, an External Relations Directorate, as well as a Legal and Treaty Department, but their nature is not known to the author.[19]

In sum, one is on safe ground in concluding that the International Department acts as the major actor concerned with the non-state dimension of foreign policy; works closely with the MFA and KGB in coordinating intelligence and in providing assessments for the Politburo; and acts as the Politburo's orchestrator of foreign policy tasks, particularly in the realm of propaganda.[20] Finally, just as the Armed Forces Chief Political Directorate oversees military publications, so the ID seems responsible for the foreign affairs commentary of the prestige Soviet press. (It is also believed to control clandestine radio stations.)[21]

Two adjuncts to the International Department are international front organisations and the social science research institutes of the USSR Academy of Sciences. Historically, international Communist front organisations (dubbed 'innocents' clubs' by their founders) have facilitated the participation of sympathetic non-Communists in Soviet sponsored activities: freeing their members of the stigma they would otherwise suffer, and the rigours of Party discipline which the 'fellow traveller' has congenitally shunned. Today, front organisations enable the ID to perform a vital function: mobilising the widest possible

Table 2 Major international Communist Front organisations

	Year founded	Head quarters	Claimed membership	Affiliates	Countries
World Peace Council	1949	Helsinki	Not published	Not published	142
World Federation of Trade Unions	1945	Prague	Ca. 206 million	92[a]	81
Women's International Democratic Federation	1945	East Berlin	Over 200 million	135[b]	117[b]
World Federation of Democratic Youth	1945	Budapest	Over 150 million	Over 270	123
Afro-Asian People's Solidarity Organisation	1957	Cairo	Not published	87	Not published
International Union of Students	1946	Prague	Over 10 million	120 (?)[c]	112 (?)[c]
World Federation of Scientific Workers	1946	London	Ca. 500 000	Ca. 40[d]	Over 70
International Organisation of Journalists	1946	Prague	Over 180 000	Not published	Over 120
Christian Peace Conference	1958	Prague	Not published	Not published	At least 80
International Association of Democratic Lawyers	1946	Brussels	Ca. 25 000	Not published	Nearly 80

SOURCE: Wallace Spaulding, 'Communist Fronts in 1984', *Problems of Communism*, 34:2, Mar.–Apr. 1985.

NOTES
[a] *Flashes from the Trade Unions* (Prague), 2 Nov. 1984.
[b] *Women of the Whole World* (East Berlin), No. 1, 1984, p. 5.
[c] National student unions from Malawi and Papua-New Guinea were admitted as new members at the April IUS Congress, Sofia BTA, 16 Apr. 1984.
[d] Radio Prague, 14 Mar. 1984.

support of Soviet foreign policy objectives. The most well known and influential fronts are listed in Table 2. On the basis of considerable testimony, these organisations are under the control, and not just the influence, of Moscow. To preserve their international image, Soviet representatives are almost never found in the top two positions, but the USSR supplies the largest number of figures in overall leadership positions, with the balance filled almost exclusively with Communists, or very reliable 'progressive' figures from Eastern and Western Europe, North America and the Third World.[22] According to Ruth Tosek, a former senior interpreter for several front organisations 'all funds of these organisations, in local and hard currency, are provided above all by the Soviet Union and also by other East European satellite countries.'[23] To all but the most persistent sceptics, four features of front organisation behaviour are enough to give the game away: (1) the absence of published budgets, (2) a fortuitous coordination of positions as regards content and timing, (3) complete preoccupation with the 'peace' issue and the particular hobby horses of the World Peace Council, (4) their consistent support of Soviet policy positions.

Apart from their main purpose, these organisations and their Soviet affiliates serve additional functions: welcoming foreign delegations and dealing with foreign personalities whom Party as well as State cannot afford openly to acknowledge (like Palestinian splinter groups beyond the pale of Middle East politics and at odds with the PLO); funnelling funds to national liberation movements, acting as a negotiating channel for arms and training (both of which are key features of the AAPSO and its Soviet affiliate, the AAPSC); finally, providing background information and intelligence on MPs, Congressmen, community leaders, media personalities and others who wittingly or unwittingly participate in their forums.[24]

It is well and good for a politically active individual to say that he will not deal with Soviet front organisations, and it is not too difficult for most people to familiarise themselves with the names of 11 organisations and several major affiliates. But a legislator or Minister on the receiving end of a letter campaign from thousands identified only as individuals and an individual who joins a major demonstration may have no ready way of establishing in what sea he swims. The name WPC may sound alarm bells, but this will not always be the case for *ad hoc* organisations which their principal figures set up. In modern political warfare, as in warfare, Soviet strategy aims at making it impossible to distinguish 'our troops' from 'their troops'.[25]

The functions performed by fronts and their affiliates are assisted by the research institutes of the Social Sciences Section of the Academy of Sciences – 25 in number as of 1980 in addition to numerous 'scientific councils' – of principal interest amongst them are the Institute of World Economy and International Relations (IMEMO), the Institute of the United States and Canada (ISShAK), the Institute of Oriental Studies (IVAN), of Africa (IA), the Far East (IDV) and of Latin America (ILA). Staff of the larger institutes may number into the many hundreds. Principal functions are:

Background Research and Intelligence Collection

Staffs are sufficiently large and qualified to comb through publications in their particular areas, and to ensure that leading figures and experts are familiar with non-Soviet perspectives and the nuances of foreign debate and opinion. The collection effort is carried out through extensive participation in international forums, an intensive programme of foreign visits, and the cultivation of foreign contacts.[26] Ties with the KGB, and in some cases the GRU, are close. (A member of the Soviet delegation to the British conference of the International Physicians for the Prevention of Nuclear War in 1982 was one M. A. Milshtein, in fact Lieutenant General M. A. Milshtein, Head of the Political–Military Section of ISShAK, and Deputy Chief for Disinformation in the GRU.[27]) It is estimated that one-third of the members of ISShAK are KGB officers, including its Deputy Director, Colonel Doctor Radomir Bogdanov. According to a former staff member, the surveillance and 'collection' enterprise was greatly intensified after Bogdanov's arrival.[28]

Background briefings and assessment

The value and influence of these are much in dispute. A few senior representatives, such as Arbatov have some standing in policy-making circles. But if it *is* true that he is a principal advisor to the Politburo, he is probably at the outer rim of that privileged circle. Politburo advice is more apt to come from key figures of the ID and from Service I of the KGB, which prepares daily classified bulletins. The role of research institutes in this respect is to support the research staffs of the International Department, the Ministry of Foreign Affairs and the intelligence services. According to one student of these matters, many institute briefing papers and journals end up in Central Committee wastepaper baskets. However, the small number of leading specialists from these organisations, grouped together under Yuriy Zhilin as a full-time consultants group to the ID, is thought to provide high quality, in-depth assessments, thereby freeing ID staff to deal with a considerable day to day operational agenda.[29]

Promotion of Soviet foreign policy objectives

This is the principal function of these institutes. In a 1973 publication entitled *The War of Ideas in International Relations*, Georgiy Arbatov stated:

> Not a whit more realistic is the plan for peaceful coexistence on the basis of an 'ideological armistice', under which each would stick to his own ideology but renounce the ideological struggle. This 'project' can only be considered realistic by people who do not understand the essence of the social processes taking place in the world and who entertain the illusion that the wheel of history can be halted by mutual agreement.[30]

In publications for the institute's Western audiences (like the *The Soviet Viewpoint*) as well as in personal contacts, the tone could not be more different. A key feature of the *détente* era is the extent to which Arbatov, Bogdanov, Milshtein, Inozemtsev and others have succeeded in ensconcing themselves into international circuits concerned with advancing East–West understanding. KGB, ID and Institute personnel have participated directly in national campaigns in Europe and North America against the neutron bomb or Cruise and Pershing missiles and have featured prominently in rallies, 'dialogues', 'seminars' and 'strategy sessions'.

Of the Soviets who applied for visas to attend a disarmament conference sponsored by the National Academy of Sciences in Washington in January 1982, roughly half were known intelligence officers. The State Department refused entry to most of them. Nevertheless, of those who came, almost half were co-opted KGB agents or International Department operatives.[31]

Whereas fronts target a broad sweep of individuals, institute intellectuals tend to focus on élite groups and their ostensible Western counterparts.

THE CURRENCY OF INFLUENCE

For many, the Soviet propaganda offensive in NATO countries is an unsavoury subject, lending itself to hyperbole, conspiracy theories, witch hunts and other postures and practices discomfiting not only to the liberal mind, but the civilised one. Dissension in NATO is not the product of Soviet active measures or of the Soviet Union's 'unwitting tools'. The lion's share of those at odds with NATO policy are a loyal opposition: the NATO establishment of today is in large measure composed of yesterday's outsiders. Debate is not only unavoidable in a democratic alliance; it is the mechanism which enables a collective entity of sovereign states to function. The contradictions within NATO – the products of geography and history – have not been put in place by the USSR, although the changed correlation of forces since 1970 has thrown them into sharp relief. What can be said is that the USSR has done its utmost to aggravate these contradictions – insidiously and continuously, at times with stupendous ineptness and at times to its immense advantage. In the process it has become more difficult for Western governments to distinguish its 'adversaries' from its 'critics'.[32]

Stanlislav Levchenko and Ladislaw Bittman are but two of a growing number of participants to confirm what many have believed for years: the importance attached to active measures by the Soviet leadership, the central role of the Politburo in initiating and monitoring active measures campaigns, and the success attributed by the leadership to its efforts.[33] Anti-Americanism in Europe, French withdrawal from NATO, the reversal of the neutron bomb deployment decision and the present furore over INF, the nuclear freeze and SDI are developments which many Western commentators (including to a large degree this author) consider to be home grown creations.[34] The CPSU Politburo for its part seems to believe otherwise. All that can be recorded here in modest proportion is the nature of the Soviet effort and of the USSR's own understanding of it. It must fall to others who are so inclined to indict their fellows for complicity or foolishness.

Soviet practitioners themselves recognise that active measures have their best chance of succeeding if they are built upon authentic anxieties and grievances. This is not to suggest that the USSR limits itself to fishing in troubled waters. As T. B. Millar once put it, she is as wont to trouble the waters and then fish in them.[35]

Marxist–Leninists, like old Tories, believe that it is the élite, not the mass who determine the course of things. (Hence, the need for 'vanguards'.) Not surprisingly, the lion's share of the propaganda effort is directed at those in positions of prominence and authority; and yet it is those whom one supposes are best equipped to grasp the reasoning behind this activity who write off Soviet propaganda as crude bombast and miss its real thrust.

When most think of Soviet propaganda campaigns, the ritualised jargon of *Pravda, New Times* and other Party mouthpieces is what comes to mind. But the principal function of these utterances is coded communication between élite factions within the Communist political world, not propaganda for international audiences. The opaque and Delphic *lingua franca* of the international communist movement, however, performs a second role: it drops a veil of inscrutability over real deliberations and forces everyone to strain to catch the informed or inadvertent hint. What other country could inspire newspaper columns and outpourings of hope by revealing that one leader has a liking for jazz and that another has a sense of humour? At the time of the KAL affair, the technique proved most effective. One acquaintance of the author in Moscow was told 'in confidence' by an ISShaK representative that, 'of course', there was no way of knowing that 007 was a spy plane at the time, but that irrefutable evidence to this effect had come to light since; the same month, a second acquaintance was told 'in confidence' by an East European ambassador to the United Nations that 'of course' everybody understood that 007 was *not* a spy plane, that the Russians were sorry as well as chagrined and would even consider paying compensation – but as their reputation could not survive an admission of such incompetence, was it not in everyone's interest to tone down the protests and help them get off the hook? The purpose of the 'big lie' is not always to be believed, but to inspire a search for a plausible truth.

When the mask suddenly drops and a Soviet spokesman speaks in normal tones, almost anyone would think the truth is at last being revealed to the world. This is where the Arbatovs of this world acquire their importance. The content of their arguments may be thoroughly pedestrian, but this is secondary to the fact that a Soviet spokesman has spoken in a recognisable idiom and revealed himself to be 'really human after all'.

'Disinformation' is less a matter of purveying falsehoods than of communicating information, true and false, which is intended to deceive. Soviet visitors who tell anti-Soviet jokes, and snipe at *Pravda* for being 'simple minded' are better for the purpose than those who do not: a 'line' to be believed must not sound like a 'line'. Disinformation may mix truth with fabrication or simply distort reality by placing true statements in a false context. A recurrent theme amongst institute Russians is the chronic complaint about 'our own hard liners'. This, presumably, is not meant to remind the listener that policy argument in the USSR is shaped by democratic centralism and a peculiarly Leninist set of assumptions, but instead intended to conjure up the thought that behind the green baize door, there is a policy-making world not unlike our own, and that 'reasonable and moderate' men in the West have allies in Moscow who need their help. (Very difficult indeed to find a Soviet representative who claims that *he* is a hard liner).

Soviet spokesmen over the years have learnt to cut their cloth to fit the customer. There is a world of difference in tone and substance (though more in tone than substance) between the Arbatov who wrote *The War of Ideas in International Relations* and the Arbatov who wrote *The Soviet Viewpoint*, as one reviewer remarked:

> The eerie thing about *The Soviet Viewpoint* . . . is that Georgiy Arbatov seems to be impersonating Cyrus Vance. What the book stunningly reveals is Arbatov's sophistication about American liberalism. He knows its peculiar gullibility, and he speaks its idiom with near-perfect nuance.[36]

In some contrast, a different sort of audience – which is to say this author and, on a separate occasion, the Director of his Institute – were told by Soviet spokesmen that, 'of course', armaments do not cause wars, and that any 'realist' understands the folly of negotiating from anything less than a 'position of strength'. The code of practice remains unaltered since Felix Dzerzhinskiy, Chief of Lenin's Cheka, first established it: 'tell them what they want to hear!'[37]

Many assume that, in seeking to influence opinion or recruit agents of influence, the Soviet aim is to convert and that the target is always on the left. To the contrary, the object is not necessarily to convince, but sow doubt. In ideological war as in shooting war, neutralisation of the opponent is sufficient to render him useless. In this enterprise, the Centre and right of the spectrum are not only fair game, but prized quarry. This, after all, is elemental Leninist logic:

> One can only conquer a more powerful enemy by the greatest exertion of forces and by the compulsory, careful, thoughtful and skilful use of every, even the smallest, split between the enemies;

[and by utilising] any ally for oneself, even a temporary, unsteady, unreliable, conditional one.[38]

The agents of influence recruited by Stanislaw Levchenko were one-third Marxist or of the left, one-third of the Centre and one-third of the right. According to Ladislaw Bittman, former Deputy Chief of the Disinformation Department of Czech intelligence,

the objective, of course, is not to recruit solely on the left, but rather across the political spectrum. The Social Democratic Party [of West Germany] was deeply penetrated, but we also had agents among the Christian Democrats. . . . In West Germany, for example, if you were working with an individual on the political right, German nationalism, US domination and manipulation of West Germany, and similar themes were stressed. . . . Every institution with foreign activities was employed, including trade organizations and associations, transportation organizations, journalist groups, and social groupings (such as, victims of Nazi aggression).[39]

Many who have no illusions about these activities believe on reflection that such contacts, properly handled, have their uses and can advance understanding. It can also be said that Soviet spokesmen are not unique in wishing to see the interests of their country advanced. Both points are true enough, but each in its way obscures critical distinctions. Whereas a Western industrialist, publishing executive or academic may, as an individual, wish to see his own country's fortunes prosper, that is not invariably his purpose in discussing the state of the world with a Soviet visitor. To his Soviet counterpart, however, advancement of foreign policy objectives is precisely what the discussion is meant to achieve; moreover, it is foreign policy interests as defined by the Politburo which are to be advanced, not the preferences and aspirations of the individual concerned. In that sense, 'discussion', understood as a mutual exploration, enrichment and adjustment of view, is often a misnomer for what is taking place. Secondly, understanding in the sense of 'intelligence', may well profit by such contacts. A serious exploration of views will help a Soviet visitor understand the strength of support for official positions, the terrain of argument over political issues in the local country, and lines of cleavage between and within tendencies of opinion. That may be useful for us as well as for him. But rather than reflect upon what is said by one's Soviet interlocutors, one would do better to reflect upon the purpose and to ask oneself why things are said. In any event, the key to genuine Soviet opinion is what is communicated to Soviet élites, not to our own.

DOES IT REALLY MATTER? A CASE IN POINT

Janos Berecz, Chairman of the Hungarian Communist Party's International Department, has boasted that 'the political campaign against the neutron bomb was one of the most significant and successful since World War II'.[40] This judgement has been echoed by Levchenko and Myagkov.

In 1961, when the possibility of developing such a device was first mooted in Western defence circles, Nikita Khrushchev declared:

> the neutron bomb as conceived by American scientists should kill everything but leave material assets intact. . . . They are acting as robbers who want to murder a man without staining his suit with blood so as to be able to use his suit.[41]

These remarks were the obvious forerunner to the Soviet media's description of the late 1970s: 'the archetypal capitalist weapon . . . a weapon which kills people without destroying property'. It would be interesting to know how this epigram migrated from Radio Moscow to the Western media, in as much as it bears scant resemblance to the bomb's characteristics and has no relation to its purpose.

As the date of Khrushchev's remarks indicates, the ERW has been the product of extensive research; however, only in the mid-1970s was its feasibility established. For years, NATO defence planners had laboured with the challenge posed in the Central Region by massed Warsaw Pact tank formations – all the more so after Khrushchev's departure, as improved firepower and mobility of conventional forces became a priority for the Soviet General Staff. Even the more devastating retaliation against Warsaw Pact choke points, staging areas and second echelon forces might not stave off defeat if its first echelon forces were strong enough to overcome NATO's defences. Rather than 'killing people and sparing property', the ERW was designed to engage armoured formations in open country (where, by virtue of the laws of physics, tank armies are obliged to concentrate). ERW therefore promised to free NATO governments from the 'MAD' choice between defeat and a Pyrrhic victory. Not even the most callous commander could have another purpose in mind, because the advantages of the ERW over other nuclear devices only come into play over distance. Targetted upon a city, the 'neutron bomb' would produce unacceptable damage by any standard: probably equal to that of a 'conventional' fission warhead, once secondary effects are taken into account.[42] Indeed, in the absence of such a defence against a well armed adversary, NATO would probably confront the prospect of Pyrrhic defeat, as the cost to life and property of a conventional attack which accomplishes its objective could well surpass the damage, direct and collateral, of a nuclear defence which halted the enemy. It is easy to appreciate the violence of the Soviet reaction to NATO's plans. Deployed in the Central Region, ERW would force the opponent to disperse his forces; it would diminish the shock and momentum of an attack, restore the initiative to the defender, and, indeed, afford him a real chance of accomplishing his objective by conventional means. Given such handicaps, an opponent would have far less incentive to cross the threshold of war in the first place.

The Ford administration's approval of deployment was prompt. Over the course of 1976, preparations proceeded without public clamour and without outcry from the USSR. But Ford's successor, Jimmy Carter, regarded the issue with ambivalence. In the summer of 1977, as the United States Congress authorised funding for the ERW, Carter announced that he would reconsider the merits of deployment. This step seems to have provided the USSR with the opportunity she sought. Within a month, the active measures apparatus mobilised for what turned out to be its most ambitious campaign since the Stockholm Peace Appeal of the early 1950s. President Carter's cancellation of the ERW programme in April 1978 is, from one point of view, encouraging testimony to the *limits* of Soviet influence. Despite the magnitude of the campaign, Carter's three principal advisors – Harold Brown, Zbigniew Brzezinski and Cyrus Vance – backed deployment to the end. NATO governments publicly confirmed their endorsement of the decision and, in the very week of cancellation, America's two leading liberal newspapers, the *New York Times* and the *Washington Post*, endorsed deployment.[43] But Carter's final decision reveals the extent to which the entire question of influence is governed by imponderables. Of some things there can be no uncertainty: cancellation did not restore the warmth of *détente*, and it had no effect on the momentum of Soviet nuclear deployments in Europe.

Within seven years, NATO has born the brunt of three massive propaganda offensives, launched in response to deployment decisions.

The techniques utilised during the 'neutron bomb' affair of 1978 resurfaced in the nuclear freeze campaign (1980–81) and, more recently, over INF deployment (1979–1985). Each campaign has been the product of a combined arms approach; like the General Staff, the ID has deployed overt and covert means in pursuit of its strategy: an unremitting Soviet media offensive; personal appeals (by scientists, trades unionists and other professionals to opposite numbers, by Deputies of the Supreme Soviet to Western legislators, and personal letters from General Secretaries Brezhnev and Andropov to NATO Heads of Government); forgeries; penetration of the Western media; and 'agent of influence' operations. But more than any single, measure, the various undertakings of the World Peace Council have probably had the greatest impact. That activity in itself has been both overt and *sub rosa*: demonstration under the WPC's own colours; demonstrations, 'seminars', petitions and 'dialogues' under the cloak of *ad hoc* committees and fronts; and the infiltration of independent, non-Communist peace organisations. Thanks to the WPC's willingness 'to utilise any ally, even the most conditional', representatives of the ID have even been welcomed into the US Capitol building itself.

Each campaign has shrewdly articulated a message which, in its contradictory form, speaks to a public caught between its own ambivalences: war is impossible today (hence, weapons modernisation is wasteful and unnecessary); war is all too possible (hence, weapons modernisation will hasten it). The USSR, as Brezhnev's and Andropov's letters have stated, 'threatens no one', but deployment will have grave (but unspecified) consequences. It is not easy to see how the proponents of present policies are to proceed against this pungent mixture of moods. Should NATO's spokesmen aim to reassure the public, or (in the words of a late American Senator) 'scare Hell out of the country'?

Definitive answers are unlikely to emerge about the extent of Soviet influence in Western debates, and it is not our purpose to produce them here. But what questions would be asked? 'Whose opinion has been changed by Soviet propaganda?' is not a fruitful question. Even if the answer were an impressive one, that in Leninist terms would be a small prize. Rather than ask whether Soviet activity has altered opinions, we would do better to consider whether it has magnified certain opinions in our own perceptions. It is not too difficult to envisage how this would be accomplished. Participatory democracy is bursting with joiners, but in the normal course of events producers only a finite number of organisers. The entrance of the Politburo's active measures apparatus into our pluralist world is like the intervention of a state bank into a market of individual buyers and sellers. Demonstrations are the product of planning, organisation and funding: they do not arise spontaneously even if the decision to join them is a spontaneous one. The greatest prize for the USSR would be to distort our perception of our own society and persuade us that the centre ground of debate lies leftwards of its true position. To date, polling data suggest that, in spite of the tumult, the centre ground has not moved very far. But this could change if the 50 per cent come to confuse themselves with the 5 per cent. The Orwellian aspect of social intercourse is that people genuinely wish to believe what is appropriate; the Orwellian aspect of communication is that questions frame their own answers. Once 'we all know that the arms race is the greatest danger we face', some solutions become difficult to propose, and a good many problems disappear from view. The best course for the NATO establishment might be to trust its public: to be more fearful of articulating banalities (to which the hysteria of hysterics, the pressures of collective responsibility, and its own inbred reticence drive it) than of articulating its honest dilemmas. It should avoid buying into its opponent's assumptions, and it should realise that its supporters need as much reassurance as its critics. But however NATO governments conduct themselves in future, the Soviet Politburo will continue with its efforts as long as it considers them effective.

7 Conclusion

It was not before our culture, bureaucratised church, or wealth and prosperity that the world bowed. It bowed before our power. And when – with a significant degree of exaggeration – it appeared that we were not as strong as everybody thought and that Russia was the colossus on clay legs – the picture immediately changed. All our enemies – both internal and foreign – raised their heads and the neutrals began to pay no attention to us.

Sergei Witte

It has been said that the civilised mind is a museum of contradictory truths. This adage stands as both a comfort and a warning to those who would assess the Soviet challenge. At the very least, the terrain to be negotiated is full of unfamiliar truths, not readily perceived with a Westerner's sextant and compass. In Europe and North America, three paradigms about Soviet conduct have contended for influence, summed up respectively by the words 'insecure', 'imperial' and 'revolutionary'; each frequently, if not always happily, associated with a 'defensive', 'pragmatic' and 'expansionist' reading of Soviet policy. These paradigms are at best like primary colours: only when combined do they enable one to see properly.

For all the striking exaggerations of the phenomenon by Soviet rulers, the legacy of vulnerability in the USSR is real enough, and insecurities about the outside world have deep and authentic roots. Soviet history, however, offers more in the way of warning than encouragement for those who would ask that the West 'give a lead' in compromise, conciliation and restraint. Weakness as well as success in surmounting it have only confirmed the 'who, whom' of Leninism, the perception of politics as struggle, and the belief that 'progress' can only be achieved through vigilance and strength. It is also well to remember the influence of internal threats on Soviet attitudes and the potency of the connection between the country's internal and external security problems. The seizure of power, the triumphs over deviationists, White Guardists, 'Basmachi'; the 'trials' of collectivisation; the suppression of Vlasovites, Banderists, collaborators and 'cosmopolites' have also shaped a view of how to protect oneself, deal with opponents, and 'get things done'. To suggest that a policy of unilateral gestures and restraints will somehow talk the USSR out of this view of the world betrays a lack of respect for its resilience and sophistication, a far-fetched notion of the abilities of Western policy-makers and an even deeper misunderstanding of their responsibilites.

But there is equal warning in this history to those instantly ready to characterise all Soviet activity as aggressive and expansionist. Far-reaching ambitions and immutable hostility do not give the lie to the claim (most recently advanced in Chernenko's obituary) that the 'primary concern' is the 'consolidation of the achievements of socialism' and the development of the 'cooperation and cohesion of the socialist community'. 'What has changed in the world?' a Soviet diplomat recently asked. He supplied his own reply: 'We are not afraid of you.' We have heard such things before, but the Soviet mood has always oscillated between confidence that movement in the correlation of forces is firmly in train and wary apprehension that the adversary will again turn the tables and snatch it all away. The Soviet rulers, active in the enemy's rear, attach by Western standards an inordinate concern about the security of their own. The challenge for the future may be a USSR both strong and insecure. In such circumstances it will be difficult to keep her 'between her hopes and her fears'.

For a second set of people – including much of the foreign policy establishment – the USSR is not so much a Leninist power as the last multinational empire in a world which has convinced itself that the age of empire has passed. To them it is more conclusively Russian than Leninist, more national than Communist and in many respects conservative despite itself: willing to deal with us in the currency of *Realpolitik* but for the fact that we ourselves have disowned it. Within its own terms this is a worrying appraisal, owing to the role which potent nationalisms have played in igniting conflict, particularly when put under threat: the international state system's track record in managing the decline of empires is a poor one. Yet the terms themselves are wanting. There is no contradiction between Russianness and ideology. Orthodoxy, messianism, a sense of exclusiveness and of destiny are all staple to Russian culture; Leninism, with its 'scientific' approach to problems – its ruthless schematising of means and ends – has disciplined rather than displaced the traditional Russian mind. For all the cynicism attributed to them, the Soviet rulers are likely to read crisis as 'climax' rather than 'miscalculation' and, presented with opportunity, are always likely to read the hand of God ('history') into it. The 'White Revolutionary', Bismarck, understood as a strategic as well as a tactical proposition, that 'genius is knowing where to stop'. Imperialist Soviets believe that politics tends towards primacy, not equilibrium, and like the last German Kaiser, they may not know when to stop.

Still, without the *Realpolitik* and 'imperial' perspective, we cannot understand what is essential to the Soviet predicament: ambivalence, the need to have one's cake and eat it. The USSR now understands what she did not fully grasp in the 1920s: that when instability threatens, she will not be its automatic beneficiary. She therefore seeks an end to history at home and controlled instability elsewhere: the best of the conservative and revolutionary worlds. It is this ambivalence that makes it possible to 'do business' with her.

Perhaps a greater basis for optimism on this score is Leninism itself. By looking starkly into what *is*, by 'judging everything according to the correlation of forces', the USSR has found it possible to manage its affairs with prudence, which in turn has made it possible for us to co-exist in safety. If the 'wheel of history' should turn against her in some decisive fashion, our safety may depend on whether the astringency of Leninism is strong enough to hold the *amour prôpre* of Russian imperialism in check. Leninism inspires confidence that the USSR will remain rational to the end, just as it ensures that she will remain hostile.

Many of the author's bedfellows in the 'ideological camp' are guilty of reading too little into their own insights: Leninism is not only a blueprint for expansion but a strategy for coping. A principal theme of this study has been the distinctiveness and resilience of the Soviet outlook. Many who have sought to draw attention to this ideology have described the problem in such stilted and stereotyped terms, and an adversary so single-minded, as to make their subject not only distinctive, but implausible. The continuities of Leninism with the Russian outlook, its 'fit' with the complexities of Soviet and Russian history are the things which have given it its reality and guaranteed it a long life. It is interesting how even Soviet *émigrés*, determined to demonstrate the ideological bankruptcy of the USSR, succeed instead in impressing a Western audience with Russia's yearning for ideals. When those who most loathe the CPSU and all its works themselves express a who–whom, two-camp and apocalyptic view of the world, one is able to appreciate the depth of the divide which separates East and West in the 1980s.

A second objective of this study has been to bring out the institutional sub-structure of Soviet power. The basic indicators of intention are normally taken to be words and action. To these, following in Lenin's footsteps, we have added a third: organisation. It is through the instruments and mechanisms of policy that one can discern the actors and priorities in policy formation, the scope for countervailing interest and argument, the limits to reform in the Soviet economy and to diversity in Eastern Europe, and the meaning of '*détente*'. In the Soviet Union as elsewhere, personalities matter in politics. But so long as the institutions of democratic centralism and the vetting, pruning and filleting of élites (*nomenklatura*) survive, policy-making and policy-makers in Eastern Europe as well as the USSR are likely to reflect a set of orientations and commitments alien to Western thinking and broadly hostile to Western interests. To be sure, there is a spectrum of opinion in the Soviet élite on most questions of moment, but that is not to say it is one which reproduces our own. Whether or not Gorbachev will be able to proceed with Andropov's vigour in revamping the apparatus, his link with Andropov is sufficient to remind us that in Russia discipline has been the complement to reform, chauvinism to modernism, and decisiveness to flexibility. Like the previous leaders in the 'energising' tradition, Gorbachev's advent to power may presage a new boldness and shrewdness in foreign policy, today as in the past defined as the advancement of Soviet power, not the 'reduction of tension' for its own sake. The Stalin–Khrushchev succession serves to remind us of how much these interests can change and yet remain the same. *Rapprochement* with Tito, the wooing of the Third World, 'peaceful coexistence' and the shelving of the thesis of 'inevitable war' all knocked away the pillars of the edifice of Stalinist foreign policy, but only to restore and rejuvenate its Leninist foundations. That experience shows as well how likely it is that new dangers will accompany new opportunities. The process which nurtured and promoted Gorbachev, more bureaucratic and 'institutionalised' than in Khrushchev's day, make it unlikely that he will depart nearly so dramatically from the policies of his predecessors.

A second set of institutional indicators is the command economy, the meshing of civil–military concerns in education, industry, and the Military District; the dominating role in the planning process of the Defence Council and Military–Industrial Commission; and the ubiquitous priority system. These provide very clear indication of how society interprets its basic tasks as well as how it performs them. They remind us, above all, that the USSR *is* a society with basic tasks, not one where private and collective needs are left to bargain with one another in an open political and economic marketplace. True enough, the 'achievements of socialism' to be 'consolidated' embrace more than defence; the 'struggle for strengthening the economy and defence might of the motherland' demands investment in human capital as well as material infrastructure. It is enough to say that the institutional structure 'biases' the allocation of resources and that the more directly individuals and enterprises relate to defence and security, the more they will be favoured. It is not only the behaviour, but the existence, of these institutions which sees to this. If priorities are to be altered – a prospect which for reasons of security is very much in doubt – the litmus test will come not in speeches and exhortations, but in concrete structural changes. One cannot ask a 'military representative' in an enterprise to be fair to its other priorities, but in the interest of other priorities, one can dispense with 'military representatives'.

Finally, a particularly illuminating set of institutional indicators is the 'active measures' apparatus: the International Department, KGB and GRU, and the infrastructure of paramilitary training and assistance. The mere existence of the Comintern and its successors is enough to call into question the allegiance of the USSR to a diplomatic order of diverse sovereign states. The expansion of this apparatus in time of *détente* provides more concrete indication than anything else of why 'reduction of tensions' is desired and what it is meant to accomplish.

What is noteworthy in every sphere is that the institutions which most distinguish the USSR from ourselves have, in the fullness of time, shown the greatest expansion and development. This may say more about the prospects for East–West convergence than the 'common problems' which we allegedly face.

A third theme of this study is that the West tends to underestimate the Soviet Union. This is, perhaps, a curious point to make: in academic and many policy-making circles, it has by now become almost a convention to assert the opposite. Even the right falls into this category with its belief that all would be well if we lost our illusions about *détente* and 'took the gloves off'. In the post-war years, in the wake of Korea, China, not to speak of the *coup de mains* in Central Europe and the ending of our atomic monopoly, there was necessity as well as reason to stress 'the limits of Soviet power' – and again in the late 1950s when, thanks to inadequate intelligence assessment, Khrushchev's blusterings were taken at their word. It has been a long while since the USSR was seen as the source of a Red menace spreading over the world like indelible ink, or as an impulsive tyro ready to turn the tables on the West. The received wisdom of today is that the USSR is a flawed society, weighted down by military expenditure and its own inertia, governed by weary and cantakerous men whose inscrutability is a front for weakness and whose inevitability expresses cynicism more than hostility. Without all those tanks, a good many people think that the game would be up. This comparison may reveal less of how the Soviet Union has changed than about the ease with which images go in and out of fashion in our own society. We have tried to suggest that just as Soviet strengths are hackneyed and stereotyped into harmlessness, the USSR possesses the virtues of its own real weaknesses: hence the reason these weaknesses are so incorrigible.

STATE AND SOCIETY

Revolution is an uncommon occurrence in the industrialised world all the more so when élites are cohesive and present a united front to challenges from below. Stagnation in the standard of living, ossification of social mobility and demographic changes provide an agenda of worries. But order in the USSR will remain a function of whether the regime is respected, not whether it is liked. Dread of weakness and anarchy retain a hold on the popular psyche; patriotism promises to remain deep and unquenchable: one senses that there remains much in this account upon which Gorbachev and his successors will be able to draw. For all this, Russian society promises to remain a form of stand-off between the unpolitical 'we' (*obshchestvo*) and a political 'they' (*gosudarstvo*): the regime is a bane, but authority is like that; it is something to be coped with rather than questioned. As a political culture, the USSR will continue to reconcile what for us are incompatibles: cynicism about the system and patriotism; lethargy and endurance; resentment of 'them' along with a visceral admiration of decisiveness and strength.

Within the past decade or so, the West has discovered the Soviet nationality problem, but in the USSR it is nothing new, nor without its compensations. In the Muslim borderlands, Sovietism has corresponded with modernity; those with the education and ability to get things done tend to be the least interested in their own national traditions and the most 'clubbable' as far as mainstream Soviet culture is concerned. It is in the most European regions of the country – the Baltic republics and the western Ukraine – that resentments promise to explode, but it is not these populations who threaten the demographic balance, nor do they possess the numbers and wherewithal to bring down the regime. As the position of Great Russians becomes imperilled, identification of the Russian population with the established order promises to become greater rather than less.

A further buttress to order is that the Soviet élite, perhaps unique in European society, is not ashamed of being one. It is imbued with a quality still celebrated in the West, if refined out of existence by our civilising history: will. As the record of American–Soviet strategic competition shows, the Soviet Union is willing to run twice as fast to stay in place; as Afghanistan and the latest Polish crisis demonstrates, if the challenge matters the regime is willing to double the stakes and 'tough it out'. The USSR's rulers will consider it essential in the interests of public order and élite interest to retain both the appearance and substance of power: irrespective of the justice of the grievance, dissent must be seen to be futile. It is when élites become unsure of themselves and begin to bargain that they invite trouble. This has its counterpart in foreign policy: in times of stress, international reverses have usually set the ball of revolution rolling. By the same token, the regime must retain its monopoly of the distribution of privileges and perquisites (a Petrine innovation) and of resources (a Soviet innovation). These imperatives will place stringent limits on the degree to which foreign policy can become relaxed, diversity can be tolerated abroad, and economic authority devolved at home. But this approach to authority is apt to ensure stability and encourage opportunism rather than opposition in Soviet society. It is an error to downplay the strength and resilience of Soviet society: an error Hitler committed in 1941 and one which the democratic West may repeat.

ECONOMICS

The structural problems embedded in the economy are likely to remain lodged there. Whilst strain and stress are an appropriate vocabulary for discussing economic prospects, breakdown is not, and there is little in these problems, or even their momentum, to suggest that the Soviet Union soon, or in the forseeable future, will lose the wherewithal to remain a Superpower. The broad range of tasks by which *we* assess performance is in the USSR performed cumbersomely, inflexibly and poorly. For power political purposes, however, what matters is that in the international states system the economy remains best at fulfilling the finite number of things relevant to a country's international aims. The USSR is in this respect not only a worthy competitor, but also in a position of some advantage. Deficiencies in technology – especially in electronics and data processing – must be set against an impressive ingenuity in stretching technologies, in improvising and in making do. Growth rates, GDP comparisons and imbalances in the economy disguise the fact that the USSR may be able to outproduce the West in the material of war: a function of heavy industrial infrastructure and not simply of an obliviousness to social costs.

When it comes to international leverage and dependency, the legacy of the 1970s has been bitter-sweet, and it has left the West with fewer levers that it once possessed. In this game, we have noted that the USSR possesses levers of its own. By cost accountant's logic, the USSR suffers more than the West if grain, pipe-laying equipment and heavy machinery are embargoed. But the political logic is that the 70 per cent of the Soviet population who suffer from meat shortages may have fewer cards to play that the 3 per cent of Americans, comprising their suppliers, against an elected government in an election year. It is in the overall Western interest that trade-offs in the Soviet economy become more difficult rather than less and that present policies become more rather than less expensive to sustain. But this calculus must be reconciled against the cohesiveness of the Atlantic Alliance and the imperatives and pressures of democratic politics if it is to be turned to good effect. There is otherwise a risk of shooting ourselves in the face in order that we might shoot the opponent in the foot. Even if we avoid these pitfalls, the dividends accruing from economic pressure are apt to be modest. It is ironic that those who most appreciate what is distinct about Soviet politics and priorities are often the first to insist that the USSR will make Western-style choices (such as diverting resources from the military sector) when the squeeze is on.

Finally, any balance sheet for the future must include possibilities as well as limits. An 'energising' leadership may conclude that, for all the tinkering of the past two decades, the system has not been put through its paces. Whilst the underlying impediment to modernisation and efficiency is the system itself, a real, if ancillary, problem are the many corrigible deficiences within it. In the short to mid-term, progress remains possible even if 'solutions' are not. Within any politically significant timespan, it seems unlikely that the USSR will be definitively eclipsed or put out of the competition. For the long term, trends may be working against the USSR, but there are others (economic restructuring and the whittling away of heavy industrial capacity) that may work against the West – though one suspects that our most serious deficiencies will lie on the political and psychological fronts.

MILITARY POWER

The vaunted Soviet ability to produce tanks, ships and aircraft may be less impressive – and in the crunch less critical – than attention to the art of war and the closest possible study of its adversary's attributes and failings. Military power is not strictly a function of men and material, but the interaction between strategy, organisation and these two things; by the same token, quality is not defined by technology, but by the meshing of men and machines into an effective fighting organisation. The Soviet approach to war has shown integration and planning, calculation and forethought. Soviet strategy draws on a tradition distinct from our own: a tradition which regards peace and war as complementary, not antithetical entities. To date, Western strengths and Soviet predicaments have made war unattractive, and Soviet successes have made it unnecessary. But if this equation should change, the weakest link in our armour may not be the adequacy of our nuclear systems or of our conventional war-fighting prowess, but our ability to meet the challenges of transition between peace and war. Moreover, the initiative, creativity and virtuosity which are staple to Western societies may be mixed blessings in general armed conflict, particularly that which the USSR would plan to conduct. The notion that the intangibles would favour NATO in crisis or war is one which warrants the most painstaking re-examination.

Finally, we have drawn attention to aspects of power not normally included in the portfolio of Soviet assets: a cultivation over the years of non-military means of influencing change and, in all things, a concerted and multi-dimensional approach. 'Active measures' seem largely unmatched and also unappreciated in much of the West. In a world of pragmatists and problem-solvers, the USSR has shown a strategic grasp, a capacity for sustained and serious thought about political problems, and she has proved herself a manipulative as well as a cunning adversary: past master at dividing and misleading opponents, and surprisingly adept at gaining adherents to her cause. The fruit of her experience in matters of power and organisation have made her support and tutelage attractive not only to the most ruthless, but also to some of the cleverest and most capable élites in the world's more volatile regions. The USSR possesses influence as well as power in the world. She is likely to remain a going concern and a continuing challenge.

Part II

Perceptions of Soviet Power

8 Perceptions of Soviet Power and Influence

HELMUT SONNENFELDT*

Concepts like power and influence, however precisely they might be defined, have many intangible elements. I hope therefore you will be tolerant of my imprecisions and impressionistic judgments. Moreover, the notion of perceptions has become a fashionable way to describe any problem or inconsistency – one simply says: 'that's my perception and somebody else may have a different perception'. Nothing is what it really is; it is only a perception. Thus that part of my topic, too, lends itself to a certain amount of vagueness.

Let me nonetheless make some comments about Soviet power and Soviet influence as I see them. Inevitably, I must cast my vision backward a bit because I think the present circumstances and any prognostication for the future are bound to be influenced by one's view of the past. In the early period after the Bolshevik Revolution, the power and influence of Russia as it came to be the Soviet Union were due far less to physical strength than to its reputation, for better or worse, as a revolutionary power. For some, what had happened in Leningrad, Moscow and then Russia as a whole between 1917 and the early 1920s was the wave of the future. Someone – the Webbs reputedly – said they had seen the future and it worked.

This was the inspiration for similar movements in other countries, mostly Western, European, in the post-First World War era. Obviously, for the same reason, to some, what had happened in Russia was the source of subversion and political upheaval and was seen as a threat rather than an inspiration and a hope. Yet it was basically a weak country in a military sense, although huge and clearly capable of absorbing enormous physical hardship as it had demonstrated during the war.

The view of Bolshevik Russia as a source of revolution and a guide-post to the reorganisation of society, whether one saw it as a

* Guest Scholar, The Brookings Institution, Washington, D.C.

181

hope or a source of subversion, was exaggerated. It was neither as much of a model for a better life nor as serious a source of subversion as many people in those days thought. Indeed, the Soviets themselves, even when Lenin was still alive and certainly afterwards, with all their ebullience at having won what they chose to think of as a revolution, soon felt encircled by the outside world. And well they should have, since they were challenging the status quo and represented themselves as prophets of a new order in the desolate circumstances of the post-First World War scene. But as time went on, their power, weight and strength did not become such that Hitler, even allowing for his irrationality, could not feel capable by 1940–41 of making a run at destroying the Soviet Union. And there were not a few in the West, who thought that he might just do so; or that at the very least both Germany and Russia would exhaust each other to the benefit of the rest of the world.

The failure of the Hitlerian adventure – the Russian–Soviet capacity to dip deeply into some physical as well as non-physical resources, and the coincidence that others were also fighting Hitlerian Germany, did turn the Soviet Union into a victor power at the end of the Second World War after enormous exertions and sacrifices and suffering. Although severely damaged, and set back in the programme of forced industrialisation which Stalin had initiated in the 1930s, Soviet Russia emerged as the most powerful land power in Eurasia after the Second World War. It sought in both the *de jure* and the *de facto* peace arrangements after 1945, to buttress its security through zones of control and influence around the periphery, as well as the maintenance of massive military power. The Soviets early in the post-war period and perhaps even during the war, unlike the United States which was the other power that had the real option, decided not to demobilise and dismantle its military establishment but to maintain it.

In the process of surrounding itself with a satellite empire and other zones of influence or control and in the process of maintaining a massive military establishment, Stalin sowed the seeds of many later difficulties, not least in Eastern Europe and with China. And, of course, the policies of seeking from the outcome of the Second World War the maximum feasible security guarantees beyond the border of Soviet Russia provoked Western reactions. Above all, they helped to bring about a fundamental change in the traditional American aloofness from international affairs which was at best episodic and produced American involvement in Europe and the indefinite presence of American military power on the Eurasian land mass.

The Soviets in this period retained some of the aura of a revolutionary and progressive power. But perhaps more important, and in many ways more unfortunate, was that in the West there tended to be widespread acceptance of the Stalinist myth of the irreversibility of 'revolutions'. If they had been properly understood in the West, the events in Russia in 1917 were not so much a revolution as a *coup*. Likewise, Soviet domination of Eastern Europe was achieved by a series of forcible take-overs of governments by communist groups and Soviet controlled security forces. Perhaps this accounts for the sense of irreversibility which ingrained itself so much on the Western mentality as it did during that period. This sense amounted to a substantial bonus to the physical power that the Soviet Union represented in the post-Second World War era. The idea of irreversibility, incidentally, was not shared by the enunciator of the policy of containment, George Kennan. In those days, he spoke, as some Reaganites do today, about the fundamental instability of the Soviet system and the presence within it of the seeds of its own destruction, especially if its expansionary propensity could be contained.

Stalin, for his part, seeking to consolidate the gains from the Second World War, was in fact cautious about excessive expansion. One of his main disagreements with Tito concerned precisely that issue and this was not properly perceived in the West at the time. But Stalin disguised his caution. It was difficult to recognise it because he was interested in frightening or even terrorising the outside world. He wanted to see firmly fixed the notion of irreversibility, of historical inevitability. It was both a shield and a sword for the Soviet Union in attempting to preserve and promote its own interests.

Stalin apparently saw few, if any, opportunities for expansion in the decolonisation process that began in the aftermath of the Second World War. He considered very little in that process as worth the risk to Soviet security. Indeed, he and his ideological acolytes questioned whether what was happening in the European empires was in fact genuine decolonisation. Thus, at the end of the Stalin era, Soviet Russia was a major continental power on the Eurasian land mass. It was widely accepted as a great world power. It sat in the UN Security Council with a veto and in the United Nations itself with three seats. Few people questioned that it was one of the great post-war actors and should be so regarded.

Stalin had concentrated much of his effort on rebuilding and consolidation, though in a context of increasingly Byzantine and debilitating power struggles and manoeuvring for his succession. It is difficult, at least for me, to discern what in fact was Stalin's own concept of a future world order or whether he had one. Of course, it involved power for the Soviet Union. But this was the man who had invented the notion of socialism in one country, partly out of preference and partly out of necessity. I find it far from clear how or even whether, despite the irreversibility myth, he envisaged a world populated by socialist powers on the Soviet model. He could not conceive of any socialist powers on any other model. That indeed was part of the problem. More likely, his vision of the world was one of struggle as his vision of the Soviet Union itself was one of struggle, of suspicion, of police power and of constant concern about security in the personal sense, a vision of struggle for the survival of the regime and of the Soviet Union. With this obsession Stalin probably never got around to having an operationally significant concept of a world order dominated by the Soviet Union and emulating it. In that sense, it may be said that containment worked, although in the West this judgment was far from clear and unchallenged. We did after all have to face the problem of the Korean War and the Soviet Union was far from passive.

We will probably never know what Stalin's own expectations and plans might have been with respect to regions beyond those where the Red Army had halted or where other arrangements, subversive or otherwise, had been made for the installation of Soviet power. But in the post-Stalin period a significant development, in terms of the range and scope of Soviet power and influence, has been the breaking out of the continental mould. Militarily, the USSR did so by acquiring weapons and military implements with a reach beyond the Eurasian land mass, aircraft and then missiles, and, of course, a navy which gradually in the 1950s and 1960s became 'blue water'.

Moreover, Soviet military programmes in the 1950s, 1960s and thereafter were designed to begin and then to accelerate a process of undermining what had become the Western concept of defence for Europe, that is, the reliance on American strategic and nuclear power to offset the advantages of continental (that is, Eurasian continental) Russia *vis-à-vis* the West European peninsula. As the Soviets came to challenge American strategic power and mobility, they challenged the very concept, which the West in its wisdom and with the constraints under which it operated, had come to decide was the safest and best way of protecting Western Europe. That is a problem which clearly remains with us. The Western defence concept is in question because of what the Soviets have achieved militarily.

Politically, the Soviets broke out of the continental mould by adjusting their views of decolonisation and finding and exploiting opportunities to expand their role, influence and, selectively, their presence in regions more remote from Russia. Their methods were to support the grievances of groups of people around the world, particularly against the metropolitan powers but also among each other, to supply them with arms, and to provide a certain political backing, as well as some economic support. Psychologically and ideologically, as they broke out of the Stalin mould and continental limits, the Soviets of Khrushchev's day seemed genuinely to believe that they could be a model for the emerging countries, with their theories and experience of struggle, industrialisation, modernisation and social and political organisation, Soviet leaders thought they had an answer that would be appealing in the 'Third World'. They adjusted doctrinal formulations to meet these aspirations and pretensions, and what they thought were the aspirations, among peoples in the former colonial regions and those still under colonial sway which were emerging as part of the international arena of independent powers.

Thus the assertion of Soviet power and interests began to assume a global character. The revolutionary mystique seemed to have a second wind in this period. Americans may have taken this Soviet plunge into the world's fringes beyond Eurasia more seriously than others. Certainly in the Kennedy Administration it was considered to be the biggest challenge of the day. Indeed, the Kennedy Administration made perhaps the most extensive US commitments, 'Fight any foe, support any friend', in the context of the new Soviet expansionism, although the Kennedy Administration was in fact schizophrenic in its approach to the Soviets. (The ambivalence was manifested in the famous speech at American University by John F. Kennedy in 1963. The first half was about Soviet expansion and its dangers, the second half dealt with how the United States must deal with the Soviet Union in order to cope with the common danger of nuclear conflict.)

Still, the Europeans seemed to be less impressed with Soviet global involvement. They were preoccupied with their own affairs and, I suppose, they had seen empires come and go and were not quite as struck by the Soviet imperial plunge as the Americans. Curiously enough, too, in the Third World, if I may use that bad shorthand term, by and large, people were also less impressed by Soviet involvement in their affairs. Of course, they wanted what help they could get from the Soviets. Sometimes that was considerable in the political and military realms, and, for individual countries, quite substantial in economic terms. But most of them did not consider themselves particularly vulnerable or enticed by the appeals of Soviet communism. In fact, few proved to be very susceptible to the appeals of Soviet communism. There was a variety of reasons for this, having to do with both the inherent character of Soviet communism and the skills, talents and temperaments of the practitioners of Soviet communism.

But, interestingly, while the Americans took the Soviet push seriously and the Europeans and Third World countries did less so, the Chinese took it very seriously; they indeed set about, starting in the late 1950s, to challenge the implications of Soviet policy in the Third World by contesting Soviet hegemony in the entire communist world. This in turn served to undermine the Soviet notion, whatever its precise content, that philosophically at least, it was possible to envisage a harmonious world of diverse communists.

Stalin had had no such notions. But once he had died there were Russians, Khrushchev among them, who did. The Chinese severely challenged that notion under the impact of the Soviet imperial impulse, which asserted itself in the 1950s. Along with this, the East Europeans repeatedly demonstrated what I have in the past referred to as the unnatural character of the Soviet empire as a base for a global order shaped by Soviet example. Again and again we have seen that it is not and cannot be such a base, as long as the Soviets insist on organising affairs in Eastern Europe as they do.

In the 1970s, the US, for reasons involving American over-extension, domestic dissension and many other factors, sought a *modus vivendi* with the Soviet Union based on containment of Soviet military expansion but also on acceptance of a global Soviet role, albeit one characterised by mutual restraint and caution. The United States, in this period, expected other international actors – Europeans, Chinese, Japanese and others – to play a role in maintaining global balance by participating in the containment of Soviet expansionism. But, of course, it was seen as a balance in which the Soviets were bound to be a major actor.

The nature of Soviet power is such that if military instruments are constrained, that power is likely to contract. The other elements of Soviet power have far less weight. Thus, when the US and Europeans were distracted, the Soviets did in fact use, in the latter part of the 1970s, various forms of military power, sometimes via proxies, to manoeuvre for geopolitical gains. Some of these were impressive.

It may be said retrospectively, that the period from 1970 to about 1977, under Brezhnev, was something like the golden age of Bolshevik

Russia. Its interests and ambitions fared reasonably well, for the reasons I have indicated, in the world at large. There was a certain stability within the Soviet Union; stagnation was not yet obvious. There seemed to be a general acquiescence in the regime's policies, at least among the bulk of the population. The élites were reaping the rewards of being élites. Perhaps one of Brezhnev's greater achievements was that, under him the average age of the Politburo became higher than the average age of the Soviet population, which it had not been in the past.

Soviet foreign activism in the 1970s did in due course produce a reaction in the United States, during the last part of the Carter Administration and then in the Reagan Administration. First, to readjust the military balance by correcting deficiencies in strategic forces, in long-range intervention forces and in the European nuclear and conventional balance. Second, particularly in the Reagan Administration, a more robust, though still quite cautious, policy to reverse Soviet global expansion. Third, and most important from the standpoint of the Reagan Administration, an effort through non-inflationary economic growth to make it possible for the United States to maintain its defence obligations. The question of whether the Reagan Administration is succeeding continues to be debated both in America and in the international community in general.

There are now some serious questions about the future character of the Western Alliance and the ability of the West to reach and maintain common approaches about how to cope with Soviet power in the future. In my view, there is greater fluidity in the European area than for many years, not in the sense of the fears of the 1940s – that is, of Soviet takeovers and Communist Party subversion on behalf of the Soviet Union – but there have developed new attractions between East and West in Europe, particularly between the two parts of Germany.

There are serious and, I think, more than tactical and procedural differences between the United States and the West Europeans, allowing for differences within each, over the matter of East–West economic relations. This is important because for the Soviets, Western Europe represents something of an economic arsenal, important to support the economies of the East Europeans and to help the Soviets avoid basic shifts in their own economic and political priorities.

I may note here that differences between Americans and Europeans on economic relations with the East are to some extent encouraged by the possibility that the Europeans will fall behind in the area of high technology, and will find that the best customers for both their efficient (or even not so efficient) traditional industries are in the East. Meanwhile, there are signs that the Soviets themselves are over-extended in their Third World ambitions. It is not clear at the moment how much they can and will invest to promote these ambitions, and to exploit fluctuating American fortunes in the Third World.

In a sense then, Soviet power and influence are on a plateau, a high plateau no doubt, but seemingly stalled. How then to reach a final conclusion concerning Soviet objectives?

It is always said that interests are permanent and that the Soviets know their interests perhaps better than others. That may be true, but, interests and objectives are not identical.

Broadly speaking, a major current Soviet objective must be to address the domestic issues of stagnation, apathy, inefficiency, generational change, and demographical change. All of them pose more questions than answers. It is a partial list, but I would guess that any Politburo and Secretariat – the 28 or 30 people that make up the top group in the Soviet Union – must somehow have those issues on their agenda and it would seem that the new leadership has firmly put them there. Second, to keep control of Eastern Europe; again an objective that hides within it a bundle of complexities, choices, dilemmas and trade-offs. Thirdly, as already indicated, to enlist Western Europe for economic support and to prevent it from being or becoming in the future an arena that applies significant military constraints on the Soviet Union. Fourth, since they are involved there now, to keep an acceptable regime in Afghanistan at tolerable cost; to preserve options for Soviet policy in post-Khomeini Iran. Fifth, to modulate the conflict with China. But above all, to build an infrastructure in the Soviet East as a long term barrier against China. And, in that context, to prevent a US–China–Japan alliance. (Europeans, as well as Japanese, should ask themselves to what degree they want to be partners in the Soviet effort to industrialise Siberia, largely as a bulwark against an emerging China and as a means of supporting the Soviet military presence in the Far East and in Central Asia which is now extraordinarily expensive because of the long line of communications). Sixth, to avoid over-exposure in remote regions while seeking whatever influence they can maintain and obtain there. Seventh, a *modus vivendi* with the United States, if possible by inhibiting American military programmes. Even before the ugly, sulking manner of the Soviet leaders gave way to Gorbachev's more open and robust approach, I believe that there had been a desire to seek a *modus vivendi*. I do not mean by that a 'Peace of Westphalia'.

I mean a distant *modus vivendi* in which the Soviet Union feels that it will be left alone to pursue its own vast agenda. Finally, and possibly contradicting many of the above points, to preserve the party élite monopoly and to contain and, where possible, to exclude, intrusions from the outside world that undermine that monopoly. That may not be altogether feasible if the Soviets really wish to rely on the Western industrialised world to make up the gap in their investment and to support their ambitions with respect to the industrialisation of Siberia.

These goals may strike you as being stated in a rather conservative fashion. My stress on consolidation and on avoiding over-exposure is not intended to suggest passivity. The dynamism of Mikhail Gorbachev is testimony enough to that. But despite his willingness to tackle some underlying problems – indeed perhaps because of it – his priority will lie on building power over the long haul. The Soviets will undoubtedly resist encroachments. But I do not see them having now or in the forseeable future a grand vision of how to organise a congenial world. They will still see themselves basically in a hostile and uncongenial world with at least as many dangers as opportunities.

Such attitudes, well suited to the temperament of the oligarchs who ran the Soviet Union before Chernenko left the scene, may just as much suit the long-term interests of their younger and more radical successors. They no doubt could lash out if they felt excessively challenged, if some opportunity beckoned or if they felt that they were not properly treated as a great power. That is always a danger. But so is the danger that the West, and others, will squander their own assets and that the Soviets, despite the enormous flaws in their power, would by sheer tenacity and staying power become the world's single greatest power. I think this too is unlikely. But if there is a Soviet vision nowadays it may well be that somehow they will out-last all others and somehow emerge in such a way that they can say that they are reasonably secure. But I do not think the Soviets see that as around the corner, if indeed they see such glowing prospects at all.

(*Presentation given to the RUSI as part of its Main Theme Study, 'Soviet Power and Prospects' and subsequently updated.*)

9 Europe and the Security of Russia

EDWINA MORETON*

It is my contention that Europe's influence on how secure the Russians feel is a key element in understanding Russia's role in European security. I am told that it was a Tsarist foreign minister who once coined the expression that 'the only safe border is one Russia is on both sides of'. Who knows what the Tsarist gentleman had in mind. Today the expression would most likely be trotted out to point to the potential threat posed to the world outside by an expansionist Soviet Union. And it could apply to almost any border. There is, of course, a less cynical interpretation – that Russia (and for my purposes here, the Soviet Union) has never felt secure with its neighbours. Without getting into an argument with myself over whether the Soviet Union is by nature an aggressive power or just a misunderstood defensive power, I would argue that when it comes to feeling insecure with its neighbours, the Soviet Union's border with Europe presents the biggest headache of all. And by Europe I mean both parts of it – East and West.

Of course, as any Russian will tell you at the drop of a hat, the western borders of modern Russia have been tempting targets for hostile armies, from Napoleon to Hitler. Today the Warsaw Pact's western front – NATO's eastern front – is littered with one of the greatest concentrations of weaponry in the world. The battle-lines were drawn long ago. The two military Blocs have solidified against them. And the effect has been to produce a quite remarkable period of military stability, if not exactly peace, in Europe.

But it is not the military dimension of security I had in the front of my mind when thinking about this talk. Rather it was the political one. Because, whatever the military disposition of Russia's Western neighbours, from Peter the Great to Karl Marx, the Russians have either gone in search of Western ideas or had Western ideas thrust upon them. From the October revolution to the present, from Stalin to

* Dr Edwina Moreton is a correspondent for 'The Economist'.

190

Gorbachev, through periods of at times considerable hostility, the same process is still at work. Take, for example, the word Yalta. Depending on which side of the issue you take, Yalta may be convenient shorthand for the legitimate division of Europe into two halves, or for the unacceptable Soviet claim to dominion in Europe's eastern half. No prizes for guessing how the Soviet Union sees it. But Yalta and the lines drawn and since fortified in its name have been unable to solve the Soviet Union's problem with Europe.

I mentioned that when I used the word 'Europe' I had in mind both parts of Europe – East and West. I would first like to take a look at Eastern Europe's role in the problem before making the link to the wider issue of European security and the Soviet Union's role in it. The Soviet stake in Eastern Europe can be broken down into four main parts: the physical, or geographical stake, the economic, the military and the ideological. The first of these – physical security – is straightforward. Since the 1940s, the states of Eastern Europe have formed a physical security buffer along the Soviet Union's western borders. But the Soviet stake in Eastern Europe has grown considerably since then. As the Comecon economies have developed, traded with each other and come to rely on each other in that peculiarly inefficient way Comecon has of creating mutual dependence, the Soviet Union too has come to depend on its Comecon allies. Though by far the largest economy and in many ways self-sufficient, the Soviet Union has come to rely on the colonial system in reverse: in the 19th century colonial powers used political dominion to gain economic benefit. In the Soviet case the reverse has happened: the Soviet Union uses its economic dominion to bolster political control.

The countries of the northern tier – East Germany, Poland and Czechoslovakia – are of special importance to the Soviet military stake in Eastern Europe. They form the first strategic echelon in Warsaw Pact military strategy. Since the 1970s, the Soviet Union has been putting much greater emphasis on military integration within the Pact. To some extent the pressure for greater coordination in military affairs has increased the room for mischief-making by the East Europeans. Romania, which criticised Soviet handling of the Geneva talks and missile deployments in Europe, is a case in point. Naturally, Romania's voice is studiously ignored in Moscow, which of course demonstrates how limited that room for real mischief-making really is. And the Soviet Union would not tolerate the withdrawal of any of the East European states from the Warsaw Pact. But while Pact membership is a necessary condition of Soviet tolerance of limited diversity, the Soviet reaction both to the Czechoslovak Prague Spring in 1968 and to the Polish crisis and solidarity have demonstrated that it is not on its own a sufficient one.

That leads us to the fourth – and to my mind the most important – Soviet stake in Eastern Europe: the political and ideological one. It is important for two basic reasons. One, because Soviet control over Eastern Europe is the practical basis to its claim first to regional and then later to global Superpower status. And two, because Eastern Europe is now the only region in the world where the Soviet model has taken root, however inadequately. The importance of Eastern Europe to the Soviet Union has grown with each new ideological challenge, first from China and then from the Eurocommunists. The continued loyalty of the East European regimes is both the symbolic and the practical basis for the Soviet Union's claim to leadership of the world communist movement. A challenge to the Soviet model in Eastern Europe becomes a fundamental challenge to Soviet authority around the globe.

But having established how important the eastern half of Europe is to the Soviet Union, we come up against a series of paradoxes that face Soviet leadership. To feel secure, the Soviet leadership needs a set of stable and loyal allies on its western borders. Most Western economists agree that one of the greatest stabilisers in the long run in Eastern Europe would be economic reform. Yet it is hard, if not impossible, to talk of major systemic reform because that in itself is a challenge to the Soviet Union. Although we anticipate some limited reform in the Soviet Union, it is of course too early to say whether Gorbachev's boldness will extend to allowing Eastern Europe to become a laboratory of reformist experiments. But to date, with the exception of Hungary, such reform as there has been has amounted to tinkering, not a major overhaul. The longer the East Europeans dither, the greater the pressures from disgruntled populations who have seen their standard of living decline relatively and, in the case of Poland, absolutely. 'Have we reached real communism or is it going to get worse?' is the joke in Eastern Europe.

The East European regimes are caught between pressures for change and pressure from the Soviet Union to hold the ideological line. The command economy, it was claimed, would at least shield Eastern Europe from the cyclical crises of capitalism: unemployment, inflation and the rest. Having in most cases hoisted the East European regimes to power, the Soviet Union may now be the biggest threat to the security of those regimes. In this desire for both stability and loyality, the Soviet Union cannot afford to dominate Eastern Europe, and it cannot afford not to. The consequence is that each of the East European regimes, in its own way, has been forced into some sort of national deviation in the search for self-preservation. Hungary has developed furthest in the direction of economic reform, though is careful to stay inside the ideological lines that require the continued apparatus of party control over the economy. Romania has developed the model of socialism in one family: a flamboyantly disrespectful foreign policy, combined with a deadening Stalinism at home – martial law in all but name. Czechoslovakia tried its brand of socialism with a human face – in order to bolster communist party authority, not undermine it – only to have it trodden into the dust. The immobility which has followed has had its own impact on an increasingly stagnant economy. In Poland, attempts to buy off the need for reform led eventually to a political explosion as Marx's irresistible force, the working class, collided with Lenin's immovable object, the communist party. 'There's no sausage in Poland', which was true for a time, was probably the main barrier to the early spread of the Polish shock-wave through more of Eastern Europe.

Poland has been the worst case in some ways, although this time the party itself was pushed into whatever reforms were carried through before and since martial law. And Poland showed up two other paradoxes. The first, that although Soviet military power has increased enormously since the war, it has been unable to translate that power into corresponding political control – especially in Poland, where the pressure for change came not from a small group at the top, but massively from below. The Soviet Union's one effective tool, the armed forces, is the least suited to defend its most vital stake in Eastern Europe: ideological loyalty. If it had been the only force left to hold the line in Poland, the Soviet Union would have used its armed forces anyway. It was mightily relieved it did not have to. With a hostile Solidarity on one front and China at its rear, there was a time in 1980–81 when the Soviet Union had the dubious distinction of being the only state in the world to be surrounded by hostile communist powers.

And secondly, the most damning paradox of all: that it is not the fall of capitalism like a ripe plum that the world has now come to expect, but upheaval in Eastern Europe, born not out of the spark of revolution with the energy released by rapidly changing ideas, but out of social decay. What we can expect in the late 1980s and 1990s is probably not the final crisis of capitalism we have been warned about for so long, but a crisis of faith among communist parties in power who see no way out except continuing to muddle through.

I have always felt that what Eastern Europe needs is a loyal opposition. That role is played more subversively, in the least cynical sense of the word, by Western Europe. If all the Soviet Union had to cope with were the problems it faces in Eastern Europe, it would have its hands full. But it has the problem of Western Europe too: not just as a reference point, a yardstick against which East Europeans can compare their own standard of living, and grumble. Western Europe and Western policy towards Eastern Europe are a direct challenge, politically, to Soviet control over Eastern Europe. Take some of the code-names for that policy as they have changed over the past two decades: peaceful engagement, bridge-building, change through *rapprochement* (a West German variant), *détente* and the Helsinki process, and for want of a catchier phrase, the differentiation of the sort Vice-President Bush talked of in his speech in Vienna in 1983. In no instance was the West aiming at overturning the status quo in Europe by military means. The military purpose has been to preserve stability. Yet politically the purpose of Western policy has been change: the loosening up of Eastern Europe and the relaxation of the Soviet grip on Eastern Europe. With each successive new policy the precise means have been different but the underlying purpose has been consistent: change.

So the sort of change Western policy has aimed at presents the Soviet Union with a second set of dilemmas. Let me highlight just one or two issues to illustrate what I mean. Take, for example, the German question. The time is long past when the Soviet Union dithered over whether it preferred a united or a divided Germany in the heart of Europe. Now West Germany plays a crucial role in Soviet strategy both towards Western Europe and the Western Alliance in general. But how far can the Soviet Union go in trying to manipulate its relationship with West Germany – possibly by offering enticements in intra-German relations, without destabilising communist party control in East Germany. Already closer contacts between Germans are having a considerable impact in East Germany. It is not just that two-thirds of East Germans can now see the world outside reflected through the eyes of West German television cameras. East Germans are gradually being brought back into the mainstream of European history and culture. The regime is happy to go along with that, just so long as it remains in control of the process. But that kind of process is hard to control. The German question, to the extent that it remains open, poses as many problems for the Soviet Union as it does opportunities. Consider the fiasco of Honecker's aborted visit to West Germany in 1984. That episode exposed more clearly than any other the fallacy of always characterising the East Germans as the brake on East–West *rapprochement*. On straight-forward economic grounds, if nothing else, the regime in East Berlin desires a controlled expansion of state-to-state contacts with West Germany. On the other hand, it is jealous of its special ties with Moscow, while still nervous sometimes about its international identity and worried about being upstaged by Bonn. The Soviet Union for its part, whilst desiring also closer ties with West Germany, wishes to insulate the GDR from its fellow Germans or at least remain the arbiter of their relations. All parties are trying to have their cake and eat it. But the levers, inducements and constraints which shape inter-bloc and intra-bloc relations are not entirely of any one party's making or within any one party's control.

The German question is closely linked to the wider Soviet strategy towards Western Europe. Another example of the problems this poses in the Helsinki process itself. What the Soviet Union wanted and got out of Helsinki was first, formal recognition of the territorial status quo in Europe, and second, benefits of East–West trade. But although borders in Europe may be unalterable by force, yet again that does not mean that they are impermeable to East–West communication and the flow of ideas. Along with the trade the technology and the finance, the Soviet Union and Eastern Europe imported other, less welcome, Western influences. Who knows, without Helsinki maybe the Polish economy would have sunk beneath the waves more slowly and Solidarity, if it had appeared at all, might have been easier to manage.

A third example of the sorts of difficulties the Soviet Union faces in devising a coherent political strategy towards Western Europe, is the issue which was the real focus of East–West attention for many months: the deployment of new NATO missiles in Europe to offset the imbalance in medium-range missiles. During the 1970s, the Soviet Union seemed happy enough to accept the involvement of the United States in Europe as a fact of political, economic and military life. Since then the picture has changed quite dramatically. The breakdown of the arms control process, the reaction to the Soviet invasion of Afghanistan and the election of a more actively anti-communist president in the United States have all played a part. Now the main Soviet aim seems to be wherever possible to divide Europeans from Americans. The Soviet Union did not manufacture the divisions which have appeared in the NATO Alliance, but it has sought to use them for greater leverage. In the first half of the 1980s the point at which most of the pressure was exerted was on the NATO deployment decision; in the second half of the decade it is likely to focus on Reagan's SDI initiative. But partly because so much Soviet propaganda has focused on the United States and its supposedly riding roughshod over the reluctant West Europeans, partly because the nuclear issue is an emotive one whatever your language or ideology, the propaganda has begun to boomerang.

There are nascent anti-nuclear groups in several East European countries, including East Germany and Czechoslovakia where the Soviet Union is deploying new short-range nuclear weapons in response to NATO. These Soviet deployments, made public to put more pressure on the European–American divide has undercut Soviet peace propaganda at home in the Warsaw Pact, as well as abroad in NATO. East Europeans have begun to ask themselves why a nuclear weapon in the hands of a capitalist Superpower in Europe is any more threatening than one in the hands of a Superpower claiming to be socialist. But a Superpower nonetheless. The answer is hardly comforting to the Soviet Union or the regimes in power in Eastern Europe.

Détente brought considerable benefits to the Soviet Union and Eastern Europe, but it also magnified Soviet dilemmas in coping with the two Europes on its front doorstep. If you follow that thought through to its logical conclusion, then the sharp cooling of East–West relations, often regretted in parts of Western and Eastern Europe, has been a boon to the Soviet leadership. The Brezhnev era, which once seemed full of promise precisely because of its gamble on *détente*, may in future be handled more harshly by Soviet historiographers.

But then, if there is a bottom line to what I have said, it is this: faced with all these dilemmas in its handling of the two Europes, East and West, the Soviet Union's priority will remain the ideological security of Eastern Europe – in other words the maintaining in power, by force if necessary, of communist parties loyal to Moscow. But the Soviet Union's attitude to European security hinges on that. If anything, from what we have seen so far from his attitude at home, Mr Andropov is a man inclined to draw the lines around Eastern Europe more sharply than his predecessor, and to try to make sure that any 'bridges' from West to East in Europe are closely watched. His protégé, Mikhail Gorbachev, will run up against these same dilemmas – all the more so if he proves more successful than his predecessors at driving wedges between the United States and Western Europe. Good relations between the Soviet Union and Western Europe complicate Soviet relations with Eastern Europe: that is the corner the Soviets have backed themselves into.

Mr Gorbachev could do worse than read the thoughts of one of his predecessors, Nikita Khrushchev, on the subject. Reflecting on his own efforts in the 1950s to manage Soviet–East European relations, Mr Khrushchev concluded in his unofficial memoirs, 'You can't herd people into paradise with threats, and then post sentries at the gates'.

(*Presentation given to the RUSI as part of its Main Theme Study, 'Soviet Power and Prospects', and subsequently updated.*)

10 The Middle East, Afghanistan and the Gulf in the Soviet Perception

FRED HALLIDAY*

When it comes to our looking at Soviet attitudes towards this part of the world, there is a danger of our making a mistake about perception. The problem is not of erroneous snap decisions but of long term and unmoving illusions about the Soviet Union. If one looks at many of the arguments that have been advanced in the last ten years in academic, journalistic or diplomatic statements or analyses of Soviet policy, many are questionable – that it is a priority of the Soviet Union to acquire warm water ports; that the question of Soviet Moslems is today a major factor in Soviet foreign policy; that the Soviet Union faces the possible threat of an energy crisis comparable to that of the West, necessitating substantial oil imports; and, finally, the view that the Russians 'blundered' in Afghanistan. I do not share the view that the Russians 'blundered' in Afghanistan. They took a decision in 1979 the consequences of which they foresaw: they have paid a price for it but it was a price which they knew in advance they would pay.

Now of course all of this is said in the context of something which is evident; we do not know what the Russian leadership thinks. The USSR is a country where foreign policy is made by a very restricted group of people – the Politburo is ten, 12 or 13 people, depending on which year its composition is examined. Even within the Politburo the people who actually take foreign policy decisions may be a minority: the General Secretary, Minister of Defence, Minister of Foreign Affairs, the Head of the KGB, perhaps one or two others. We cannot say for sure what they are thinking or why they took certain

* Professor of International Relations, London School of Economics and Political Science

decisions. We cannot even go over a major Soviet decision like Afghanistan, or their attitude to Iran, in the way we can go over some Western decisions because the documentary evidence is lacking. But despite these limitations I think we can look at what they say and we can look at what they do. On that basis we can at least have some discussions, and question the assumptions that underlie much current analysis.

If the Russians look south, there are two very important points that have to be borne in mind. One is that they do not see the region as a unified whole. They take first what they call *Sryednii Vostok*, the Middle East or the Central East. These are the countries that border the Soviet Union – Turkey, Iran, Afghanistan – and also countries with which the Russians have a long historic association. This includes the fact that they have fought wars with all these countries in the past and have had fluctuating boundaries with all of them.

At the same time there is the Near East, what they call *Blizhnii Vostok*, the Arab world, Israel, the Red Sea down to the Horn of Africa, North Africa, the Arabian Peninsula and the Gulf – or the non-Iranian part of the Gulf. Their association with this area is more recent and it is much less important to them. The result is that the areas of the Middle East that are vital to the Soviet Union are not necessarily the same areas that are vital to the West. And their response to what happens in those areas is also different.

It is often said, of course, that geography is no longer an important factor in international relations. Certainly, in an era of missiles and satellites it is no longer important in the way it was a century ago. But the question of what one could call the 'vicinity' of countries, of being nearby, is very important. In fact it is in some ways more important now that it was in the past because, not just for reasons of strategy but also for reasons of ideology, to have an ideologically distinct and a hostile, even small, country on your frontier is not something the great powers like at all. You only have to look at the Americans in Central America to see that. The same goes for the Russians. So this area bordering them, this *Sryednii Vostok* area is, because of its vicinity, a very important region and in some ways has become an enhanced area of importance because of the East–West conflict.

One of the general points often raised about Soviet policy is that of economics. For the West the Middle East is a vital area because of economic factors: the supply of oil, the sale of goods and the disposition of petrodollars. The Soviet Union's trade with the Third World is much less important than the West's to its economy, and the

Soviet Union's imports from the Middle East are slight indeed. It does not import oil to any significant extent. Its one significant attempt to import gas from a Persian Gulf source ended with the Iranian revolution of 1979 and has not been restarted. Similarly, the Soviet Union sells some goods to the Middle East. It is a trading partner of Iran, Afghanistan, Turkey, and still of Egypt. But again one cannot say that such trade occupies anything like the same place that it does in Western foreign trade. Foreign trade as a whole is much less of a factor in Soviet than it is in Western foreign policy.

The central Russian concern about this area is strategic: to prevent the West from gaining an advantage there. The number one Russian question about any Middle Eastern crisis is: what is the West going to do here, are they going to gain an advantage? If one looks at their attitude, for example, to the Lebanese crisis the central Soviet issue was the presence of a US and Western peace-keeping force in Beirut. From the Soviet point of view NATO forces were being deployed in Beirut. That is what the Russians were really concerned about. Likewise, the Soviet attitude towards the American naval task force at the mouth of the Persian Gulf is determined above all by this attitude. If one is looking for a guiding principle of Soviet policy it lies in the first instance in this concern with strategy and with prevention of Western gains, rather more than with the Soviet Union actually gaining their own foothold. Like everybody else, the Soviets will take advantage if certain opportunities arise, but their main concern remains to block Western advances.

They have a second commitment, one which Afghanistan bears out very clearly, namely the commitment to ideology. If one asks why the Russians invaded Afghanistan, the answer is that there are two basic reasons. One is that Afghanistan borders the Soviet Union and from mid-1979, the Russians were worried about a hostile government coming to power there by overthrowing the Amin regime. The other reason, equally important and a necessary condition for the Russians to invade Afghanistan, was that a pro-Soviet communist party was in power there already and there was a danger of it being ousted. That specific combination of ideology and geography produced the Afghan crisis and reminds us that if and when communist parties come to power elsewhere on the Soviet frontier, but not necessarily further afield, then the Russians will be very likely to respond in a similar way.

These, then, are some very general reflections on Soviet policy in this area. Now let me move on to the particular countries involved.

First of all, Iran. It is generally established that the Russians had no role in the Iranian revolution except in a negative sense, that because Iran bordered the Soviet Union, it was even less likely that the West would have ever intervened in force to support the Shah. The main reason that the West did not intervene was because it was quite impractical to do so, as anybody who has read Sir Anthony Parsons' memoirs or those of the American Ambassador, William Sullivan, will know. The 'we could have saved Iran by a show of force' argument which is sometimes heard in the West, especially in Washington, is quite insubstantial. The local preconditions for a Western intervention in Iran in late 1978 were not there. But had there been such a possibility, on internal Iranian grounds, then certainly the fact that it bordered the Soviet Union would have constituted an additional deterrent factor.

After the revolution the Soviet Union tried to establish a working relationship with Khomeini. They wanted to develop economic ties and they sought to steer Iranian foreign policy in a pro-Soviet direction. But a whole number of factors prevented this from happening. First of all the Iranians do not need the Russians. They can sell their oil to the West and they have, at least until recently, acquired arms on the free market or from countries like North Korea, which has a great need for foreign exchange. Secondly there is the issue of Afghanistan. Although the Iranians are not playing a major role in aiding the opposition, they are playing some part in aid to Shi'a guerrillas, and their propaganda and diplomatic posture are outspokenly hostile to the Soviet Union. Then there is the Iran–Iraq war. Here the Soviet Union has, especially since July 1982, supported the Iraqi position on the grounds that Iran should stop the war now that it has won back its national territory. So as soon as Iran entered Iraqi territory the Soviets ceased to be indulgent towards Iran, as they had been when the war first began in 1980. Then there is the persecution of the Tudeh party in Iran and the arrest of thousands of its members since early 1983. Now, the Russians have not responded violently to the suppression of their allies inside Iran. As is evident from other cases, they are willing to tolerate local communist parties being suppressed, even when they support those regimes. Nasser locked up his communists and killed some. The Iraqi Ba'th certainly liquidated quite a few communists too. So the mere fact of the Tudeh being suppressed is not, in itself, a factor that will lead to a breach in relations with the Soviet Union. But it has led to serious deterioration in relations between the two states.

The Russians now have two basic concerns about Iran. One – which is in some ways shared by the West – is to limit the spread of the Islamic revolution, especially to Iraq, a country which they are now supporting very substantially. It is Soviet ground-to-ground missiles which are landing on Iranian towns such as Dez Ful, Andimeshk and Abadan. The Russians want to stop the Iranian revolution spreading to Afghanistan through propaganda and financial aid, and of course to stop it spreading to Soviet Central Asia. In Central Asia there would not seem to be a major pro-Khomeini movement, but the number of women wearing chadors in the streets of Dushambe and Tashkent in Soviet Central Asia has reportedly risen in the last four years. The Soviet Politburo took a decision not to allow Khomeini to open a consulate in Soviet Tajikistan, where the language is Persian and his diplomats might have had a particular impact. In this limited sense the Soviet Union shares the view, which the West has, that the Islamic revolution should be contained, although they share it for very different reasons. But there is a second Soviet concern which is quite serious, and which the Russians, at least in private, emphasise even if we do not hear so much about it in public. It is this: the Russians reserve the right to invade Iran if they feel their national security is threatened. This, they argue, is inscribed in the 1921 Iranian–Soviet Treaty.

Now, there are many ifs and buts about this, and many different interpretations of the Treaty. The Iranians have, under Khomeini, repudiated the relevant sections of this Treaty on more than one occasion. The Russians refuse to accept that repudiation and they insist that the Treaty is still valid. I have heard Russians say they think Iran is the one area in the world where there is a serious possibility, a serious danger, of a direct East–West conflict, of a Soviet–American conflict; that they would be prepared in the event of what they would regard as an American intervention in Iran – covert or overt – to intervene themselves. I have heard it said they would act 'decisively, massively and immediately'. This may be an overstatement. But I certainly think that the Soviets do look at Iran and say, 'Well, we've got Khomeini. He is enough trouble, enough of a problem. But were there to be a serious Western involvement in Iran, were we to think that the West was regaining a foothold in Iran then we would do something about it.' It is true that the Soviet forces on the Caucasus frontier are said not to be at full strength. We have not seen anything substantial to indicate the Russians are, as it were, building up forces or even using the threat of troops on the Iranian frontier in any way. But just as there is in the West's mind a long term goal and a long term anxiety about what happens to Iran after Khomeini, and what happens if the Russians get involved there, so in the Soviet view Iran is high on their list of world concerns. It is the one area of the Third World where they might not back away as they have in Southern Africa or the way that they may be playing a low profile in Central America. Iran is part of this *Sryednii Vostok*, the area that lies on their frontier with historic, economic and strategic importance.

Therefore the fact that a US takeover in Iran is not an actual concern now should not conceal the possibility that it could become a major one in the future. One only has to remember a very simple fact about where the cold war first began. It was not in Poland. It was not in Berlin. It began in Iran, in 1946, over Azerbaijan. It may be that the world will see some more East–West confrontations over Iran in the future if the Khomeini regime falls apart, and I do not see much prospect of Iran's government collapsing in the near future. But this certainly is a major Russian concern, and will remain so.

Turning now to Afghanistan, my views of what the Russians are thinking and doing are not held by most experts in the field. I think that the Russians knew when they invaded in 1979 that they would face an uphill struggle and pay an international price. But, faced with the alternative of seeing a communist party, a loyal pro-Soviet communist party, being overthrown by the Moslem rebels they took their decision. And they are quite willing to sit it out. I do not believe that the Russians will withdraw from Afghanistan and abandon their allies there in return for certain compensations elsewhere in the world. I do not believe that they would seriously, through the United Nations negotiations or anything else, agree to a substantial dilution of the current regime. In their view, the Afghan 'revolution' is irreversible. They might get rid of Babrak Karmal. They might bring in some non-party people. They might cobble together some new party called the Afghan People's Freedom Front or something. After all, some of the ruling Eastern European parties are not called communist parties. But the fact of the matter is they have in Afghanistan a state, a party and increasingly now an army which they have formed and which, if not loyal in ideology, is loyal in interests to them. That may be an important distinction. The majority of the Polish officer corps are not necessarily pro-Soviet but they know which side of the bread their butter is on and they have remained loyal to the Jaruzelski regime. A similar type of calculation may apply in Afghanistan.

What the Russians are doing in Afghanistan is building up a central state. It does not matter so much if half the country is in the hands of the rebels for the time being. No Afghan central government has ever controlled the whole country and it will take a long time to do so. It does not matter if bombs go off in Kabul. They go off in Belfast; it does not lead to the overthrow of the British Government. Similarly it does not matter if there is fighting in the mountainous province for some years to come, and if it is filmed by foreign TV crews. What the Russians are concerned with is building up a party, which they have expanded from under 20 000 in 1978 to over 100 000 now; building up the communist mass organisations around them, the trade unions, the women, the youth and so forth, all of which have memberships in the tens of thousands. They are training up in the Soviet Union thousands of young Afghans whose security and careers largely require a continuation of the regime and who are not so tainted by the interparty squabbles of the first years of the communist regime. They are also seeking to create an economic apparatus which has nothing much to do with communism or socialism, but which binds more and more of the country into a central state for reasons of self-interest. The Russians in their publications will argue – I have no way of testing if it is true but it is an indication of what they think – that 20 per cent of the economically active population of Afghanistan is now in one way or the other on the government's payroll. They will point out that a substantial amount of the trade done between the Soviet export firms and Afghanistan is done on the Afghan side by private traders.

What they are also trying to do, and in many ways have been successful in doing, is in getting economic factors to break down the barrier between the area which they control and the area which the rebels control. Many people who have been in the rebel areas report that there is quite a lot of substantial trade between the two sides; and that there is in some ways a more unified Afghan economy than there is a unified polity. Kabul itself is rather an extraordinary place to visit because while it is the capital of a communist party, and the capital of a Soviet-occupied country, it is one in which there is a free exchange of currency. There is no black market. The Afghan currency is a free-market currency. And you can get anything you want from the West, a Mercedes car or a refrigerator or anything else. The Russians and their Afghan allies have therefore since 1979 deliberately played down social reforms in order to try and consolidate this relatively free economy. Of course the Soviet army and the officer corps benefit from this through all sorts of corruption and import deals of their own, but that is another story. We can discount at least 50 per cent of what the

Russians say about what they have achieved in Afghanistan. But an analysis does indicate something about their strategy. First of all, they are willing to sit it out as they sat it out in Central Asia in the 1920s and 1930s. Secondly they are not so bothered by what happens in the remoter mountains: they are not going to do what the Americans did in Vietnam and go chasing the guerrillas into the highlands and lowlands of the interior. That is not such an important factor for them.

In one way they have fallen back on the old Moslem division between the part of the country you can govern, and the part you cannot govern. The part you can govern comprises the cities, the economically exploitable areas and the plains in the north near the Soviet frontier. And through that partial control gradually built up, a state and party apparatus emerges. The most controversial aspect of this process concerns the Afghan Army. We have all heard that they are having immense difficulty in getting people into the army, and in keeping them there. But the Afghan Army is doing a lot more fighting than it did in 1979 or 1980. Western diplomatic reports on the spring 1984 offensive in the Panjshir Valley give a figure of about 12 or 13 000 Soviet troops involved there and about 8 000 Afghan troops. These are Western figures; I have no idea of whether they are accurate. But the idea that the Afghan Army does not play a role in the fighting and garrisoning in the countryside is an outdated one. And the figure I have from one non-communist source in Kabul, who was there for three years, is that the Afghan Army now contains well over 100 000 men of which half are willing to fight. This may be an exaggeration: but it suggests a very different picture from the magical 30 000 that one has heard for several years now.

The Russians stress the fact, as they stress it for other countries in the Third World, such as South Yemen and Ethiopia, that a substantial proportion, a majority of the officer corps are members of the communist party. Whether you can see the officer corps as being represented in the party or whether in fact you see the party as more being an extension of military is debatable. But there is certainly a very close interlock of the officer corps and party, and in that way the military is bound into the state apparatus.

If the Russians are looking for a compromise in Afghanistan it is going to be a compromise very much on their own terms. They believe that sooner or later the Pakistanis will come round to accepting the Babrak Karmal regime. Indeed they even believe that it may be the Pakistani Army as much as their own army or the Afghan Army which will finish off the Mojahidin when the time comes. That is probably five or ten years away. But the idea that the Russians will be ousted from Afghanistan or that they will accept a phased withdrawal leading to – in the delicate phrase – a 'decent' interval, is very dubious indeed. It is not the way they have operated in the past, and it does not seem to tally with their intentions. I could be wrong: only history will tell.

Let me cover more briefly two other areas of concern. One is the Arab–Israeli dispute and the other is the Arabian Peninsula. The Russians have had very little role in Arab-Israeli diplomacy for many years. They broke relations with Israel in 1967, a break which some Russians in private now say was a mistake. The Russians have an interest in re-establishing relations with Israel but even if they could do so it would not give them significant influence on Israeli diplomacy or reduce the US position there. Since the Vance–Gromyko joint statement of October, 1977, there has been no bilateral US–Soviet policy on the Middle Eastern question. The United States has monopolised Arab–Israeli diplomacy, and the Soviet response has been predictable. It has been to criticise all American attempts even if in practice, as in the September 1982 Reagan plan, it was rather like what the Russians would like to see, or what the Russians in private would be willing to accept. This criticism derives from the fact that these US proposals are seen as giving unilateral diplomatic advantage to the United States.

Instead the Russians have dug in. They have done so, first of all, in Syria. I doubt if the Russians will go to war for Syria. It is not a country ruled by a communist party, and it is too far from their frontiers. Therefore Syria, unlike Afghanistan, does not meet either of the two major conditions for the USSR to help it. But with many military personnel there and with substantial supplies of military equipment sent after the 1982 war, the Russians have certainly declared their support for Syria. They do not agree with the Syrians on many things. They do not agree with Syria on Lebanon, an issue on which they have criticised Syria on more than one occasion. They do not agree with the Syrian attitude towards the PLO. But if they have to choose in their old fashioned way between allies that are states and ones that are liberation movements, then the Russians have no doubt that they will choose states. In that sense if they are forced to choose between the Syrians and the PLO they will choose the Syrians.

The longer-run Soviet hope is eventually that through Syria the USSR can exert its influence on the wider process of Middle East diplomacy. The Russians must hope too that Syria can exert its leverage in Lebanon to enforce a new peace settlement there, one that would both permanently establish Syrian influence in Lebanon, and equally permanently exclude that of the Israelis and of the USA. The Soviet Union gained one enormous benefit from the Western involvement in Lebanon, namely that the USA was, after declaring its commitment to the Gemayel regime, forced to pull its forces out. The contrast with the Soviet role in Syria, and even more so Afghanistan, could not be more evident. But, having seen the Americans re-embarking and sailing away, the Russians would now like to see the Lebanese conflict subside and a stable, more neutral, regime emerge. They would not like to become involved themselves in such an unstable situation, not least because their forces would become targets for Lebanese Christians, and the Israelis.

It has been very interesting in the past two years how they have backed away, not so much from the PLO in general as from Arafat in particular. They supported Arafat publicly in the 1982 war with Israel. They supported Arafat when the PLO mutiny began in May 1983. But once Arafat went to Cairo to see Mubarak and once it became evident to the Russians that the split within the PLO was as deep as it was, then Arafat's position in Soviet protocol, statements and commentaries went down considerably. There were even those rather blatant messages to Arafat from Brezhnev and then later from Andropov, warning him on two counts: about the risks involved in the division of the PLO and about the danger of seeking diplomatic resolution of the Palestinian question by going to the Americans. That second warning points to a basic Soviet anxiety that, as the Russians would say, the Arabs are unreliable. They go to one lot of people and smile at them. If they do not succeed there they will go somewhere else. This is the strong, very often rather racist, animosity towards the Arab states often found in the Soviet Union. There is a fundamental fear that Arafat is only talking to the Russians because he cannot get the ear of the Americans, but that if he could do so, that would be the last the Russians would see of him. But they would not support Abu Musa and Abu Saleh, the dissidents within the PLO. They know very well that they are just puppets of the Syrians. But they certainly are not giving Arafat the support that he previously was getting.

One other interesting aspect of Soviet policy on the Arab–Israeli dispute concerns Egypt. The Russians are great believers in history and in 'historic' ties. At the Aswan Dam there still stands a monument to the eternal friendship with the Egyptian and Soviet peoples, somewhat dusty I suspect at the moment. The Russians hope that sooner or later some opening to Egypt will become possible. They have established low level dialogue with the Mubarak government. They have eased some of the economic relations with Egypt. But they are also sceptical. They want to see what Mubarak is actually going to do about changing relations with the Americans, hosting the Rapid Deployment Force, and keeping relations with Israel. He is still very much talking to the United States. He is still keeping a low profile on relations with the USSR. Sadat died in October 1981, and nothing substantial has happened since. So that is a measurable element of scepticism about Egypt, one offset by a recognition of Egypt's central role in the Arab world, which nothing can displace. There is, secondly the hope that sooner or later Egypt will turn back to the Soviet Union, but not as it did in the days of Nasser – that is something which the Russians do not want anyway as that would involve them in massive economic aid to Egypt and because they know that the social character of Egypt has changed since Nasser's death in 1970.

Now to say something briefly about the Gulf. The Russians in their old-fashioned and stubborn way insist on calling it by its traditional name, the Persian Gulf, *Peridski Zaliv*. There is no nonsense about the 'Arab Gulf', or any of the euphemisms which have become common in the West in recent years. The fundamental Russian view is that the central question in the Gulf is Iran. And this is the main thing that they are worried about. They do not import oil from the area. It is a long, long way from any Soviet home ports, particularly if the Suez Canal is closed. It is about the furthest place on the earth in fact from home ports like Odessa if the Canal is closed.

But the Russians are clearly concerned at the way in which local conflicts have given diplomatic openings to the United States. Very practically, they are concerned about the way in which the Iraqi attack against Iran in September 1980 was the occasion for the deployment of American AWACs planes in Saudi Arabia. They can observe perfectly well that it is increasing Arab anxiety about the Iran–Iraq War which has led to the deployment of the US carrier force at the Straits of Hormuz. In general they think that the ways in which the United States has justified its Central Command, RDF deployments, and its prepositioned equipment are invalid. The Russians see the deployment of those forces there as directed not at the region but as having a use in future operations against the Soviet Union. So they want to deny the West opportunities to increase its influence. What is striking is the degree to which the Russians have sought not to inflame local tensions, but to encourage their local allies in that area to 'normalise' their relations with other states. In the 1960s when they were at loggerheads with the Shah of Iran and on good terms with Iraq they nonetheless remained neutral in the Iran–Iraq conflict that broke out then in 1969–70.

They have long sought to establish diplomatic relations with Saudi Arabia, so far without success. The Saudis seem to imagine that the mere threat of opening diplomatic relations with the Soviet Union can influence American policy. I do not think it would do anything of the kind, but the Saudis seem to imagine it will.

Even in dealing with South Yemen, a state with which they have very close relations, by far the closest relationship with any Arab state, they have urged the South Yemenis to be more cautious. The idea that the South Yemenis are radical, or calling for revolution in the Arabian Peninsula because the Russians tell them to do so, is quite mistaken. The Russians have urged the South Yemenis to normalise their relations with Oman and publicly welcomed the fact that relations were established in October 1982. The Russians have never supported the South Yemenis in their attempts to overthrow the government of North Yemen, far from it: the Russians have carried out what can be called an 'Afghanistan in reverse' in North Yemen. It is the Soviet Union which has armed the North Yemini Army and so enabled it to crush the left wing pro-South guerrillas of the National Democratic Front in North Yemen, who were defeated in the spring of 1982. The Russians have good relations, rivalling those of the West, with North Yemen, and these directly impinge upon and harm the interests of South Yemen. If one looks at the communiqués which the Russians have signed with the South Yemenis going back ten years or more the phrase comes up again and again, that the Soviet Union 'looks favourably upon the efforts being made to normalise the situation in the Arabian Peninsula'. At the same time they have in South Yemen a political and military investment. And South Yemen is useful to the Russians for reconnaissance, for transit and servicing and changing the crews on their ships.

Despite what many reports allege, the Russians do not have a base in the proper sense of the word in South Yemen, if by this is meant a sovereign area with their own troops in the country. They do have facilities which are of considerable use to them. But I think the South Yemen is of greater use for another reason which is that of a diplomatic ally in the Arab field as a whole, where South Yemen despite its limited resources plays quite an active role.

To conclude with one final observation: there is a conflict, a rivalry between East and West in the Middle East. This involves competition for states, for social groups and for ethnic groups as allies. But there is also a rivalry for diplomatic advantage and for success in solving diplomatic problems. Now, the consensual Western view, certainly since October 1977, that is, since the breakdown of the Vance–Gromyko understanding, has been that it conflicts in the Middle East, be they the Arab–Israeli dispute, the Horn of Africa or the Iran–Iraq war, the diplomatic solution should be pursued in such a way that the Soviet Union is excluded from participation in negotiations. The Russians are not to get any credit for being involved, and the Russians will, we are told, only use their role in the negotiations to push out the West or gain an advantage, so the West, and the United States in particular, should pursue peace-keeping activities on a unilateral Western basis.

This is a consensual Western view and not one which, despite a few ifs and buts, the Western European governments oppose. The Reagan Administration has, on some occasions, hinted that it might depart from this policy but no consistent alternative has emerged. The Soviet view is clearly the opposite. They are willing to play a role in diplomatic negotiations, they are willing to sign an international agreement on security of shipping in the Persian Gulf, they are willing to participate in a Geneva conference in the Arab–Israeli dispute. Their views on the Iran–Iraq war are really not that different from those of the West in terms of how it should be solved. But the Russians are not going to support Western peace-keeping initiatives, even if they are well-intentioned or intrinsically positive, if they are themselves excluded.

Now, this situation reflects a choice which the West has made. It cannot be derived merely from the fact of rivalry. Just as the West looks for advantage when advantage arises, as they clearly did in Egypt in the 1970s, so the Russians look for it as well. And no rules, codes of behaviour or legal agreements can be devised to solve this problem. Some balance between rivalry and bilateral negotiations in East–West relations will remain the pattern because ultimately you can neither control the countries of the region themselves or abolish the deeper causes of East–West competition. But I would myself question whether this currently predominant Western preference for a unilateral approach to Middle Eastern problems is really the best way to go about them. A different view of Soviet policy may bring more stability and progress in the Middle East, as well as the East–West relations as a whole.

(*Presentation given to the RUSI as part of its Main Theme Study, 'Soviet Power and Prospects', and subsequently updated.*)

11 Power in the Kremlin: Politics and the Military

MALCOLM MACKINTOSH, CMG*

The aim of this discussion on the relationship between the Communist Party in the Soviet Union and the Soviet Armed Forces is first to try to describe the machinery through which these two organisations operate together in the Soviet system, and then to see how the relationship is working together at the present time. We have to recognise that any judgement of the power and influence of the Armed Forces over Party decision-making in military affairs or domestic and foreign policy is bound to be speculative since Army–Party relations have always been a particularly secretive matter in the Soviet Union. In this situation it may be helpful, therefore, to say a little about the historical background of the relationship so that we have some indication of the Russian as well as Soviet traditions in this field on which to base our discussion and possibly our conclusions.

Military power has always played a dominant role in the development of the Russian state – partly because of the open and exposed nature of Russia in geographic and military terms and partly because of the urge to expand which became almost instinctive in Russia as the country grew from a small Grand Duchy to the Empire of the Tsars which was overthrown at the time of the Revolution in 1917. All Russian leaders, however, made strenuous efforts to control their military forces by subordinating them rigidly to the authority through which the Tsars ruled, and by restricting the choice of military leaders to those whom they knew they could trust. This, incidentally, was one of the reasons why, although Russia produced ample numbers of experienced generals, the Tsars frequently recruited military leaders from abroad in, for example, the 17th and 18th centuries – placing the armed forces under men who had no personal or political motive to try to usurp power for the military in the Russia of their day.

As a result of these protective measures, no serious or successful attempt by the Russian military leadership to seize power, carry out a

---

* Malcolm Mackintosh works in the Cabinet Office, specialising in Soviet affairs.

coup d'état or even acquire dominant influence over the political leadership of the country took place in Russia during this historical period. There has grown up a deep-rooted tradition of military obedience to the political rulers of Russia, which has been quite different from attitudes in other Slav and East European nations. The top-ranking Russian soldiers and sailors have long been brought up to regard themselves solely as professional commanders of the nation's military forces, and to 'stand to attention' when facing their political masters. This is a long-standing tradition which, I think, still has great potency today within the Soviet Armed Forces.

After the Revolution in 1917 and the long-drawn-out Civil War which followed, both experience and ideology led the Soviet regime, especially under Stalin, to redouble their efforts to subordinate the Red Army to the Communist Party. Harking back to the French Revolution, the Soviet Party leaders expressed their fear of the emergence of 'Bonapartism' in the Soviet Union, and the early reorganisation of the Red Army High Command enabled the Party leaders to dominate the military decision-making machinery – then called the Revolutionary Military Council. It also established Party control throughout the Forces through the appointment of Political Commissars at all levels and the extension of the Secret Police network, then known as the Cheka or OGPU into the Armed Forces. Even the General Staff – the one military organisation which had, partially, at least, survived the Revolution and retained many of its professional officers – was tightly controlled by the Party.

Stalin was so insistent that the leadership of the Red Army, on which the security of the Soviet Union depended, should be in the hands of men whom he trusted, that he decimated the Army and Navy High Commands in the 1937–39 military purges in what he probably regarded as a 'pre-emptive strike' against a rival power base – in addition to his personal jealousy of those who had led the Red Army to victory in the Civil War. As he was later to find out in Finland in 1939 and in the German invasion of 1941–42, his fear of 'Bonapartism' deprived the Soviet Armed Forces of a competent and experienced military leadership when the real trial of war came upon him.

The experiences and the final victory in the Second World War brought the Soviet Army to the height of its prestige, authority and popularity. But Stalin took urgent measures after the war to re-establish the strict Party and Secret Police control over it which characterised the pre-war years. War heroes such as Marshal Zhukov were dismissed in disgrace, or despatched abroad or to distant parts of the Soviet Union between 1946 and 1953, and only four senior officers were advanced to the next rank of four-star General or the equivalent. The Command of the Moscow Garrison and the Military District was entrusted to NKVD (Secret Police) rather than Army Generals; and with a continuing process of purging within the senior officer class, it is no wonder that the Military High Command virtually cowered in an atmosphere of fear and suspicion of the Party and even their own colleagues. Nor is it surprising, as a former Chief of the General Staff publicly noted, that during Stalin's post-war years not one work of original military thinking was written or published in the Soviet Armed Forces, even within their own restricted military journals.

Khrushchev's period of rule from 1955 to 1964 opened up a new chapter in Army–Party relations based largely on the selection of a new military and naval leadership composed of officers with whom he had served as a Political Commissar during the war. These years were also noted for Khrushchev's readiness to trust his Service Chiefs to a greater extent than before, to support their recommendations in the rapid Soviet advance to strategic nuclear missile and global naval power, and even to permit a modicum of debate on defence issues to appear in published journals.

The title of this article forbids me to go into detail on this fascinating and turbulent period in Soviet politico–military history. On one important occasion, however, we see the resurrection of the old fear of 'Bonapartism' in Khrushchev's mind, and the Party's immediate and drastic action to counter it, which I think is worth recording. In mid-1957 Khrushchev was faced by a majority revolt in the Poltiburo against his policies by the so-called 'Anti-Party Group'. To defeat his rivals he summoned a meeting of the 600-odd membership of the Party's Central Committee, and turned to Marshal Zhukov, the Defence Minister, to use the Armed Forces, primarily the Air Force, to bring a 'healthy' majority of pro-Khrushchev members to Moscow from distant provinces and from abroad in time to attend the meeting – at which Khrushchev 'routed' the opposition and arrested the 'Anti-Party Group'.

Though the evidence is circumstantial, it seems almost certain that Zhukov sought, as a *quid pro quo*, increased military representation in the Higher Military Council, a high-level committee composed of Party officials and one or two soldiers, responsible for the formulation of military policy in the Soviet Union – whose role I shall return to shortly. Khrushchev and the Party leaders were horrified, rejected the proposal out of hand, and proceeded to dismiss Marshal Zhukov from all his posts – and even deprive him of some of his medals. Not only was this action taken swiftly and effectively – and against someone who had just saved Khrushchev from defeat in the Politburo – but not one professional Service Chief rallied to Zhukov's support. Many, indeed, wrote or signed vituperative articles against him and his wartime reputation.

This incident is, I think, important, because it is a clear indication of the readiness of the Party to act against the Armed Forces in the event of the slightest suspicion of military ambitions to increase their influence over the Party. It also shows, incidentally, that in these circumstances the Soviet system does not allow professional loyalty any role in challenging the decisions of the Party even when the career of a famous war hero is at stake.

Against this background, let us now examine Army–Party relations and military influence on decision-making today, subject always to the scarcity of reliable and detailed information which I mentioned at the beginning of my talk. First of all, the organisational structure. As in the case of all Soviet decision-making on domestic issues, the economy, foreign policy and ideology, final decisions on defence and all military matters is reserved to the Politburo: now composed of 13 full voting members and seven candidate members. To advise and make recommendations on defence to the Politburo there is a Defence Council, whose members are appointed, according to the Soviet Constitution of 1977, by the Presidium of the Supreme Soviet. The Defence Council's chairman is the General Secretary of the Party, Mikhail Gorbachev.

We do not know precisely who are the members of the Defence Council, which appears to be the old Higher Military Council of the Khrushchev era renamed, but there is good evidence that of about ten or 12 members, all but one, the Chief of the General Staff, Marshal Akhromeyev, are civilians. They are either full or candidate members the Politburo or of the Secretariat of the Central Committee or the Council of Ministers – for example, the Foreign Minister, the Defence Minister and senior officials concerned with the Armaments Industries. From historical evidence, it seems likely, however, that the Secretary of the Defence Council is a senior serving officer from the General Staff.

The composition of the Defence Council indicates how closely the Party leadership exercises its control over decision-making or even recommendations on defence issues. These include, though we have no firm evidence, military doctrine, strategy, force levels, weapons and their allocation within the forces, and, in broad terms, arms control. From the Defence Council, Politburo instructions go to the Ministry of Defence. The Minister is, as already mentioned, a member of the Defence Council; the present minister, Marshal Sergei Sokolov, a 74-year old professional soldier, may be an interim occupant of the post. His predecessor, Marshal Dmitri Ustinov, who died in December 1984, was a civilian and an experienced armaments expert and engineer. He showed himself to be a Party leader and a member of the Politburo first and foremost. When Brezhnev, just before he died in November 1982, summoned a meeting of the leaders of the Armed Forces – apparently to assure them, whatever their doubts, that the Party was giving the Forces all the resources they needed – Ustinov clearly supported Brezhnev on this issue.

Within the Ministry of Defence, the Minister chairs two senior bodies; the Collegium and the Main Military Council. All Soviet Ministries have a Collegium, which is a committee of senior officials who advise the Minister, primarily on formal occasions and on issues relating to honours and status. It seems to have no vote in the decision-making process. The Main Military Council's duties are somewhat unclear. But they are probably similar to those of the Military Councils at the headquarters of Military Districts and Fleets at a lower level in the Soviet Union. These Councils include the senior officers of these formations, who, together with the Chief Political Officers, and, where appropriate, a senior civilian regional or urban Party Secretary, meet to discuss current defence issues. The Councils also act as disciplinary authorities within their formations. They, and probably also the Main Military Council in the Ministry of Defence, provide yet another point of access, if not control, for the Party within the Armed Forces.

Finally, in this structural picture there is the Chief Political Directorate of the Armed Forces, which was for 23 years under Army-General Yepishev, and now in the hands of Colonel-General Aleksei Lizichev, formerly head of the Political Directorate of the Group of Soviet Forces in East Germany. This Directorate, which under the Soviet Constitution has the status of a Department of the Party's Central Committee, controls the huge network of the political officers throughout the Armed Forces, from the Main Military Council to the smallest unit in all the five Branches of the Forces. Each political officer is expected to play an active role in the Military or Naval programme of his unit or formation: many in the Air Forces, for example, are qualified pilots or air crew. But their primary role is political indoctrination; and while they have no formal responsibility for the security or loyalty of their troops or sailors – that falls to the KGB – they are an important instrument of the Party in the Forces, and contribute significantly to the control of the Armed Forces by the Party.

At the same time there is the interesting question as to how far, if at all, current Soviet military leaders can express their opinions or exert influence on the Party through the press. It seems very likely that the leaders of the Armed Forces, especially in the age of advanced technology and 'weapons of mass destruction' – to use the Soviet phrase – have their own views on defence and defence-associated foreign policy issues – such as arms control – as well as on resource allocation and procurement. It is occasionally possible to sense that in some of their published articles and statements some military leaders sometimes hint at disapproval of party policies. But the research that I have been able to undertake on this fascinating topic has failed to reveal reliable evidence of such disagreements. And when we recall that all material published or quoted by serving officers in the press, on television or at international conferences is cleared with the Chief Political Directorate, I am forced to the conclusion that while differences of opinion probably exist and style and emphasis may change, the military's *public* stance on these issues is at one with the Party's.

To summarise this picture of the organisational structure of the Army–Party relationship: final decision-making on defence issues and the role of the Armed Forces is taken in the Poltiburo, usually after debate in the Defence Council. The Politburo has no serving soldier, sailor or airman in its full or candidate membership, and the Defence Council has, at present, only one: the Chief of the General Staff. Military access, except through approved channels, to the decision-makers on defence issues, including arms control, let alone on foreign or internal policies, is very limited and tightly controlled by the Party. Moreover, the Party has, through the Chief Political Directorate, the political officers at Military Council level and the KGB, machinery by which it can monitor and check any unusual activity, any criticism on political or military issues or the foreign policy of the state which might appear within the Armed Forces. The basic fear of 'Bonapartism', I believe, however remote it may seem to be at any particular time, still exists in the Soviet Party leadership, and the military leaders are well aware of the situation, and accept it for traditional as well as current practical reasons.

You may think at this point that I have perhaps down-graded the status of the Armed Forces in the Soviet Union by outlining their subordination to the Party and the Politburo. In this final section of my remarks I would like to say a little more about their position in Soviet society and their role in Soviet policy-making and in the life of the country.

Of the three main power bases in the Soviet Union today the Party, the Armed Forces and the KGB, the Armed Forces, after the Party itself, is the most numerous, the most prestigious and the most important. They still enjoy the reputation created by their victory in the Second World War, and a massive publicity campaign still pays tremendous attention to the experiences, sufferings and achievements of the Soviet Forces and people in that war. Moreover, many members of the current Soviet military leadership participated in the war, including Admiral Sergei Gorshkov a Deputy Minister of Defence and Commander-in-Chief of the Soviet Navy. There is no reason to doubt, in my view as a former liaison officer with the Soviet army during and after the war, that the awareness of the war and its effects on Russia are still very vivid in the minds of the Soviet people.

The size and deployment of the Armed Forces throughout the Soviet Union makes the existence of the Forces a real factor in the lives of the peoples of Russia. The Forces number, according to IISS figures published in the West, some 3 705 000 men, together with 500 000 KGB Frontier Guards and Internal Security Troops (now under a KGB General as Minister of the Interior), and national service involves two years for them in the Army and the Air Force and two to three years in the Navy. This means that virtually all able-bodied male Soviet citizens have some experience of service in the Forces, including professional and technical training and political indoctrination. There is every reason to believe that military service is, though not popular, generally regarded as essential to the security of the homeland among the Soviet people, and that entry into the military or naval profession as a career officer is prestigious and highly respected among the Soviet professional classes.

The Soviet Army, in particular, is widely involved in both the educational and the economic life of the country. The normal school system includes indoctrination in the 'military virtues', and Second World War veterans take classes in simplified infantry tactics as well as lecturing on their experiences during the war. The Soviet version of part-time military service, DOSAAF, is a thriving organisation which encourages students to undergo pre-national service military or naval training, including, in some cases, parachute jumping, flying and military–medical first aid. National Servicemen normally continue some form of service each year until their 60th or 65th birthday. In the economic field, servicemen are required to take part in harvesting of the grain crops and in maintaining farm buildings in the Collective or State Farms – though even the official Soviet military press admits that this activity is sometimes open to abuse.

As far as defence expenditure is concerned, precise figures and demands are hard to find because of Soviet secrecy, but everyone in the West agrees that the official Soviet annual figure of six per cent of GNP is totally inaccurate. The best British figure I know is about 13 per cent, with an annual growth rate of two to three per cent, though some higher percentages have been quoted by NATO governments. From our point of view today, I think the most interesting question is: is there any evidence that the military estimates of essential defence expenditure are challenged, for example, in the Defence Council, the Council of Ministers or the Politburo, on the grounds that they are exaggerated, inflated or damaging to progress in civilian economic projects or to planned rises in the standard of living of the ordinary Soviet people?

I wish we knew more about the debates on resource allocation and defence expenditures than we do in order to answer this question. We understand that a Military Industrial Commission exists attached to the Council of Ministers, which is responsible for coordinating military procurement policies between the Armed Forces and the Economic Ministries, and that the Commission may be represented in the membership of the Defence Council. But we do not know how authoritative its recommendations are in the Defence Council or as they move onwards to the Politburo. If Soviet and Russian traditions are anything to go by, advocates of civilian priorities in resource allocation and cuts in defence expenditure have an uphill struggle in the Soviet leadership. The chances are that unless the Politburo decides for political or international reasons to reduce defence expenditure or reject the requests of the Armed Forces on resource allocations – which has happened occasionally in the past, with some evidence of rigorous opposition from the Soviet Chiefs – tradition will give the military broadly speaking, what they want. The civilian consumer in the Soviet Union is the first to have to tighten his or her belt.

This, then, is the main picture which I have of Army–Party relations in the Soviet Union today. Perhaps the most recent evidence on how the relationship works was in connection with the Korean airliner tragedy. It has been said that this unhappy incident indicates that in recent years the influence of the military over the Party in decision-making has greatly increased; that the shoot-down was a deliberate initiative by the military leaders to display their power and their capacity to force the Party and Government into an international crisis of their own, military, choosing.

In my personal view there is no evidence to support this interpretation of the tragedy. From all available evidence it is clear that when the Korean airliner – for whatever reason – crossed into Soviet air space, the Soviet Air Defence authorities in the Far East put their 'standing orders' – their 'rules of engagement' – into effect, and everything that happened after that for the two-and-a-half hours – with the errors and failures that apparently were committed – was a purely military defensive action for which no higher authority was needed, according to Soviet military practice, than the Air Defence Headquarters in the Far East or in Moscow. I do not believe that the Poltiburo or Andropov were either informed or aware of what was happening; and I categorically reject the view that the Armed Forces deliberately 'set up' the crisis to demonstrate their power or authority over the Party leadership.

Once the aircraft had been shot down with such an appalling loss of life, and international publicity for Soviet responsibility for the tragedy had become widespread, no Soviet Government would have dreamt of apologising, accepting blame or paying compensation to the families of the victims. This would be a totally unacceptably 'unpatriotic' gesture on Russian as well as Soviet grounds; and the only conceivable way of responding was, therefore, to brazen it out and blame other countries. Moreover, Party, Government and military unity had to be displayed in public: hence the Press Conference in Moscow, chaired by Marshal Ogarkov, who was then the Chief of the General Staff, and including a senior Party official, Leonid Zamyatin and a Deputy Foreign Minister, Georgi Kornienko. Such a demonstration of unity will not prevent, of course, severe punishment of any serving officer or military Chief held responsible for the professional failures committed during the Korean airliner's flight through Soviet air space; and I expect that such action has been taken long ago.

If the tragedy has any lesson to teach us on Army–Party relations in the Soviet Union today it is that the Armed Forces' standing and prestige remains as high as ever. Indeed, in the Soviet system it cannot be queried or challenged in front of a Soviet or foreign audience – on patriotic grounds. But if, as I assume, those responsible have been punished behind closed doors in the Soviet Union, the Party will have had one more opportunity to show to the Forces that it is they who rule.

Finally in this brief look at Army–Party relations in the Soviet Union today let us consider possible developments under the leadership of Mikhail Gorbachev. There is no evidence so far available that Gorbachev intends to change the system or reduce the ultimate control of the Party over the Armed Forces: and no military leader at present in charge would expect him to do so. Gorbachev's main aim will probably be to replace some of the older officers, like Chief Marshal of Artillery V. F. Tolubko, the Commander-in-Chief of the Strategic Rocket Forces, who is 70, by younger men, like, in this case, Army-General Yuri Maksimov, aged 61. Other changes may be under consideration. But it is certainly significant that one of Gorbachev's first appointments was to bring a new and younger man into the Chief Political Directorate of the Armed Forces: Colonel-General Aleksei Lizichev, aged 57, clearly a move indicating the importance Gorbachev gives as Party leader to this key post in Army–Party relations.

(*Presentation given to the RUSI as part of its Main Theme Study, 'Soviet Power and Prospects' and subsequently updated.*)

12 Soviet Maritime Power

ADMIRAL SIR JOHN FIELDHOUSE, GCB, GBE, ADC*

We, as a nation, have travelled through a period of misguided unconcern about maritime matters. I can only reflect that the populace of our country, which comparatively rarely these days travels by sea – except to cross the Channel or go silver-sea cruising – has largely forgotten about its dependence upon the oceans for our material needs and our standard of living. Indeed the immensity of the ocean, still infinitely impressive if you should happen to find yourself upon it, even in a large ship, together with the extraordinary power it can generate, and the opaqueness of its depths to systematic penetration by detection systems, is entirely lost on the air traveller. We Europeans seem to have been going through a period of 'sea blindness' – most inappropriately, for in East–West terms, Western Europe is, we should realise, a subcontinental island – but I really do believe that the scales are at length beginning to fall away.

I have alluded to the strategic importance of the ocean as a medium for the transport of goods and resources. It is as well to remind ourselves of its importance not just as a medium, but as a provider of goods and – increasingly important – raw materials as well as sources of energy. Thus it provides not only a means by which maritime power itself can be deployed, in a manner well understood for centuries by seafaring nations, but it is also increasingly a victim of resource competition – and indeed abuse. The relatively recent international appreciation of all this has found expression in the 1982 United Nations Convention on the Law of the Sea and I am indebted to Dr Ken Booth, Department of International Politics, University College of Wales, for questioning whether we yet appreciate fully the implications of the Law of the Sea. He points to the increasing territorialisation of the sea and the degree to which the 200 mile Exclusive Economic Zone will gain status as a national asset: a possession to be exploited, guarded and controlled. He writes:

> When warships carry out supportive tasks in waters of associates their presence will have been explicitly welcomed . . . equally . . .

---

* *Chief of the Defence Staff.*

221

the impact of a coercive gesture will be enhanced in waters in which warships have definitely not been welcomed. But since coercive naval diplomacy is designed to send a disturbing message to the coastal state or its associates, the changed status of the water in which the ships are sailing will strengthen the signal which it is hoped to transmit . . . rather than marking the end of naval diplomacy, the territorialisation of the sea will open up a new era . . .

For, as we have known for generations, naval forces, in what I would describe as their 'presence' role, may advance, withdraw, concentrate or disperse without violating frontiers or abandoning ground.

Study of the Soviet Navy and the way in which it has developed during the remarkable tenure of Admiral Gorshkov, tells me that the Russians have sustained, true to their character, a far more logical appreciation of these developments, and what they portend, than have we – despite our maritime heritage and what remains of its material and human expression. In the United States Naval Institute *Proceedings*, Professor Norman Friedman has, with illuminating perception analysed the steady development of the Soviet Navy – a process not always as imaginative as we might expect against our Western model, but remorseless with deliberation and intent. In *Proceedings*, Professor Friedman has defined a clear future need for the Soviet Union to turn to the worldwide resources of the sea, certainly to satisfy its own requirements when the need should arise – as it will – and quite possibly with a view also to limiting Western access. Since the Soviet Union is markedly more self-sufficient than the West for many key raw materials, and indeed a current exporter of energy, this is a very nasty prospect. President Brezhnev once reputedly remarked to the President of Somalia that 'Our aim is to gain control of the two great treasure houses on which the West depends – the energy treasure house of the Persian Gulf and the mineral treasure house of central and southern Africa'. This remains an important factor in Soviet policy-making. Surely, Russia's unequalled maritime exploration effort can hardly indicate lack of interest in seabed treasure worldwide.

It may be argued that power politics is the key to future Soviet foreign policy. I would not wish to argue with that. But we do know that for whatever reason – paranoic fear, aggrandisement, sheer momentum, or all three – some 14 per cent of the Soviet GNP is devoted to arms. Moreover the profound caution of the Soviet leadership cannot be taken as any lack of determination to achieve their strategic aims in good time, whatever these may be. They take the long view. It is my belief that the situation in which they find themselves at home and globally, and the very existence of their massive armed forces, will between them dictate the way they go. One of Lenin's maxims was to probe with the bayonet; if it meets with steel withdraw, if with mush proceed. It can, or course, be either a conscious or a reflexive process, but nevertheless the Soviets are pragmatic opportunists. They are faced with a strategic balance on the ground in Europe which it would be exceedingly dangerous to disturb. Numerous little setbacks on the ground in direct imperial initiatives, greedy surrogates, and the approaching paucity of resources nationally and worldwide – all these factors together may even now, in the elephantine evolution of Soviet policy, be making a global maritime strategy, for which Admiral Gorshkov has prepared the ground so painstakingly, increasingly attractive.

I do not need to remind you in much detail of the expansion of the Soviet Navy from a coastal to a global force, achieved in the main within two decades. By way of illustrative figures, between 1971 and 1981 there was a 26 per cent increase in total hull numbers of submarines and major surface warships in the Warsaw Pact area; in absolute terms this order of battle increased by 43 major surface units and 34 long range attack submarines. The even more impressive increase in capability which should be superimposed upon this simple arithmetic, moved the former Secretary General of NATO, Dr Luns, to say in December 1983:

> The expansion of the Soviet Navy has been an equally disturbing development (to the strengthening of Soviet offensive capabilities in Eastern Europe), as it not only threatens our capability to reinforce but also it has allowed Soviet influence to be seen and felt in parts of the world hitherto beyond Soviet reach.

There is no doubt that there is a Russian preoccupation with the defence of the homeland, which is prerequisite to any other activity. Consequently the two primary missions of the Soviet Navy are to protect territory and home waters, including SSBN patrol areas, and to neutralise Allied maritime forces which could threaten the Soviet Union and vital associated military operations. Enormous effort is devoted to exercising the necessary degrees of sea control and denial in pursuit of these aims. They must keep at arm's length, such forces as NATO submarines, some of which could be armed with cruise missiles, and the USN Carrier Battle Groups. In practice, this would mean in war excluding NATO forces from the Norwegian Sea – a herculean undertaking which we must strain every sinew to make it impossible for them to achieve. Additional major wartime tasks would be to attack Allied reinforcement shipping and to support land operations on the flanks. But whereas these set-piece scenarios proclaim, probably with some accuracy what would occur during the catastrophe of total war, there are the soundest of practical reasons for supposing that provided our deterrent preparations are sufficient – as they must continue to be – such an event, with all its extreme dangers, is unlikely. But what about the continuing workaday situation now, and to which we refer increasingly as the 'violent peace'?

There is the school of thought which proclaims that in total war, defensive roles will continue to absorb the lion's share of Soviet naval resources under a 'ring-of-steel' concept of operations, but I do not agree. The evidence is that the Soviets are striving to build beyond this basic defensive requirement. It is thus especially interesting that in 1984, at a time when relations between Moscow and Washington were generally acknowledged to be in poor order, the two largest operational Soviet warships recently in the Soviet Northern Fleet, the Fleet that worries us most, were absent from their northern waters and showing themselves further afield on the high seas – the carrier *Novorossiysk* with a task group leaving the Indian Ocean going east, and the nuclear powered battle cruiser *Kirov*, with her formidable missile armament, were in the Mediterranean. Can it really be said with confidence that ships such as these are intended primarily to augment a strong defence of the homeland? What, moreover, is to be the role of a new class of larger aircraft carriers, comparable conceptually to those of the USN, which will be ready for operational service in the 1990s?

This burst of activity needs, of course, to be viewed in the overall context of continuing out-of-area presence to which, with its ups and downs, we have been accustomed. Loitering is a Soviet naval pastime, often at anchor over banks or in partial shelter – very different from our Western habits. There has also been continuous attention at various levels to, for instance, Cuba, Mozambique, Angola, the Horn of Africa, Socotra, the Seychelles, our old base at Aden, Cam Ranh Bay and Conakry, not to speak of the Antarctic and the activities of the merchant and fishing fleets. Some of this is just presence, some support for the surrogates they find it convenient to employ.

The merchant and fishing fleets are a subject in themselves. Make no mistake, the merchant fleet, (which is state subsidised and centrally controlled from an operational point of view under naval auspices), is able to undercut Western competition, and note should be taken of the contribution it has made, and continues to make, to the decline of our merchant marine. In addition, with the fishing fleet, it is ubiquitous; it has access nearly everywhere, with the capacity to eavesdrop; act as a naval auxiliary and play a major part in replenishing Soviet naval vessels around the world.

The vein of departures from precedent is continuing. As long ago as early 1984, the Sunday press reported that additional Soviet SSBN patrols had moved from northern waters into the Atlantic. Soviet SSNs have been regularly reported patrolling off the US eastern seaboard, possibly armed with cruise missiles. There are authorities who would previously have regarded such moves as almost unthinkable. This leads me to a most important concluding principle – and that is the distinction between capability and intention. Whatever moderate and reasonable intentions we may read into our potential enemies – even if these appear well established under the present leadership and for the foreseeable future – it is essential to look beyond at the capability that can be wielded, for it is this that we must not fail to match in any plausible circumstances that could arise. Let me give you a pertinent example from that most alarming force, the Soviet nuclear submarines. It is sometimes alleged that the bulk of these will be held back for ASW in Northern Fleet waters and will not, therefore, be available to attack Allied forces and shipping in the Atlantic. Such an assumption, dangerous at best, is based upon one scenario surrounding that relatively unlikely event of total war. I have always been wary of scenarios, and I must tell you that in one very small recent war – our Falklands experience – there were perhaps a dozen major events which cured me of any lingering addiction to scenarios for ever. Let us take two of them – both well known. Had the Argentines not misread our intentions and failed to appreciate our capabilities, they would never have invaded the islands. Had we not possessed the capability to move by sea (there was no other way), in sufficient force, we could never have re-possessed them. Capabilities bequeath options, and for the Soviet Navy the options increasingly are worldwide.

So what are the challenges? Above all we must get the balance right in what appears to me to be a simultaneous equation of which the main variables are areas of strategic interest, absolute danger, and levels of probability.

We must avoid the common mistake of identifying strategic interest with current activity. There are areas of great strategic interest to the

West which do not, at present, attract much obvious Soviet threat. For example, the Cape shipping route is important to Europe, even if there is little evidence of a direct Soviet threat to its operation. I would, however, mention the interesting development of the Trans-Siberian railway – a strategic feature we can do little about, although it has more to do with the Cape route than may be obvious. Between 1972 and 1979, the Trans-Siberian (offering cut rates like the Soviet merchant marine) has raised its share of all Far East–European freight from 4.4 per cent to 24 per cent. Strategic features, and threats to them, are not always immediately obvious.

Next we must avoid being too preoccupied, almost to the exclusion of anything else, by total war in well-worn scenarios of direct NATO–Warsaw Pact confrontation. We must, of course, always ensure that steel is confronted by steel, and that there is a sufficient edge on the blade. But, with a considerable measure of personal responsibility for ensuring sufficient deterrence on the Northern Flank, I see it as important to our security as the Central Region, and I would say the same for the Southern Flank for which we have less direct responsibility. Note that failure on the Northern Flank turns on the Baltic and Centre, brings the front line to the Faeroes and Shetlands, and would extend the Soviet reach directly into the Atlantic and around the central axis and lifeline of the Alliance.

But it is elsewhere that the bayonets will meet the really soft mush, and I hope I have stirred enough unease about the profound global uncertainty and competition – inevitably competition – that faces us in the medium and long term. Remember that weapon systems and platforms being conceived now must see us through at least the first two decades of the next century. In resisting the fascination with the stark blacks and whites of direct confrontation in Europe, appreciate that it is not such answers that drop out of the simultaneous equation in every-day terms – recent history confirms that. What faces us in reality is an infinity of shades of grey. It is these mainly, I predict, that will trouble our lives, not war in Europe, providing, that is, we are sufficiently alert and resolute. The activity will be elsewhere, and often on, under or over the sea. It will concern our allies as much as ourselves – as we must strive to make clear to them.

We may find that Thermistocles was being even wiser than we knew when over 2400 years ago he coined the adage 'he who controls the sea controls everything'. The Soviets may have perceived the lesson while we temporarily mislaid it. Now we are recovering from our sea blindness, let us also recover our bearings.

(*Presentation given to the RUSI as part of its Main Theme Study, 'Soviet Power and Prospects' and subsequently updated.*)

13 Morale, Motivation and Leadership in the Soviet Armed Forces

AIR COMMODORE E. S. WILLIAMS, CBE, MPhil

Most people who write or speak about the Soviet Union like to start with an apt quotation from Lenin. I shall resist the temptation. Instead I shall quote Trotsky, since he is unfashionable and does not get much of an airing these days. But it was indeed Trotsky who encapsulated the whole essence of military morale when he wrote:

> First of all you must build the morale of your own troops. Then you must look to the morale of your civilian population. Then, and only then, when these are in good repair should you concern yourself with the enemy's morale. And the best way to destroy the enemy's morale is to kill him in large numbers. There's nothing more demoralising that that.

Well, there is a lot in what he wrote – and it was Trotsky who was responsible for the morale of the Red Army. In the chaos of 1917, he spread his agitators through the remnants of the Tsar's army and rallied them to the Bolshevik side. To the civil population he sent more military agitators in special propaganda trains, whistle-stopping over the whole railway system to preach the Bolshevik message. It was the only medium available other than rumour. Newspapers were not being printed, Popov had not really invented the wireless so there was not any reliable medium other than face-to-face propaganda. And it worked, the Red Army was built on promises – it did not matter that they later turned out false – and the white armies were beaten – killed in large numbers.

And that is how it has been going for almost 70 years. The media have improved but there is still a heavy reliance on face-to-face agitation – and the message is very little altered. Soviet propaganda preaches that the people and the army are one – are united in a mystical

* Lately Defence and Air Attaché, Moscow

trinity of the peasants and workers, the intelligentsia, and the armed forces. Together they stand invincible against the capitalist enemy. The armed forces are continuously hyped as the sure shield of the homeland with, also, an internationalist obligation to protect the gains of socialism wherever on the globe they are threatened by imperialism, neo-imperialism or internal reaction. Soviet media claim incessantly that the Soviet soldier (and they mean the sailor and the airman as well) is the proud inheritor of the traditions of the great October Revolution, of the Red Army in the civil war and in the greatest war and victory of all military history, the Great Patriotic War of 1941–45 and that he now serves in the office of a line of fortifications protecting these glorious achievements, *et cetera*.

This is all very well, but what we want to know is, 'Does it work? Is he any good? Will he advance on day one of World War III or will he flee the field at the first trumpet blast from NORTHAG or 2 ATAF?'.

On 26 October 1949, Major General Richard Hilton spoke at the Royal United Services Institute for Defence Studies. He had just returned from the Soviet Union having done the job I was to do 30 years later. The Chairman on that occasion was Earl Wavell. General Hilton would have agreed with my views. He judged that Soviet military morale is a curate's egg – no reason to think that it is all bad but whether it is really sound would depend on the circumstances of any test. He suggested that their principal motivation was a harsh discipline, maintained by the NKVD/KGB and that leadership in all the Soviet services is of a doubtful quality – that officers lead neither from the front nor from the back. That in most respects they do not lead at all. They tend just to ignore the troops and actually get on themselves doing the jobs that have to be done. And if the system as a whole is not working as well as it should, then the remedy is more and yet more political education.

Those were broadly General Hilton's conclusions. I was strongly tempted to change a few names and include the transcript of his lecture as printed in the RUSI *Journal* for 1949. Nothing essential has changed it seems over the last 37 years. I find that I can only echo those conclusions. And a most interesting thing was that Earl Wavell in his summing up on that day in 1949 said that nothing appeared to have changed since he had been in Russia for the annual manoeuvres of the Tsar's army in 1911 and 1912.

What can we make of it then? In spite of all these seeming deficiencies, we know that the Russian soldier of the First World War was renowned for great courage and stoic endurance, that the Red Army during the civil war proved to be a match for the whites and the foreign interventionists – and I do not need to mention how in the Second World War, after near-fatal reverses they were able to recover, rebuild and manage the largest army the world has ever known – and do what they did to the Germans. It is a record that may not be quite as glorious as Soviet history claims, but it is mightily impressive nevertheless. Could they do it today?

For a start, Afghanistan is not proving much of an advertisement for Soviet military power – the first reckonable demonstration of its capability since 1945. We have it on good evidence that military service in Afghanistan is not all that popular – that living conditions there are bad, that morale has reached such low levels that soldiers have murdered officers, that crime of all description is rife, the desertion rate is high, and dereliction of duty a commonplace. There is drunkenness when drink can be got hold of, hashish is grown and smoked as a substitute, arms and accoutrements are bartered on a large scale with the civilian population – bartered for drink and other comforts. And that is not the end by any means of a long and sordid catalogue.

But the catalogue is in no way confined to Afghanistan. The same general sort of picture has been seen in the Group of Soviet Forces, Germany for years and indeed in the Soviet Union itself, and these are peacetime situations. *Émigrés* who have actually served in the Soviet forces are obviously a prime source of information on such issues and their commonplace tale is a pretty sorry one. They tell of a mindlessly harsh discipline untempered by human feeling, sadistic punishments – often inflicted by their fellows and equals, widespread corruption in all ranks and a ludicrous general inefficiency as the principal characteristics of the Soviet Army. One stream of such testimony decries it as a scarcely viable force – but others are not so dismissive, being of the opinion that the right motivating circumstances will generate the same quality of morale as that which took them all the very bloody way to the Elbe in 1945. In Afghanistan today, these motivating circumstances are absent – the cause is unpopular and there is no credible threat to the homeland. But fighting NATO – that would be another matter. Well – would it?

Our difficulty is where to put our money between these two poles of opinion – poles of native-born Russian opinion formed from first-hand experience and therefore both demanding of respect. To say that the truth lies somewhere between the two is a facile answer and at some given time not necessarily true. The compound weaknesses of the system could in certain circumstances trigger the collapse of the whole regime. In others, they might be of no significance in great swells of heroic patriotism leading them on to the final victory in the struggle with the dark forces of capitalist-imperialism. 1945 all over again.

But let us leave the answer somewhere in the middle while we look at some of the factors affecting morale, and ideology is an important one – but how important is it? General of the Army Yepishev, Chief of the Political Directorate, and his successor, Army-General A. I. Lizichev think it is supremely important – and all the massive output of its military publishing house and its many thousands of political officers and political workers are devoted to the cultivation of ideological understanding. It has been calculated that Lizichev's staff is somewhat larger than the whole of the British Army of the Rhine – all these people devoted to what they call 'ideological steeling of the soldier's will'. Ideology has to be important. We in the West are well accustomed to hearing that the 'Soviet soldier is heavily indoctrinated' – but we are not very often told what he is indoctrinated with and to what extent. And we would not believe it anyway – we certainly would have difficulty in appreciating the extent of the process, in believing that 30 per cent of a conscript soldier's training time is devoted to the 'ideological steeling' of his will. But it is.

We get a clue what it is about from reading the political officer's own training handbook. We read that his terms of reference charge him with the task of 'indoctrinating his unit with a spirit of high idealism, diligence and selfless devotion to the homeland'. This is the first and greatest commandment, that is 'to indoctrinate personnel with a hatred towards the nation's enemies'.

That is the nub of it – and in these instructions we have seen only another expression of the general two-strand Soviet political propaganda line as peddled to the whole country in all its 15 republics – the line glorifying the Communist party and all its works while at the same time vilifying the capitalist enemy with a degree of corrosive calumny that we cannot credit – so we just tend to laugh at it.

But the majority of Soviet soldiers do not laugh at it. Remember, it is not the first time they have come across the message – they have in fact been hearing it from birth almost. From the earliest days in the nursery school, they are surrounded by the aura of Lenin and learn about the beneficence of the Communist party. Lenin is God, Jesus Christ and Father Christmas all in one, only more so. They are constantly reminded of their extreme good fortune in having been born in the Soviet Union and thereby immediately entitled to enjoy the privileges of the Soviet constitution. Throughout all their subsequent education, their Communist 'world-outlook' is developed further by reiteration and repetition until the general lines of the doctrine are burned into their souls every bit as deeply as Christianity was burned into the souls of European children in earlier generations. Not only in schools is the child subjected to this process. He gets it also in his free time – if you can call it free time – in the Pioneer Palace and in the KOMSOMOL programme (the Young Communist League), and in the pre-conscription, paramilitary training organisation known as DOSAAF. Marxist–Leninist propaganda stares him in the face wherever he looks, and there is little or nothing by way of counter view to stimulate any doubts that might arise in the youthful breast – and certainly questioning doubts do arise.

Between the end of his pioneer days and before the young man joins the armed forces – in his KOMSOMOL days in other words – zeal for the Communist cause cools somewhat and he goes in one of three directions. He might become a dissident, the path chosen by very, very few – and even so this does not necessarily mean he abandons Marxist–Leninism. He might choose the second path, this time with very many of his contemporaries and become an *apparatchik*, a party functionary, and he chooses this way either because he retains a faith in the system or because he recognises this as the only route to the few glittering prizes that the Soviet Union has to offer, and he is prepared to pay unlimited lip-service to get up the ladder. And, thirdly, by far the greatest number of them drift along the path of political apathy, of obedient, conforming apathy, following a profession or trade, earning a living, careful not to rock the boat.

But before he gets far along any of these roads, the 18-year-old male is called up to do his two years conscript service – that is if he is not clever enough to get exemption on educational grounds. A million-and-a-half each year do not manage this and end up in the army. And every year also between 50 000 and 60 000 of them avoid conscription by becoming regular officers, avoiding persecution by becoming persecutors and gaining status in society into the bargain. As officers they will also get, by national standards, very handsome rates of pay rather than the conscript's pittance which does not cover tooth-paste, but the snag is that normally they will have to serve 20 years at least – become career professionals in fact.

The plain essence of it is that not many young people want to serve in the army these days. The Slav elements by and large suffer conscription as an inevitable thing and accept it with resignation. The others – the Uzbeks, the Tadzhiks, the Lithuanians, Estonians, Georgians, Armenians – are more truculent and just do not want to be in the Soviet Army.

A lot of people ask about this ethnic problem and how it affects discipline. It is no small problem. To begin with, there is the language. The armed forces operate exclusively in Russian and so there is no alternative if you are Uzbek or Tadzhik but to get by in Russian. In theory, you are able to speak Russian because the Soviet schools' curriculum is universal and every child in a minority republic will have been taught Russian. In theory, that is. In practice, this is effectively true only for the larger towns. In the more rural areas, it is not at all true and there are lots of children who do not go to school at all except in the most perfunctory way. Because of this, it is the town children who are going to get the educational exemptions and so the army gets lumbered with a lot of *chuchmeks* who either cannot speak or will not speak Russian. The Tsar's army never faced this problem. They had sufficient Russian-speaking Slavs to excuse the minority races from conscription. Now, manpower levels and demographic trends will not permit this. The Soviet Army has to have its cohorts from those other races. It has to have them in spite of the difficulties and certainly it understands the problem and takes steps towards reducing it but it is not going to disappear.

The problem is far from being just a matter of language. There are severe racial tensions between several main groups and the Russians – it is particularly intense between Russians and Georgians, but there are lateral rifts too. Armenians do not like Georgians for instance, and although the Baltic groups do not care much for each other they are united in their loathing for all the other constituent peoples of the USSR put together. Here again, the authorities are aware of the problems and seem to be trying to hold them in check by a divide and rule policy, since it is not only individual racial animosities that worry them but also a paranoid fear of nationalist aspirations and secession movements.

So they ensure among other things that conscripts do not serve together in ethnic units, nor do they allow them to serve near their own homes. In earlier years, they did raise ethnic units – but they were never completely trusted. The fact that the Georgian division based in its own capital, Tbilisi, was specifically not used to quell the 1956 riots in that city because its reliability was suspect owing to its local affiliations – this illustrates the difficulty. Nowadays, as one young man said to me with a shrug, 'If you are an Uzbek, you serve in Russia – if you are a Balt, you serve in Uzbekistan'.

But, apart from natural 'fed up and far from home' considerations, there is no apparent reason to suppose that this posting policy is of itself damaging to morale. Perhaps, insofar as it can and does give rise to friction with the local population over ethnic issues, it is damaging to some extent, but not nearly is it so serious as the damage created by ethnic clashes within units. These contribute greatly to the high crime rate in the Soviet armed forces. And I am not simply talking about staying out after midnight or breaking glasses in the NAAFI or such examples of petty crime when I am referring to crime. I am talking about real main-line crime, murder, for instance, on a grand scale, killing comrades or superiors with knives or, wholesale, with Kalashnikov automatics – major crimes of that sort.

Crime is sparked off very often and very easily it appears by ethnic collisions but the other great cause is drink – either too little drink or too much. I say too little because it is often the shortage of drink that leads to those other crimes, the bartering of tyres or motor fuel for Vodka or even the selling of weapons, since again in theory, troops cannot legally obtain drink and, drink being the Russian national pastime, they will go to criminal lengths to get it. When they do get it of course, it naturally leads to drunkenness and that produces crime as surely as night follows day. Stealing of vehicles is a popular one, but so is the knifing of one's comrades, often in connection with theft, or racial difficulty or revenge, or just for the hell of it. Violence accompanies drunkenness so often because of the nature of the beverages. When real vodka is not obtainable – and that is most of the time – the troops make up recipes for disaster out of radiator coolant or boot polish or cleaning fluids. This, however, does not lead to the mass alcoholism that some claim makes for weakness in military morale. Alcoholism is the curse of the nation, but not of its soldiery – unless they are alcoholic before conscription. If not they are pretty safe for the whole period of their conscription. It is not that they have any particular rechabite tendencies – it is just that they cannot easily lay their hands on drink and because the gruelling nature of their training allows them little or no leisure; and hence little time for drinking. On those occasions when they do manage it, inebriation comes swiftly and crime occasionally follows but drunkenness among 18 to 20-year-olds is not alcoholism.

But officers are another story. I saw very few drunken soldiers in the

Soviet Union, but drunken officers are ten for a kopec in public places: hotels, trains, airports – even, I understand, on duty but that I did not see personally. It is credible, though, because the officer cadre is no more than one sector of a society which is wholly plagued by the scourge of alcoholism. And officers can get all the drink they need and moreover they can make time to drink it. As a result, there is indeed alcoholism among officers and that cannot be good for morale. The officer corps is probably the target of a current anti-alcohol campaign in the military press, part of a greater, national campaign against alcohol abuse. But Gorbachev's drive against alcoholism is unlikely to be significantly remedial, certainly in the short term. 'We despised our officers', one conscript said, 'because they tormented us when they were drunk – and that was most of the time.'

And yet everything depends on the officers. If the backbone of the British Army is the NCO, the backbone of the Soviet Army is the officer. Simple aircraft refuelling and re-arming is done by an officer, all tanks and APCs are commanded by officers, and routine jobs about the ship are done by officers. The conscript bulk of the forces are expected to obey these officers in fighting, fetching and carrying and little is demanded of them by way of initiative. Obedience is the requirement not initiative – an iron discipline. And this is the nature of Soviet military discipline, a discipline based upon fear, with, in accordance with the Soviet military oath, the promise of certain punishment if the code is broken.

Without an effective NCO corps, this discipline would be difficult to enforce – so the practice has grown up over the years of letting the senior, second-year, conscripts control the first-year new boys with little supervision from officers. These seniors exert their loose authority often with mindless, sadistic and arbitrary punishments – and these are depressing to morale to say the least, and the system is reflected in the high suicide and desertion rates. And try as they have, the Soviet forces have so far not managed to build an efficient NCO corps – it just does not fit into their structure.

But in officers, initiative is required and calls are constantly being made in the Soviet military press for greater levels of it. That they do not seem to be able to get it is a psychological snag of the Russian make-up. The word *initsiyativa* does not quite equate with our 'initiative'. 'Initiative' in their book does not convey the idea of making the right decision and taking action off one's own bat. The Russian asks himself, 'What is the commander's plan for this contingency?' It is a difference of nuance perhaps rather than of significance, but when you read that this divining of the commander's plan is to be done from Marxist–Leninist principles, perhaps it is of significance. A dread that he might read his commander's mind incorrectly results very often in the Soviet officer taking no action at all – with the consequence that whatever the mission it fails with heavy collatoral damage to unit morale. Russians say *initsiyativa nakazuyema* – 'initiative is punishable' and this has serious implications. The fear of the authorities is of *rastyerannost*, of coming apart at the seams, a corporate loss of will, paralysis and a complete disintegration of the system. To prevent the collapse, they rely on constantly practiced drills, on maintaining control centralised at as high a level as possible and they wisely teach that operational orders should be as all-embracing as possible, covering the remotest contingency. But for the encouragement of true initiative their only prescription thus far – and just as General Hilton reported – is to call at frequent intervals for yet more ideological training.

These, in sum, are a few of the weaknesses of the peacetime Soviet military machine. While I suggest we should study these weaknesses a little more urgently, nevertheless will it really matter if it comes to war? Will ideological doubts, low morale arising from the boredom of peacetime soldiering and poor pay be of any significance if the homeland were to be attacked? Probably not. The young men of today are considered to be a bit softer than their grandfathers, those legendary heroes of Berlin, but they would, I am sure, display the same qualities if convinced of the justice of their cause. I am equally sure that they would be convinced of their cause. The political officers would make certain they were. Overnight they would transmute the cartoon stereotypes of the Western anti-communist forces into the real live enemies attacking the homeland and the 'ideological steeling of the will' would flip over into 'patriotic steeling of the will'. This would have a far greater galvanic effect than would all the whole 'collected works of Lenin' lain end to end. And we might find that although lack of initiative and that sort of thing might make for some sclerosis in the command and control system and a consequent loss of cohesion among units or even formations, it would be unwise of us to expect that the soldiers' wooden discipline would collapse merely from the strain of battle. The Germans know the Russian soldier better than we do. They were not bemused by a 'ten-foot tall' image of their enemy in the Second World War. They were well aware of warts and judged him accordingly. Nevertheless, they seem unanimous in assessing him as a tough enemy, courageous and enduring beyond the normal human measure. And among their own German troops there grew up the demoralising notion that Russian soldiers have to be killed twice before they die and that the Red Army could never be beaten.

I must finish on this ambivalent note, suggesting that the Soviet serviceman is not the ten-foot-tall superman of the common myth, nor the alcoholic wooden moron of the alternative popular misconception. He rates somewhere between the two but to which end of the scale he inclines will depend on circumstances.

In the West, we rather take morale for granted. We find it difficult to understand why morale is the overriding obsession of Soviet military writers. Is it simply a reflection of Russian culture, of Tolstoy's conviction that people are ultimately more important and powerful than weapons? Or does it imply recognition of the fear that Soviet ideology of itself would not naturally generate the level of morale necessary for winning a war and that frequent dressings of propaganda fertiliser are therefore required? The answer is obstinately obscure, governed by many factors, only a few of which have been presented here.

(*Presentation given to the RUSI as part of its Main Theme Study, 'Soviet Power and Prospects', and subsequently updated.*)

14 The Soviet Navy in Transition

NORMAN FRIEDMAN*

My subject is the way the Soviets view their own navy: not so much how they would use it against the West, rather the way it is apt to develop over the next ten or 20 years. Those who build navies must contend with a very complex series of factors within their own countries. Navies are extremely expensive. That is why in peacetime, in the past, they have often fared very badly in inter-service rivalry: because they are so *obviously* expensive, and because fewer and fewer people understand that material still travels by sea, even if people no longer do. If you speak to someone who is not concerned with maritime matters, he actually believes that you can move heavy goods by air, which is very regrettable because the Messiah has not yet arrived, and the laws of physics are still in effect.

If we examine the Soviet navy, and the role of Admiral Gorshkov in particular, we can observe the efforts of a service which, traditionally, has done poorly in Soviet terms, to explain why it should be allocated a very large share of resources, and even, perhaps, an ultimately dominant role. I am not suggesting that the Soviet Navy has such a role at present; I am suggesting that Admiral Gorshkov's logic, if followed, will provide it with this role.

Before proceeding further, it is worth noting that there is a rather fortuitous correspondence between Admiral Gorshkov's logic and the Soviet image of future war. In Soviet ideology, we are the ones who attack them. In practice, what the Soviets may describe as 'counter-attack' may look surprisingly like aggression. But however self-serving and far-fetched, the fact is that when Soviet strategists discuss war or 'the struggle', they must remember that they, by definition, are the injured party. Soviet psychology matters because, in the end, the Soviets must justify what they do in their own terms. In Stalin's time, the Soviets held the view that war with the West was inevitable. The West ('Imperialism'), realising that the USSR ('Socialism') was

---

* *Formerly Deputy Director of National Security Studies, Hudson Institute of New York.*

destroying it, would strike out and destroy the revolution. However, Stalin also believed that the sheer size of the USSR would make it impossible for the country to lose a conventional war. Whilst this perception was largely responsible for his failure to anticipate Germany's attack in 1941, it also is a key to a lot of what has happened since. When Stalin died, and the Soviet military began to discuss nuclear weapons on a large scale, they concluded that the armed forces were in the midst of what came to be called 'the Revolution in Military Affairs'. The content of the Revolution, in essence, is that nuclear weapons are decisive. From a Western point of view, the conclusion which follows is that the Soviets would begin any war with heavy use of nuclear weapons. But in the light of Stalin's assessments and doctrinal 'defensiveness', nuclear weapons are 'decisive' in Soviet eyes because they provide the sole means by which the Soviet Union would be defeated in war. There are two possible responses to this challenge: the 'minimalist' one of straightforward deterrence, which was Khrushchev's objective, or as we have seen since Khrushchev, a search for usable means and strategems below the nuclear threshold once such deterrence is achieved.

It is here that the navy comes in. Once it is strong enough to accomplish its basic task of protecting the homeland, it is available to strike out elsewhere in the world. If nuclear war in Europe can be deterred by nuclear means; if, secondly, the Soviet Union need not fear defeat in a conventional war, there is a conclusion which readily follows: that 'progress' in the world can be advanced in limited places, outside the main axis of NATO–Warsaw Pact confrontation. This is Gorshkov's logic. I do not think he has sold that logic yet, by any means. But I do think that he has been trying rather hard.

Moreover, the logic of Gorshkov's thinking is supported by the logic of naval expansion. Navies are long-term investments; ships take a long time to build, and they are very complicated. It is very difficult to cancel a programme (more so in the Soviet Union than elsewhere). Very often, the political masters who approve a ship are not really aware of its capabilities or its potential. They may rule out those missions which navies aspire to, but once the ships exist, options are open, and views can be changed. Therefore, when we speak about what the Soviets will or will not do, we must consider three things: their statements, their hardware and the options it affords them, and the internal logic of their ideology, which they cannot ignore. I have never been certain whether the Soviets believe what they say, or whether they simply adopt a particular language for the sake of convenience.

However, once you speak a given language which has certain conventions – and ideologies are a language like anything else – those conventions tend to take on a certain force.

The Soviet Navy has evolved out of a rather poor background. To be sure, Russia has often built up large surface navies, but they have not performed very well in combat. Many will recall the battle of Tsushima, which must haunt men like Admiral Gorshkov. It must be particularly galling to him that he has no glorious naval history to parade before his officers. What a contrast to the Soviet Ground Forces and the volumes of historical writing it sponsors! However, when it comes to navies, the country has not been stinting with money, if for no other purpose than to buy a certain prestige in the world. We can almost imagine Stalin saying, 'we want to be taken seriously by those capitalists. To be taken seriously, you must have certain attributes, and that includes a big navy'. Once you have a navy, then it opens up possibilities far beyond the original objectives for it. Similarly, if we look at Admiral Gorshkov and the naval construction he has sponsored – or at least extracted from the Soviet leadership – that has its possibilities as well. During the Brezhnev years, the Soviet Navy regularly received about one-fifth of the Soviet military budget. That in itself suggests that Gorshkov was able to impress on the Soviet leadership a respect for the value of navies. At the very least, there has been a grudging admission that there is value in building large and expensive ships.

If one looks at some of those ships, one has to think carefully about why they were built, because they cost a great deal of money. As a case in point, Khrushchev authorised the construction of two light aircraft carriers – helicopter ships – which are always described as ASW ships. In fact, they are usually described as anti-Polaris, but two ships do not an anti-Polaris capability make. In part, these ships testify to the maxim that once a programme is in train, however ill-conceived, something must come of it. But in this case, something more is involved. Let us recall that the USSR is a large industrial system which operates on the basis of five-year plans. It is at the very least embarrassing to change the plan once it has been set, and if we consider the timescale of ship-building or weapons procurement, a major programme may represent the cumulative result of several such plans joined together. Therefore, only a brave Soviet leader will fool with the Five-Year Plan, and to fool with two or three such plans, one must be very brave indeed. The only Soviet leader in recent years to have had that sort of courage was Khrushchev. Khrushchev was willing to make trouble. He was willing to make a great deal of trouble because he felt himself constricted economically; he had real ideas; he was very enthusiastic about modern weapons, and he also believed that the USSR should move away from tradition. To him, the navy was part of this tradition, and he tried to decimate it. It is quite obvious from his memoirs that Admiral Gorshkov was appointed in the expectation that he would be a good boy and would help to destroy the Soviet surface fleet. I would think it was a great achievement on the part of the Admiral, and on the part of those who worked with him, to save the Soviet fleet from total extinction. When Khrushchev left the scene, not just the Navy but the entire defence establishment set about recovering from the nuclear obsession which he tried to impose upon it. Tank production increased, interest revived in tactical aircraft, and even a bomber like the Backfire dates from the immediate post-Khrushchev years when it became possible to consider the utility of traditional weapons once again.

Thus, after a lengthy detour, the Soviet Navy returned to the business of building great ships. If, bearing in mind the Five-Year Plans, we consider a carrier like the *Kiev*, we can see that the idea is a product of this immediate post-Khrushchev period. A planning system of the Soviet type is predicated upon long-term considerations, and it also imposes them. Decisions made now do not become publicly visible for five or ten years. If we look at a submarine like the *Alfa*, which went to sea in 1969, and consider the industrial effort behind it, it would be reasonable to conclude that the groundwork was laid during Khrushchev's Seven-Year Plan of 1959–1965. The very existence of this plan demonstrates Khrushchev's efforts to break the mould of the previous planning cycles and shake things up. A lot of what has happened since stems from the attempt to undo that shake-up. Thus, the ideas behind the *Alfa*, which we think of as a futuristic submarine, date from the mid-1950s. The basic concept must have emerged in 1957, or 1958 at the latest. One begins to see that the *Alfa* was born because, to Khrushchev, it looked like the submarine of the future. He picked futuristic projects partly for prestige, partly because he just liked them. If you are the dictator of a world power, you pick what you like.

That sort of thing has since given way to a navy much more rational in appearance and designed for more definite purposes. First, my own analysis suggests that the Soviets place a high priority on strategic missile submarines, an objective they had more or less abandoned under Khrushchev for reasons of cost. If you choose to keep your submarines in home waters, as the Soviets do, you must then protect your home waters, which in turn requires a degree of sea control, and that is a very expensive undertaking. But if we look at what has emerged since Khrushchev, we find a fleet largely designed for that purpose: controlling the approaches to the Soviet Union at a distance. That is the first change we have witnessed.

Secondly, from the late 1960s we begin to see Admiral Gorshkov talking about the need to protect Soviet interests abroad: in other words, protecting friends in the Third World and 'keeping the Imperialists at bay'. Both Britain and the United States are Imperialists. Britain demonstrated as much in the Falklands, the United States does so every day, and the Soviet Navy is there to protect 'progressive mankind' from the likes of the British and the Americans. So far, they have not devoted a lot of effort to this role, but there is a fair chance that the nuclear powered battle cruiser *Kirov* was originally conceived as an expression of this desire. Thinking again in terms of Five-Year Plans, we can see that the *Kirov*'s origins roughly coincide with those words written in about 1967 about protecting Soviet state interests abroad. At that time, limited protection is probably all that the Soviets had in mind, and they envisaged devoting limited resources to the task. Rather than set about taking on NATO's naval forces, they focused on acquiring a capability for operating freely in the world's oceans in peacetime.

But there is another, less visible, change which takes on a striking significance in the light of these developments: the improvement in command and control capabilities. Thanks to that, the Soviet Navy is at last acquiring the ability to operate anywhere in the world. In order to attack enemy ships, the Soviet Navy relies extensively upon external sensors. The *Kirov* is not expected to find a ship 200–300 miles away; it is told that there is a target, and it shoots. The same is true for virtually all Soviet warships. Classically, this has meant nothing more than dependence on a system of radio direction finders in the USSR, supplemented by radar equipped aircraft. In this manner, targets are located and confirmed, forces are regrouped, and a simultaneous attack is launched. But with target location centred in the USSR, accuracy declines with distance. Thus, even if operations take place 1000 or 1500 miles from the USSR, we are talking of a navy which has conceived of itself in coastal terms. All of that changed when the Soviets developed satellites to perform these functions: satellites with direction finders, satellites with radar (like the one which came down in Canada some time ago). From this point, it became clear that the

Soviets were building, on however limited a scale, a capability to operate wherever they wished.

Satellites and space systems are not cheap; in fact, they represent a major investment. One of my personal fears is that the US Navy will run itself bankrupt by buying exactly the kind of system which the Soviets are acquiring. Although this form of investment is difficult to observe, it is as significant as anything more conspicuous. Without it, ships are impressive only for presence; with it, tactics can be put to use far from home. Here we come back to the essential point: ships may be built for one thing and used for something radically different. Once ships are built, governments have a way of finding uses for them. For example, whilst it would be insane, given standard Soviet tactics, for the Soviets to operate ballistic missile submarines in the Atlantic on a wartime footing, that was not the point when Andropov needed a response to NATO's INF deployment. Andropov said, 'you place your missiles in Europe, we will do something about it', and the Soviet Navy became the vehicle for doing something about it.

Where is the Soviet Navy heading? It is not altogether clear. What is clear is that Soviet ships are changing. That change must have occurred some considerable time ago because, given the logic of the planning system, the building and thinking take more time in the USSR than they do here. Let us examine some ships and draw some inferences.

The *Kirov* is a ship that can operate by itself, which means that if you wish to operate far from home, it is a good ship to have. Nuclear power affords immense range, although not at very high speed; the *Kirov*'s missile system is the best which the USSR has produced, although inferior to Aegis; and *Kirov* also has long-range anti-ship capability. What it lacks is an effective shore bombardment capability. Its purpose is to sink other ships if it must, to protect itself, and to operate anywhere in the world (assuming the necessary communications support).

Let us then consider the Typhoon SSBN. Typhoon illustrates the Soviet Navy's seriousness about putting missiles out to sea. If the Soviet Navy is going to the trouble of MIRVing SLBMs – which means spending more of their expensive nuclear material per missile – then, they obviously have decided that major national assets can be deployed at sea and protected. This is a very far cry from the Khrushchev years, when cruisers were described as coffins and the sea was perceived as a kind of jungle in which Soviet ships would not survive. Thus, Typhoon's missiles testify to some far-reaching changes.

If you approach the Soviet Armed Forces from a Western perspective, you may imagine that a decision made today under one set of assumptions may be switched round tomorrow when assessments change. It is not that easy. Why, after all, do the Soviets keep producing endless amounts of military hardware in the first place? One obvious – and fundamental – reason is that the Soviet economy is not biased towards civilian production as the Western economy is. But another reason is the simple momentum of the industrial system. No one below the level of senior party member has any political responsibility. Even relatively senior Party members who work for the Party–State apparatus are constrained, and this is certainly true for those who end up managing industrial plants. The responsibility of a plant manager is to produce what the plan dictates, and perks and bonuses are tied to doing that and that alone. There is absolutely no incentive to prefer, let us say, passenger cars to tanks. If you are managing a tank plant, it is in your interest that tanks remain in production. Of course, better not be under pressure to produce more in the current plan than in the preceding one. But the preoccupation with budgets and the pressures of economics so ingrained in the Western mind simply do not exist. To us, every year is a new disaster. Every year, the US Treasury says, 'we notice that if we cut you in half, our lives would be so much better', or 'the fact is that eight new divisions for the Central Front would be more cost-effective than your new missile cruiser, so please do not bother telling us about it'. These things do not ocur in the USSR. There, the easiest course is to continue producing what has always been produced. Without countervailing forces, the system, like a mechanical monster, just keeps going forever. Moreover, the Soviets are not fond of destroying what they have already built. The result is that 'the threat' worsens even if there is no particular decision to worsen it. When there is, it worsens more dramatically. As with tanks, so with ships. As new ships are built, the fleet grows, options grow, and the real limiting factor becomes available manpower rather than economics. At some point in the months following Khrushchev's fall, the Naval establishment managed to sell the idea of increasing Soviet naval procurement. It may well be that the deciding factor was the personal connection between Gorshkov and Brezhnev. But whatever the reason, once naval procurement had been sold, it did not have to be resold.

Typhoon, then, like any Soviet ship, illustrates important themes of procurement, capability and policy. What lessons can we learn from the Victor III SSN? The principal one is continuity. Victor first appeared about 1968. Victor III is still being built now. It has been a long time, and the product has been improved gradually – but decidedly improved. The United States has officially stated that Victor III is extremely quiet. It also has a towed array in the nacelle projecting from its fin. That in itself does not mean that the Soviets will be able to find our submarines, because it is questionable just how good their signal processing is. But, let us not fool ourselves: our opponent is gradually beginning to understand the technologies that we have painfully developed over a very long period. When he really understands those technologies, and once he builds up operational experience with these devices, he will then have a much better idea of how to evade them and how to counter us. We have not been pouring the kind of money into new ideas and new technologies that he has been pouring into copying us. Americans have a shameful slogan: 'not invented here', by which we mean that we will not borrow from others. Our opponent has absolutely no such inhibitions. To be sure, his ability to copy is restricted by his industrial limitations, and those limitations are still severe. There are important ways in which the Soviet Union is still a Third World country. But it is a Third World country with an over-developed military industry, and one of the questions that Mr Andropov posed was whether this country could attempt to broaden its industrial base to the point where it could become a Superpower in a non-military sense. As I will suggest in my conclusion, Mr Andropov's death and Chernenko's succession were, for a time, the best things that could have happened to the Soviet Navy. But Chernenko's death was a considerable misfortune; Gorbachev was Andropov's protégé, and he seems quite willing to disturb the internal Soviet status quo.

When we turn to the surface navy, the message once again is that roles are changing. The Kynda class cruiser, built in the early 1960s, was an anti-ship system. Shortly thereafter, the emphasis shifted to anti-submarine warfare: in other words, to protecting those ballistic missile submarines from our own SSNs. As time went on, the ASW ships became smaller. If one is counting upon close-in protection of SSBN operating areas, the trend towards smaller ships is a highly rational one. However, at the present time, we are increasingly seeing larger individual units: units which can go further from home, or sustain themselves on station for longer periods of time. The Udaloy class destroyer, for example, gives every appearance of being a US Navy Spruance. It can carry out anti-submarine operations and do so very far from home. In theory it represents a more ambitious counter to our SSN threat. In practice, its ability to achieve its objective will depend on the quality of its equipment. But it will depend just as much on the tactics which are developed. For the analyst, the latter is a most significant point.

Traditionally, Soviet naval tactics have not been orientated towards fleet operations as ours have. Fleet operations demand special purpose ships designed to work with others. Soviet ships in contrast, are designed to perform multiple capabilities: ASW, AAW, occasionally anti-ship, but mostly anti-submarine and anti-air. But the Sovremennyy class destroyer, with its anti-ship and anti-air configuration, is a departure from this mould; and it suggests to the Western analyst that the Soviet Naval establishment may be looking more seriously at fleet operations. If so, it would be an important change.

Interestingly, the *Slava*, the successor to the *Kara*, has also moved away from the anti-submarine and anti-air role. The *Slava* has the same anti-aircraft missile as the *Kirov*, but in place of the *Kara*'s anti-submarine rockets, we see a row of anti-ship weapons: a tremendous battery in fact, and a very impressive one. It is not easy to see what role such a ship would perform in a major war. But *Slava* may be one indication that the Soviet Navy is thinking less of all out war with NATO, and more in terms of something more limited. If they are thinking in terms of storehouses of energy and raw materials; if they are thinking of something simpler, like protecting their friends, the configuration of *Slava* is easier to explain.

Thus, there are numerous signs of change, numerous intimations of fresh potential. What does it all amount to? Our first conclusion must be that the Soviet Navy represents not so much a force coherently designed for a specific purpose, but an organic growth – a weed, if you like. As an organism rather than a purpose-built entity, it is in large measure what political, strategic and bureaucratic influences have made it, and these influences have not always been consistent.

Historically, the Soviet Navy has been the junior service, and to this day the lion's share of its efforts go into fulfilling some fairly traditional functions: coastal defence (which, we must not forget, has an internal security dimension) and, from the late 1960s, the maintenance and defence of a sea-based nuclear deterrent. Those of us in the West who spend a lot of time looking at new Soviet surface ships should remind ourselves that the Soviet Navy is largely what it was 30 years ago: a navy of submarines and land-based bombers. The surface ships, impressive as they might be, are not the whole fleet by any means.

Furthermore, the Soviets have not built the kind of support capability at sea that we would regard as essential in a protracted war.

My appraisal is that Admiral Gorshkov always wished to enlarge his traditional brief, whilst settling for what he could get. In this enterprise he was, of course, dependent on his political masters. If we look to the recent past there are indications that Ustinov, on becoming Minister of Defence, wished to cut the Navy's share of the budget. However, Brezhnev was sufficiently pro-Navy, or pro-Gorshkov, that Ustinov was circumvented. But when Andropov arrived on the scene he, like Khrushchev, was determined to shake things up and, like Khrushchev he was not afraid of controversy. He was determined to make the economy move ahead. Andropov, it may be recalled, pledged to streamline the planning mechanism – which meant displacing the old generation of planning officials; he pledged to improve productivity – which meant raiding the steam baths to make sure that workers returned to work; and he pledged to root out corruption. Whatever this might have achieved in economic terms, in élite terms it amounted to the KGB and a section of the military party taking an axe to the non-military party-state bureaucracy: a bureaucracy which, incidentally, includes a number of shipbuilders. It is less clear with Gorbachev whether he has in mind to clean up the Soviet economy by cutting, or by rationalising, the armed forces. In all countries which are essentially land-orientated, navies worry about that kind of thing. That is dangerous to us, because in demonstrating its value to its leadership, the Soviet Navy may well claim a usefulness which it does not really have and argue itself into places which are really quite dangerous.

Another pressure on the Navy is Afghanistan. As the only war now being fought, it must concentrate Soviet military minds just as Vietnam concentrated US military minds. It is irrelevant whether it has anything to do with larger Soviet ambitions or, for that matter, with mainstream Soviet thinking about 'the war'. It is the war they have got. Whenever you are fighting the war you have got, the question basically is: 'what are you doing to help that war?' To Gorshkov's misfortune, Afghanistan is a landlocked country, and there is simply no way in which buying missile cruisers can affect the war in that country to the slightest degree. If I were a Soviet naval officer, I would curse the day the Soviet Union invaded Afghanistan. But they have done it and so how does the Navy get around it? The only way to do so is to show off what the Navy can do; and also to reiterate tirelessly that Afghanistan is one of those little hitches in the onward march of Socialism: that the decisive struggle is somewhere else – in Africa or in the Gulf, for instance. That is dangerous for us as well.

When Andropov left the scene, his successor, Chernenko, was the ideal *apparatchik*. When he became General Secretary thousands of other *apparatchiks* heaved a sigh of relief. We may now find that they have had only a brief reprise in view of Gorbachev's succession. This will only redouble the incentive for putting the Navy's case. What case is that? It is the case which we stated at the outset of this discussion and which, from the standpoint of Soviet history and ideology, it the most logical case to make. 'There is not going to be a war in Europe; let us put some of our money elsewhere'.

If we read Admiral Gorshkov's books, and we read about what navies have done in the past, those navies were not Russian. Gorshkov knows it, and it hurts. When he says that 'the United States must acknowledge that there is now a new world power', that is not the sign of a man with enormous self-confidence, but of a man desperately trying to prove himself. One can find much of the same from Admiral Tirpitz.

The Soviet Navy is a new navy – in thought at least – and it is trying very hard to show what it can do: trying very hard to tell itself that it can do the job. In the Royal Navy or the US Navy, we do not say things like that. We know that we can do the job. The fact that the Soviet Navy is nervous; the knowledge that at some point the rug can be pulled out from under it must be a driving force of extraordinary power. In the 1880s, the United States Navy was also new in modern terms. If one reads what it said then when it was not sure anyone wanted it to be in business, it sounds very similar to what Gorshkov has been saying over the past 20 years. If that is an appropriate analogy, then the future is exceptionally bleak because those tentative statements in the United States turned into very hard competence. If we give the Soviets another ten years, they may no longer be talking about how they challenge us on the world's oceans, and they may no longer need to. Apocalyptic as this prediction may sound, extravagant as Gorshkov's claims may be, this is the conclusion which follows not from fantasy, but from Soviet military theory. Other Soviet services are bound to resist, but Gorshkov has the logic of Soviet ideology on his side, and that may make him irresistible in the end. Perhaps next year, perhaps in five or ten years, when someone says, 'wait a minute, I have got to save money somewhere', Admiral Gorshkov or the next Admiral Gorshkov may reply: 'Comrade, why do you need all those ground forces in Europe when the Navy can do it so well and strangle them from the outside?' Maybe he already has.

(*Presentation given to the RUSI as part of its Main Theme Study, 'Soviet Power and Prospects' and subsequently updated.*)

Notes and References

CHAPTER 1   FIRST PRINCIPLES

1. Harriet Fast Scott and William F. Scott (eds.), *The Soviet Art of War: Doctrine, Strategy and Tactics* (Boulder: Westview Press, 1982) p. 287.
2. As stated by A. Sovetov in the *Journal of the Institute of World Economy and International Relations (IMEMO)*. *International Affairs* (no. 5, 1979).
3. An issue taken up in Chapter 6. See Richard H. Shultz and Roy Godson, *Dezinformatsia* (Oxford: Pergamon-Brasseys, 1984) pp. 12–13, 33, 35, 71–2, 102, 187–91.
4. Richard Pipes, 'How Vulnerable is the West?', *Survey*, vol. 28, no. 2 (121) Summer 1984.
5. For a recent assessment of Soviet dilemmas over Germany see E. Moreton, 'The German Factor' in Edwina Moreton and Gerald Segal (eds), *Soviet Strategy Toward Western Europe* (London: Allen & Unwin, 1984) pp. 110–37.
6. George Ball, *The Dicipline of Power: Essentials of a Modern World Structure* (London: Bodley Head, 1968) p. 264.
7. Max Beloff, *The Foreign Policy of Soviet Russia*, vol. 2 (Oxford University Press, 1949) p. 391.
8. The same point is made in John J. Dziak, *Soviet Perceptions of Military Power: the Interaction of Theory and Practice* (New York: Crane, Russak/National Strategy Information Centre, 1981) p. 63.
9. Arthur J. Alexander, *Decision-Making in Soviet Weapons Procurement*, Adelphi Papers 147–8 (London: IISS, 1978/9).
10. Thomas Wolfe, *The SALT Experience* (Cambridge, Mass.: Ballinger Publishing Co./RAND, 1979) pp. 60–1, 315 n. 48.
11. Raymond Aron, *Peace and War: a Theory of International Relations* (London: Weidenfeld & Nicholson, 1962) p. 90.
12. Martin Wight, *Power Politics*, Hedley Bull and Carsten Holbraad (eds) (New York: Holmes & Meier/RIIA, 1978) pp. 92–3.
13. On the Marxist–Leninist view of politics, see P. H. Vigor, *A Guide to Marxism and Its Effect of Soviet Development* (London: Faber & Faber, 1966) and John Plamenatz, *German Marxism and Russian Communism* (London: Longmans, Green and Co., 1954) pp. 217–66, 306–39. On the Darwinian connection, see Anthony Fleu, *Darwinian Evolution* (London: Granada, 1984) pp. 92–113.
14. The definitive analysis of Soviet views about violence and war remains Peter Vigor, *The Soviet View of War, Peace and Neutrality* (London: Routledge & Kegan Paul, 1975). Lenin quotations: on 'war as a tool of policy', see Vigor, pp. 86–9.
15. Colonel A. M. Danchenko and Colonel I. F. Vydrin, *Military Pedagogy* (Moscow: Voyenizdat, 1973), cited in Ian Greig, *They Mean What They Say* (London: Foreign Affairs Research Institute, 1981) p. 28.

16. Vojtech Mastny, *Russia's Road to the Cold War: Diplomacy, Warfare and the Politics of Communism, 1941–45* (New York: Columbia University Press, 1979) p. 18.
17. Milovan Djilas, *Conversations with Stalin* (New York: Harcourt, 1962) p. 73.
18. E. H. Carr, *Socialism in One Country, 1924–26*, vol. III, Part 1 (London: Macmillan, 1964) p. 3.
19. I. Deutscher, *The Prophet Armed* (London: Oxford University Press, 1954) p. 327. A. Ulam, *Expansion and Coexistence: a History of Soviet Foreign Policy* (New York: Praeger, 1968) pp. 126–45; J. W. Wheeler-Bennett, *Brest-Litovsk: the Forgotten Peace* (London: Macmillan, 1938) p. 227.
20. Robert C. Tucker, *The Soviet Political Mind: Stalinism and Post–Stalin Change* (New York: W. W. Norton, 1972) p. 233.
21. M. Wight, op. cit., p. 88.
22. Soviet radio (in Persian), cited in Shahram Chubin, *Soviet Policy Towards Iran and the Gulf*, Adelphi Paper 157 (London: IISS, 1980) p. 47 n 32.
23. *Great Soviet Encyclopedia*, 3rd edn. (English trans.) (London: Collier-Macmillan, 1976), vol. 16, p. 625.
24. *Rude Pravo* editorital cited in Ian Greig (ed.), *They Mean What They Say* (London: Foreign Affairs Research Institute, 1981).
25. Jan Sejna, *We Will Bury You* (London: Sidgwick & Jackson, 1982) pp. 100–18.
26. *Pravda*, 25 Feb. 1976. cited in Greig, op. cit., p. 48.
27. Ian Greig, op. cit., p. 48.
28. Ibid, pp. 48–9.
29. Jan Sejna, op. cit., p. 52.
30. Leonard Schapiro, 'The International Department of the CPSU: Key to Soviet Policy', *International Journal* (Winter 1976–77) p. 42.
31. *Kommunist* (Moscow, Feb. 1973) p. 110, cited in Adam Ulam, 'The World Outside' in Robert F. Byrnes (ed.) *After Brezhnev* (London: Frances Pinter, 1983) p. 348.
32. Genrikh Tromfimenko, 'America, Russia and the Third World', *Foreign Affairs*, vol. 59, no. 5, Summer 1981, p. 1027.
33. J. M. Mackintosh, *Strategy and Tactics of Soviet Foriegn Policy* (London: Oxford University Press, 1962) pp. 261–2.
34. David Holloway, *The Soviet Union and the Arms Race* (London: Yale University Press, 1983) p. 104.

CHAPTER 2 FOUNDATIONS OF POWER: RESOURCES

1. J. R. Killian, *Sputniks, Scientists and Eisenhower* (Cambridge, Mass.: MIT Press, 1977). Lawrence Freedman, *US Intelligence and the Soviet Strategic Threat* (London: Macmillan, 1977). Note also Khrushchev's boast that the USSR would surpass the United States in gross industrial production by 1970 and per capita income by 1980: treated with scepticism in the West, but not dismissed.

2. CIA *Handbook of Economic Statistics, 1985* (Washington, DC: 1985) p. 24. Herbert Block, 'The Economic Basis of Soviet Power', p. 138 in Edward Luttwak, *The Grand Strategy of the Soviet Union.*

3. The official Soviet figures (10–12 per cent per annum growth in the early 1950's) were revised to 6.8 per cent for 1950–58 by Abram Bergson. Marshall I. Goldman, *USSR in Crisis: the Failure of an Economic System* (New York: W. W. Norton, 1983) p. 21. The US Office of Technology Assessment (*Technology and Soviet Energy Availability, 1981*) cites average per annum growth of 6.0 per cent for 1951–55 and 5.8 per cent for 1956–60 (p. 250).

4. CIA, op. cit., p. 64.

5. Herbert Block, 'The Economic Basis of Soviet Power', p. 129, Edward Luttwak, *The Grand Strategy of the Soviet Union.*

6. OECD member countries achieved similar growth rates with a more advantageous investment share (21.7 per cent in 1979), whereas Japan's 32 per cent share for 1979 brought about growth rates almost twice as strong as in the USSR. Block, op. cit., p. 130.

7. Boris Rumer, 'Structural Imbalance in the Soviet Economy', *Problems of Communism*, (7–8/84) pp. 26–29, 31. The author also notes that growth in the electronic industry is lower than that of the economy as a whole.

8. CIA, op. cit., p. 64.

9. Dimitry Simes, 'The Military and Militarism in the Soviet Union', *International Security*, Winter 1981–82.

10. Goldman, op. cit. p. 78.

11. 1980 figures. Under Stalin, agricultural investment amounted to 13 per cent of the total; between 1956–60, 17 per cent. Goldman, op. cit., p. 76. Boris Rumer cites a figure of 38 per cent (1980) for the proportion of total investment allocated to the 'agro-industrial complex', op. cit., p. 29.

12. Angela Stent, 'Economic Strategy', Edwina Moreton and Gerald Segal (eds), *Soviet Strategy Toward Western Europe*, p. 212. This is the figure for 'food and food related imports'. Meat and grain alone account for 25 per cent of hard currency imports. Goldman, op. cit., p. 66.

13. Ann Helgeson, 'Demographic Policy' in Archie Brown and Michael Kaser (eds), *Soviet Policy for the 1980s* (London: Macmillan, 1982) p. 121.

14. Michael Kaser, 'Economic Policy', Archie Brown and Michael Kaser (eds), op. cit., p. 207.

15. By the late 1950s Soviet life expectancy was higher than in the United States, and Soviet Central Asians could expect to live 15 years longer than Iranians. Nick Eberstadt, 'The Health Crisis in the USSR', *New York Review of Books*, p. 23.

16. Eberstadt, op. cit., p. 25. Also see Christopher Davis and Murray Feshbach, *Rising Infant Mortality in the USSR in the 1970s* (United States Bureau of the Census, Series P-95, No. 74, 1980).

17. [Socialist] forms of payment for labour are in no case compatible with egalitarianism'. V. S. Kulikov in Alastair McAuley, 'Social Policy' in Brown and Kaser, op. cit. pp. 148–9. Given that the distribution of rewards is considered to be just in a 'socialist' society, it is also suggested that 'cash transfers should reinforce rather than alleviate the distribution of earnings'.

18. Dimitriy Simes, 'The Military and Militarism in the Soviet Union', *International Security*, Winter 1981–82. Similarly, a very large proportion of students in the Moscow Institute of International relations are sons and daughters of Foreign Ministry officials.

19. Rumer, op. cit., p. 29.

20. This is a major reason why, despite income supplements of up to 50 per cent, workers from the European portion of the USSR are reluctant to move to remote areas.

21. Goldman, op. cit., p. 55. In short, money helps make Western society *more* equal than Soviet society. In Britain, no one short of the necessary cash can dine at the Ritz; by the same token, anyone with sufficient cash can do so. In the USSR, only the 'right' people can do so. A comment by a Moscow lady to the American journalist, Robert Kaiser, brings home the irrelevance of money in the USSR: 'I realise that when I die, no one will know what kind of taste I had. I have never been able to buy what I liked, only what was available.'

22. The innate limitations of central planning are discussed fully in Alec Nove, 'Socialism, Centralised Planning and the One Party State,' T. H. Rigby, Archie Brown and Peter Reddaway (eds), *Authority, Power and Policy in the USSR*, pp. 77–97. 12 million products – p. 84; Computer programming – Alec Nove lecture in Oxford, spring 1980.

23. Kaser in Brown and Kaser, op. cit., pp. 193–202. Fyodor I. Kushnirsky, 'The Limits of Soviet Economic Reform', *Problems of Communism*, July–Aug., 1984, pp. 33–43.

24. Rumer, op. cit., p. 27.

25. Thane Gustafson, *International Security*, Winter 1981–82.

26. Author's interview with Captain Vladil Lysenko, former Soviet Fishing Fleet Captain, author of *A Crime Against the World* (London: Gollancz, 1984), Spring 1984.

27. Kushnirsky, op. cit., pp. 33–37.

28. Alec Nove in Brown and Kaser, op. cit., p. 179ff.

29. See K.-E. Wadekin, 'Soviet Agriculture's Dependence on the West', *Foreign Affairs*, 59:4, Spring 1981, p. 794.

30. Philip Hanson in R. Annan and J. Cooper (eds), *Industrial Innovation in the Soviet Union* (New Haven, Conn.: Yale University Press, 1982) pp. 419–20.

31. Angela Stent, op. cit., pp. 218–20, 224–33.

32. Thane Gustafson, op. cit., p. 72.

33. John Kiser, 'The Perception Gap', unpublished manuscript (1978).

34. Marshal Goldman, op. cit., p. 45.

35. Stent, op. cit., pp. 209, 212; Block, op. cit., p. 132. In the United States, also a large 'internal' economy with abundant resources, the proportion of trade to GNP was 9.2 per cent in 1980. (Block, p. 132.) Foreign trade contributes as much as 30 per cent to the GNP of some EEC countries (Stent, p. 221).

36. Thane Gustafson, *Selling the Russians the Rope: Soviet Technology Policy and US Export Controls*, R–2649–ARPA (Santa Monica: RAND, 1981) p. 28.

37. Stent, op. cit., p. 211.

38. Hanson, pp. 427–8.
39. Hanson, op. cit., p. 436.
40. Thane Gustafson, 'Selling Them the Rope?' pp. vi, 16–17.
41. Stent, op. cit., pp. 213, 216.
42. Hanson, Brown and Kaser, op. cit., p. 91.
43. Block, op. cit., p. 120.
44. David Holloway, *The Soviet Union and the Arms Race* (New Haven, Conn.: Yale University Press, 1983) pp. 118–19.
45. Aims of Industry/National Strategy Information Center Inc., *The Challenge of Soviet Shipping*, p. 6.
46. Aims of Industry, op. cit., p. 44.
47. Harriet Fast Scott, William F. Scott, *The Armed Forces of the USSR*, 3rd edn (London: Arms and Armour Press, 1984) p. 315; Victor Suvorov, *Soviet Military Intelligence* (London: Hamish Hamilton, 1984) p. 93.
48. Goldman, op. cit., pp. 34–5.
49. In the following section (to page 25), I am indebted to the comprehensive treatment of these issues provided by Arthur J. Alexander, *Decision-Making in Soviet Weapons Procurement*, Adelphi paper 147–48 (IISS, 1978–79), (pp. 6–24); David Holloway, ch. 7 of *Industrial Innovation in the Soviet Union*, Scott and Scott, op. cit., pp. 105–112, 314. As much as possible I have confined notations to other sources and to especially controversial points.
50. The Politburo has extensive support not only in the CC Secretariat, but in the personal Secretariats of its individual members. The General-Secretary himself, in addition to a large personal Secretariat, relies upon the CC General Department, headed by a CC Secretary (in Brezhnev's day, Chernenko).
51. First mention in the West of the Defence Council was in 1969 (Alexander, p. 57, n.80). The USSR did not publicly identify it until Brezhnev's promotion to Marshal of the Soviet Union on 7 May, 1976 (Scott and Scott, p. 105).
52. Although written before its existence had been confirmed, John Erickson's *Soviet Military Power* (RUSI, 1971) articulates the military's arguments for a 'supreme military–political organ' after Khrushchev's fall (p. 9). Also, pp. 7–12, 13–16, 25–29, 29–31.
53. A breakdown of the various ministries is in Scott and Scott, p. 315.
54. Alexander, op. cit., p. 23.
55. Goldman, op. cit., p. 29.
56. John P. Berman, John C. Baker, *Soviet Strategic Forces: Requirements and Responses*, (Washington DC: Brookings Institution, 1982) p. 54.
57. *Aviation Week*, 18 Sept., 1959.
58. Richard D. Ward, 'The Structured World of the Soviet Designer', *Air Force Magazine*, Mar. 1984, p. 33.
59. David Holloway, op. cit., p. 132.
60. Christopher Donnelly, *Soviet Military Doctrine* (RMA Sandhurst: Soviet Studies Research Centre) p. 12ff. (Unpublished manuscript.)
61. Holloway, ch. 8, *Soviet Innovation*, p. 385.
62. Alexander, op. cit., p. 34.

63. Kenneth Freeman, 'Soviet R & D: Implications for NATO Procurement' (unpublished RUSI research paper) p. 3.
64. Berman and Baker, op. cit., p. 65–7, 85–108.
65. Holloway in Amman and Cooper, op. cit., p. 278.

CHAPTER 3   FOUNDATIONS OF POWER: EMPIRE

1. *Constitution (Fundamental Law) of the Union of Soviet Socialist Republics*, (Moscow: Novosti Press Agency Publishing House, 1982) pp. 41–5 (Articles 70, 72, 80).
2. As of this writing, 26 countries are party to such treaties with the Soviet Union: the four countries listed, eight countries ruled by 'Vanguard Revolutionary Democratic' parties, and 14 others which, along with the USSR, form the 'world socialist system'. See *The Military Balance*, 1984–85 (London: IISS, 1984) pp. 50, 57, 74, 94.
3. See Chapter 10, Fred Halliday.
4. Finland is not a member of the Non-Aligned Movement.
5. Richard F. Starr, 'Checklist of Communist Parties in 1983', *Problems of Communism*, vol. XXXIII, 3–4/84, p. 42. Some might also wish to include the Sandinista Front of National Liberation (FSLN) of Nicaragua, which 'is organised on the Cuban model and has close ties with Cuba and other communist governments, but does not acknowledge itself to be a communist party, even though it regularly has party-to-party contacts with the CPSU'. Starr, p. 47 note u.
6. Ibid., p. 42. Cuba and Vietnam are members of CMEA but not of the WTO.
7. Jan Sejna, *We Will Bury You* (London: Sidgwick & Jackson, 1982) p. 85.
8. The Mongolian People's Republic was officially founded in November, 1924. O. Edmund Clubb, *China and Russia: The 'Great Game'* (New York: Columbia University Press, 1971) pp. 175–87, 213.
9. See F. Rubin, 'Security Concerns of the USSR and the other Warsaw Treaty Organisation Countries', RUSI *Journal*, vol. 128, no. 3, Sept. 1983.
10. The subordination of Eastern Europe did not, of course, ensure Soviet invulnerability in Central Asia or the Far East. Despite the scope of the post-1969 build-up the USSR may still have reason to ask herself how secure her flanks would be in event of war in Europe. Forces in the Far East are therefore structured to conduct independent operations for prolonged periods – not unlike the Soviet Far Eastern Army of pre-war years. A special Far East High Command (GK) was re-created in March 1969.
11. Gromyko's July 1969 statement has been one of several along these lines: 'The Soviet people do not plead with anybody to be allowed to have their say in the solution of any question involving the maintenance of international peace, and our country's extensive interests. This is our right, due to the Soviet Union's position as a great power. During any acute situation, however far away it appears from our country, the Soviet

Union's reaction is to be expected in all capitals of the world' (*Pravda*, 11 July 1969).
12. F. Rubin, op. cit., p. 36.
13. Professor A. P. Butenko (ed.), *The Unity of the Socialist Countries* (Moscow: Izdatyelstvo Nauka, 1977) p. 36.
14. The Politburo recognised that developments in Hungary in 1956 and Czechoslovakia in 1968 had aroused considerable interest on the part of Soviet intellectuals and dissidents. Jiri Valenta, 'Soviet Policy toward Hungary and Czechoslovakia', Sarah Meiklejohn Terry (ed.), *Soviet Policy in Eastern Europe* (Yale: New Haven, 1984) pp. 100, 104.
15. This was certainly the verdict of Molotov and other Politburo conservatives who tried to unseat Khrushchev in 1957. Ibid., p. 101.
16. According to Khrushchev, Bloc leaders urged prompt military action in Hungary, and Romania even offered military assistance. Even Tito accepted the need for a military solution. Strobe Talbott (ed.), *Khrushchev Remembers* (Boston: Little, Brown, 1970) pp. 417–22. On the initiatives of Ulbricht and Gomulka in the 1968 Czech crisis, see Jiri Valenta, *Soviet Intervention in Czechoslovakia: Anatomy of a Decision* (Baltimore: Johns Hopkins University Press, 1979) pp. 114–18, and Zdeněk Mlynář, *Night Frost in Prague* (C. Hurst & Co: London, 1980) pp. 152–6.
17. Jan Vanous, 'East European Economic Slowdown', *Problems of Communism*, vol. xxxi. July–Aug. 1982, pp. 7–8.
18. Edwina Moreton, 'The German Factor', E. Moreton and Gerald Segal (eds), *Soviet Strategy Toward Western Europe* (London: Allen & Unwin, 1984) pp. 111–14, 124–8; A. Ross Johnson, Robert W. Dean, Alexander Alexiev, *East European Military Establishments: the Warsaw Pact Northern Tier* (New York: Crane Russak, 1982) p. 17.
19. *Soviet Constitution* (1936), Articles I–IV; Ghita Ionescu, *The Politics of the European Communist States* (New York: Praeger, 1967) pp. 20, 22.
20. On 'democratic centralism', see *Constitution (Fundamental Law) of the USSR*, Ch. I, Article 3. On *nomenklatura* in the USSR, see Michael Voslensky, *Nomenklatura* (London: Bodley Head, 1984) pp. 1–65; in Eastern Europe, Ghita Ionescu, op. cit., pp. 60–4, and Timothy Garton Ash, *The Polish Revolution: Solidarity 1980–82* (London: Jonathan Cape, 1983) pp. 6–8. The classic exposition of the prerogatives and privileges of the Soviet and East European ruling classes is to be found in Milovan Djilas, *The New Class* (London: Thames and Hudson, 1957).
21. Z. K. Brzezinski, *The Soviet Bloc* (Cambridge, Mass.: Harvard University Press, 1967) pp. 118, 107–29.
22. Vladimir Solovyov, Elena Klepikova, *Yuri Andropov: a Secret Passage into the Kremlin* (London: Collier–Macmillan, 1983) pp. 1–25. Also Valenta in Sarah Meiklejohn Terry, op. cit., p. 103.
23. Mlynář, op. cit., p. 57.
24. 'Only those Polish officers who have attended Soviet General Staff academies (for two year courses) are allowed to take up command of Polish Divisions', C. N. Donnelly, 'Poland: the Military Significance of the Polish Crisis', *RUSI/Brassey's Defence Yearbook*, 1982, p. 11. For supervision of NSWP armed forces by the KGB and NSWP Ministry of

Security bodies, see F. Rubin, 'The Hungarian People's Army' in RUSI *Journal*, Sept. 1976, p. 65ff. Bittman in Richard H. Shultz and Roy Godson, *Dezinformatsia: Active Measures in Soviet Strategy* (London: Pergamon–Brasseys, 1984) pp. 172–3.

25. Shultz and Godson, op. cit., p. 22. Mlynář, op. cit., p. 42; quotation from p. 238.
26. For an assessment of Dubček's personality and political strategy, see Mlynář, op. cit., pp. 101–104.
27. John Van Oudenaren, *The Soviet Union and Eastern Europe: Options for the 1980s and Beyond* (RAND), p. 13.
28. On the careers of Novotný and Husák, see Mlynář, op. cit., pp. 65–71, 222–76. Olszowski is discussed in Henri Blanc, 'The Relationship between the Soviet Union and Eastern Europe', *Atlantic Quarterly*. On the disjunction between state and society, see George Schöpflin, 'The Political Structure in Eastern Europe as a Factor in Intra-bloc Relations', Karen Dawisha and Philip Hanson (ed)., *Soviet–East European Dilemmas* (London: Heinemann, 1981) pp. 61–83.
29. John Van Oudenaren, op. cit., pp. 56–57.
30. Soviet exploitation of Eastern Europe has been estimated as $20 billion for the 1945–56 period. Z. K. Brzezinski, op. cit., p. 127. Between April 1948 and January 1952 US credits to countries participating in the European Recovery Programme totalled $12 992.5 billion. Alfred Grosser, *The Western Alliance* (London: Macmillan, 1980) p. 79. For origins of CMEA see John Van Oudenaren, op. cit., pp. 5–6 and Brzezinski, op. cit., pp. 128–9, 284–91.
31. A good summary of social and economic conditions in this period is that of Daniel W. Paul and Maurice D. Simon, 'Poland Today and Czechoslovakia 1968', *Problems of Communism*, vol. xxx, Sept.–Oct., 1981, pp. 25–9.
32. Jan Sejna, op. cit., p. 24.
33. Paul Marer, 'The Political Economy of Soviet Relations with Eastern Europe' in Sarah Meiklejohn Terry, op. cit., pp. 160–2, 165. Summerscale, op. cit., pp. 20–1.
34. George Schopflin, op. cit., pp. 66–9.
35. Simon and Paul, op. cit., pp. 27–31.
36. Vanous, op. cit., pp. 1–6; Marer, op. cit., pp. 165–6.
37. Summerscale, op. cit., pp. 56–7, 69–70.
38. Rudolf L. Tokés, 'Hungarian Reform Imperatives', *Problems of Communism*, Sept.–Oct., 1984, pp. 1–2.
39. Henri Blanc, 'A Comparison between the Private Sector in Poland and the German Democratic Republic', unpublished manuscript.
40. Summerscale, op. cit., p. 59.
41. Henri Blanc, *Atlantic Quarterly*, op. cit.
42. Vanous, op. cit., p. 4.
43. Ibid., p. 8. A table charting the growth of CMEA debt can be found on p. 4.
44. The Hungarian debt service ratio is 47 per cent. Henri Blanc, *Atlantic Quarterly*, op. cit.
45. Tokés, op. cit., p. 6.

46. Peter Summerscale, op. cit., pp. 69–73.
47. Henri Blanc, *Atlantic Quarterly*, op. cit.
48. For 1981–85, the share of investment in the Romanian national product was expected to decline to 30 per cent, compared with 33 per cent for 1976–80. Summerscale, op. cit., pp. 69–70.
49. These conclusions are similar to those of Henri Blanc, *Atlantic Quarterly*, op. cit.
50. M. Marrese and J. Vanous, *Implicit Subsidies and Non-Market Benefits in Soviet Trade with Eastern Europe* (Berkeley: University of California Press, 1983). A recent study puts the total bill far higher. Charles Wolf, Jr., K. C. Yeh, Edmund Brunner, Jr. Aaron Gurwitz, Marilee Lawrence, *The Costs of the Soviet Empire* (Santa Monica: Rand R–3073/1–NA, Sept. 1983). However, 'empire' as defined in this study includes a good many countries outside the WTO and CMEA.
51. Paul Marer, 'Soviet Economic Relations with Eastern Europe', Sarah Meiklejohn Terry (ed.), op. cit., p. 171–80.
52. John P. Hardt, 'Soviet Energy Policy in Eastern Europe', Sarah Meiklejohn Terry (ed.), op. cit., p. 207.
53. A. Ross Johnson, Robert W. Dean, Alexander Alexiev, *East European Military Establishments: The Warsaw Pact Northern Tier* (New York: Crane Russak, 1982), pp. 7–10. Harriet Fast Scott, William F. Scott, *The Armed Forces of the USSR* (London: Arms and Armour Press, 1984) (3rd edn) pp. 213–15.
54. Malcolm Mackintosh, 'The Warsaw Treaty Organisation: History and Development', RUSI lecture, Apr. 1984, pp. 5–6. Sokolovskii in *Military Strategy* (1963 edn). (Englewood Cliffs, NJ) p. 495.
55. Malcolm Mackintosh, op. cit., pp. 4, 8.
56. *The Military Balance 1984–85* (London: IISS) pp. 19, 24–8.
57. Scott and Scott, op. cit., pp. 213–24.
58. Valenta, in Terry, (ed)., op. cit., pp. 102, 105.
59. A. Ross Johnson et al, op. cit., pp. 151–5. I am indebted to this publication for much of the information in this section as well as that concerning the evolution of the Polish People's Army in the 1960s and 1970s. (The reader will note that this volume went to press before the outbreak of the 1980–81 crisis.)
60. Scott and Scott, pp. 218, 220.
61. C. N. Donnelly, op. cit., p. 11.
62. F. Rubin, RUSI *Journal*, Sept. 1976. Aleksei Myagkov, *Inside the KGB* (Richmond: Foreign Affairs Publishing Co., Ltd, 1976) pp. 28, 58.
63. A. R. Johnson et al, op. cit., pp. 23–4, 70–6. Dale Herspring, 'The Polish Military and the Policy Process', Maurice D. Simon and Roger E. Kanet (ed)., *Background to Crisis: Policy and Politics in Poland* (Boulder: Westview Press, 1980).
64. Jiri Valenta, 'Soviet Use of Surprise and Deception', *Survival*, vol. X, IV, no. 2, 3–4/82, p. 56.
65. A. R. Johnson et al., op. cit., pp. 36–8, 76–89.
66. Ibid., pp. 23–9, 48–9.
67. Ibid., pp. 42–8, 143–4.
68. Ibid., p. 52. Timothy Garton Ash, op. cit., p. 144.

69. C. N. Donnelly, p. 11. Zyg Ager, 'Political Events Leading up to the Declaration of Martial Law in Poland', *RUSI/Brassey's Defence Yearbook*, 1982, p. 5.
70. T. Garton Ash, pp. 144–5.
71. Zyg Ager, op. cit., pp 5–7. Ash, op. cit., pp. 172–82.

CHAPTER 4   ARMY AND PARTY, WAR AND POLITICS

1. *International Herald Tribune*, 18 September 1984.
2. Peter Deriabin and T. H. Bagley, 'Fedorchuk, the KGB and the Soviet Succession', *Orbis*, 26:3 Autumn 1982, p. 612.
3. *Rules of the Communist Party of the Soviet Union*.
4. Major-General S. N. Kozlov, *The Officer's Handbook* (Moscow, 1971), (trans. US Air Force: US Government Printing Office) p. 63.
5. John J. Dziak, *Soviet Perceptions of Military Power: The Interaction of Theory and Practice* (New York: Crane Russak, 1981) p. 52.
6. Kenneth Currie, 'Soviet General Staff's New Role', *Problems of Communism*, (Mar.–Apr. 1984) pp. 32–40.
7. See for example Dimitri K. Simes, 'The Politics of Defence in the Soviet Union: Brezhnev's Era', Jiri Valenta and William Potter (eds), *Soviet Decision-making for National Security* (London: Allen & Unwin, 1984) pp. 74–84. (The word 'constituencies' in this context is used on p. 76.)
8. T. H. Rigby, 'A Conceptual Approach to Authority, Power and Policy in the Soviet Union', T. H. Rigby, Archie Brown and Peter Reddaway (eds), *Authority, Power and Policy in the USSR*, pp. 9–31. This distinction is introduced on p. 17.
9. M. V. Frunze, 'A Unified Military Doctrine for the Red Army' in Harriet Fast Scott and William F. Scott, *The Soviet Art of War: Doctrine, Strategy and Tactics* (Boulder, Col.: Westview Press, 1982) pp. 27–31. 'The militarization of the entire population' from his essay, 'Front and Rear in Future War', cited in William E. Odom, 'The Militarization of Soviet Society', *Problems of Communism*, Sept.–Oct., 1976, p. 34.
10. Yosef Avidar, *The Party and the Army in the Soviet Union* (Jerusalem: Magnes Press, 1983) pp. 159–70.
11. Harriet Fast Scott and William F. Scott, *The Armed Forces of the USSR* (London: Arms and Armour Press, 1984) p. 277. [Hereafter, *Armed Forces*].
12. Timothy J. Colton, 'The Impact of the Military on Soviet Society', in Seweryn Bialer (ed.), *The Domestic Context of Soviet Foreign Policy* (Boulder, Col.: Westview Press, 1981) p. 126.
13. Odom, op. cit., pp. 36–9, 44–7. He cites a 1976 figure of 13 Middle Military Schools, 125 Higher Military Schools and 23 for Academies and Institutes.
14. Colton quoted in Bialer, op. cit., pp. 122, 135.
15. Strobe Talbott (ed.), *Khrushchev Remembers* (Boston: Little, Brown, 1970) pp. 336–8.

16. Malcolm Mackintosh, *Juggernaut* (London: Secker & Warburg, 1967) p. 287.
17. Yosef Avidar, op. cit., pp. 170–8.
18. This was an unprecedented but constitutional step. The Central Committee is not known to have reversed any Politburo decisions since.
19. Avidar, op. cit., pp. 147–51, provides a concise description of how Zhukov attempted to downgrade the status of Military Councils and bring them within the *nomenklatura* of the MOD, rather than the Central Committee.
20. Some 250 000 officers were dismissed. Avidar, op. cit., p. 260.
21. By no means were the Armed Forces solidly against Khrushchev. Many senior commanders had a strong personal loyalty to him, and his reforms appealed to the vast bulk of younger, technically-minded officers, particularly in the new Strategic Rocket Forces. Yosef Avidar, op. cit. p. 270f.
22. Erickson speaks of a 'continuation and revision' of Khrushchev's policies. John Erickson, *Soviet Military Power* (London: RUSI, 1971) p. 41.
23. Roy and Zhores Medvedev, *Khrushchev: The Years in Power* (New York: W. W. Norton, 1978) pp. 143–79.
24. Scott and Scott, *Armed Forces*, pp. 293–6.
25. Ibid., pp. 190–2.
26. Aleksei Myagkov, *Inside the KGB* (Richmond: Foreign Affairs Publishing Co., 1976).
27. Scott and Scott, *Armed Forces*, pp. 288–9.
28. John J. Dziak, op. cit., pp. 56–7.
29. Ibid., p. 35.
30. John Erickson, op. cit., p. 9.
31. Scott and Scott, *Armed Forces*, p. 105. Dziak, op. cit., p. 47.
32. Sergei Freidzon, *The Soviet Defense Council* (Part I) (Washington: Institute for Strategic Trade, 1981) pp. 8–12. Quoted with permission.
33. John J. Dziak, op. cit., p. 46. Scott and Scott, *Armed Forces*, p. 107, Sergei Freidzon, op. cit., p. 4. Not all sources make Freidzon's distinction between permanent members, advisors and consultants. It is also unclear which individuals are members *ex officio* and which because of their personal prominence: e.g. it was thought by Dziak that Kirilenko (Secretary for Cadres) sat on the Defence Council in 1980, at a time when he was Brezhnev's heir apparent, but this does not mean that his successor as Secretary for Cadres would have a seat on the body.
34. On the institutions of advisers and consultants, see Freidzon, op. cit., pp. 5–6.
35. Peter Vigor, *The Soviet View of War, Peace and Neutrality* (London: Routledge & Kegan Paul, 1975) pp. 9–10, 14–23, 25–70. Also Robert C. Tucker, 'Dialectics of Coexistence' in *The Soviet Political Mind* (New York: W. W. Norton, 1971, Revised edition) pp. 243–5, 251–2, 259–60.
36. Boleslaw Wojcicki in *Trybuna Ludu*, 27 June 1972. The preceding sentence reads, '[p]eaceful co-existence in the history making thinking of the Communist Parties and in the practical politics of the Social-ist countries is, in fact, only a form of ideological warfare and of the maltifarious, world-wide confrontation between Socialism and

Imperialism, such as is appropriate to this current era'. Cited in Ian Greig, *They Mean What They Say* (London: Foreign Affairs Research Institute, 1981) p. 45.

37. *Pravda*, 9 Oct., 1970 in Greig, op. cit., p. 45.
38. Theodore G. Shackeley 'The Uses of Paramilitary Covert Action in the 1980s', Roy Godson (ed.), *Intelligence Requirements for the 1980s*, vol. IV (New York: Crane, Russak and Co., 1983) pp. 136–7. Bruce Porter, *The Soviet Union in Third World Conflicts*, pp. 216–20, 224, 234.
39. N. S. Khrushchev, 'For New Victories of the World Communist Movement', *Communism – Peace and Happiness for the People*, vol. 1 (Moscow: Foreign Languages Publishing House, 1961) p. 41.
40. Genrikh Trofimenko, 'America, Russia and the Third World', *Foreign Affairs*, vol. 59, no. 5, Summer 1981, p. 1025.
41. Stephen S. Kaplan, *Diplomacy of Power: Soviet Armed Forces as a Political Instrument* (Washington: Brookings, 1981) pp. 689–93.
42. Tomas Ries, 'Defending the Far North', *International Defence Review*, no. 7, 1984, pp. 873–80. Also *International Defence Review*, no. 10, 1984, p. 1417.
43. Probably the definitive analysis of their views in English is Peter Vigor's: op. cit., pp. 9–10, 20–57.
44. Roberta Goren, *The Soviet Union and Terrorism* (London: Allen & Unwin, 1984) p. 21.
45. Ibid., p. 7.
46. Bruce D. Porter, *The USSR in Third World Conflicts: Soviet Arms and Diplomacy in Local Wars* (Cambridge University Press, 1984) p. 7.
47. O. Edmund Clubb, *China and Russia: The Great Game* (New York: Columbia University Press, 1974) pp. 233–9.
48. Again, I am indebted to Peter Vigor's seminal work, *The Soviet View of War, Peace and Neutrality* for a number of the points which follow on pp. 18–21.
49. Ibid., p. 83.
50. V. I. Lenin, *Selected Works* (New York: International Publishers) vol. 8, p. 297.
51. John Erickson, op. cit., p. 42.
52. Douglas M. Hart, 'Soviet Approaches to Crisis Management: The Military Dimension', *Survival* (London: IISS, 9–10/1984). 'Soviet notions of crisis management appear to differ from Western approaches in several significant aspects. The Soviet Union is very event-orientated. Rather than classifying a weapons system or a strategy as destabilizing in any likely scenario, Soviet analysts tend to view action or deployment as contributing to instability within the context of a particular crisis situation.' (p. 222).
53. Bruce Porter, op. cit., pp. 147, 170–5, 205, 209.
54. Zdenek Mlynar, *Night Frost in Prague* (London: Cape Hurst, 1980) p. 241.
55. Peter Vigor, op. cit., p. 17.
56. V. I. Lenin, 'Defeat of One's Own Government in Imperialist War' (1915).

57. For example, in *Kommunist Vooryzhenyk Sil'* (Communist of the Armed Forces), July 1969; cited in Greig, op. cit., p. 66.
58. Marshal V. D. Sokolovskiy, *Military Strategy* (1963 edn), cited in Vigor, p. 55. Similarly, the 1971 *Great Soviet Encyclopaedia* asserts that 'a new world war will be a struggle for the very existence of the two opposing world-wide systems, the socialist and the capitalist. This war will decide the fate of all mankind'. In 1973 the Minister of Defence, Marshal A. A. Grechko reiterated this point. Vigor, pp. 122–6.
59. Peter Vigor, op. cit., pp. 112–13.
60. John J. Dziak, 'Soviet Intelligence and Security Services in the 1980s: the Paramilitary Dimension', Roy Godson (ed.), *Intelligence Requirements for the 1980s* (New York: Crane Russak, 1983) vol. III, pp. 96–8.
61. Lawrence Freedman, *The Evolution of Nuclear Strategy* (London: Macmillan, 1983); Alec Nove, *An Economic History of the USSR* (Harmondsworth: Penguin, 1972). Nevertheless, the initial shock was devastating, and most of the industrial losses occurred within the first few weeks.
62. The first assertion ('no winners') begs the question of how we define 'nuclear war': massive all-out nuclear conflict between East and West, or any conflict between East and West in which some number of nuclear weapons are used? If the former, the 'unwinnable' thesis may well be correct (but it is not *certain* to be correct, and even in this extremity, the USSR would aim to survive and recover). The latter eventuality – a war terminated after very limited exchanges, or after a largely conventional victory – could well be calamitous but would be even less likely to mean the end of civilisation, or even of the belligerents. The second assertion (that the USSR believes she could 'fight and win' a nuclear war) is equally unfortunate, as it suggests that it is the aim of her policy (and of her arms build-up) to do so. The purpose of Soviet policy is to avoid having to do so. But if war should occur despite this, she would aim to secure victory (ie the capitulation of an enemy and the destruction of his armed forces) and, in all contingencies, seek to survive as a political, economic and military entity. See John Dziak, op. cit., pp. 27–8 for reinforcement of these points.

CHAPTER 5   THE CHANGING SCOPE OF MILITARY STRATEGY

1. The thesis that considerations of deterrence have become divorced from reassurance in Alliance policy is put persuasively by Michael Howard, 'Reassurance and Deterrence', *Foreign Affairs*, vol. 61, no. 2, Winter 1982–83, pp. 309–24.
2. Some of the best comparisons between Soviet and Western (but particularly American) thinking are to be found in Ken Booth, *Strategy and Ethnocentrism* (New York: Holmes & Meier, 1979), Benjamin S. Lambeth, *The Elements of Soviet Strategic Policy*, (California: Santa Monica, RAND, P-6389, 1979), Fritz Ermarth, 'Contrasts in American

and Soviet Strategic Thought' in Derek Leebaert (ed.), *Soviet Military Thinking* (London: Allen & Unwin, 1981), Roman Kolkowicz, 'The Soviet Union – Elusive Adversary' in *Soviet Union/Union Soviétique*, 10, parts 2–3 (1983) pp. 153–76.

3. Harriet Fast Scott and William F. Scott (eds), *The Soviet Art of War: Doctrine, Strategy and Tactics* (Boulder Col.: Westview Press, 1982) p. ix.
4. See 'Defence Open Government Document 80/23' (July 1980) and 'Defence Open Government Document 82/1' (Mar. 1982) parts 3 and 30.
5. John J. Dziak, *Soviet Perceptions of Military Power: The Interaction of Theory and Practice* (New York: Crane Russak and Co./National Strategy Information Centre, 1981) pp. 65–6.
6. In addition to publications in n. 2, see John Erickson, *Soviet Military Power*, (London: RUSI, 1971) pp. 8–11, 42–52; John Erickson, 'The Soviet View of Deterrence: A General Survey', *Survival*, 34:6 (London: IISS, November–December 1982); Robert P. Berman and John C. Baker, *Soviet Strategic Forces: Requirements and Responses* (Washington: Brookings, 1982) pp. 27–33; Dziak, op. cit., pp. 24–9; and Scott and Scott, *Art of War*, pp. 243–5.
7. Scott and Scott, op. cit., p. 3.
8. In a 1960 address to the USSR Supreme Soviet, Khrushchev stated that 'every sober-minded person is well aware that atomic and hydrogen weapons offer the greatest danger to those countries that have a high population density'. Although in nuclear war, the USSR would sustain huge loss of life, the country would survive because its 'territory is enormous, and the population is less concentrated in large industrial centres than in many other countries'. From Phillip A. Petersen and John G. Hines, 'The Evolution of Soviet Military Thought', p. 9. (Paper delivered to joint RUSI/Boston Foriegn Affairs Group Conference on 'Soviet Military Strategy and Western Europe', Nuneham Park, Oxfordshire, 25–25 September 1984).
9. Quoted from ibid., p. 58, n 44.
10. See for example, Avigdor Haselkorn, *The Evolution of Soviet Security Strategy, 1965–1975* (New York: Crane, Russak & Co., 1978), pp. 4–20, 91–95; also John Erickson's discussion of the Soviet Navy in *Soviet Military Power*, pp. 52–61.
11. Christian Hacke and Wolfgang Pfeiler, 'Soviet Approaches to Limited War and Theatre Warfare', *Soviet Union/Union Soviétique*, op. cit., pp. 277–8;
12. Each fleet must traverse narrow or difficult waters for egress to its wartime area of operations: for the Northern Fleet, the Greenland–Iceland–UK (GIUK) Gap, for the Black Sea Fleet, the Bosphorus and Dardanelles, for the Baltic Fleet, the Danish Straits finally, ships of the Pacific Fleet based at Sovetskaya Gavan must traverse the narrow La Pérouse Strait between Sakhalin and Japan.
13. Berman and Baker, op. cit., p. 2.
14. Dennis Gromley and Douglas Hart, *Soviet Views on Escalation: Implications for Alliance Strategy*, EAI Paper 8 (Marina del Rey, Calif: European American Institute for Security Research, 1984) p. 4.
15. Gormley and Hart, ibid., pp. 1, 3–4, 5–8; Scott and Scott, *Art of War*, pp. 241–3. For such an 'extreme' American view, see Jeffrey Record,

NATO's Theater Nuclear Force Modernization Program: The Real Issues (Cambridge, Massachusetts: Institute for Foreign Policy Analysis, 1981), pp. 1–10.

16. Good discussions of the Alliance perspective regarding Soviet regional nuclear force modernization can be found in William Hyland, 'Soviet Theatre Forces and Arms Control Policy', *Survival*, 23:5, Sept.–Oct. 1981; Record, op. cit.; and Jed C. Snyder, 'European Security, East–West Policy and the INF Debate', *Orbis*, Winter 1984, pp. 914–28.

17. Record, op. cit., pp. 1–10, pp. 58–68.

18. Raymond L. Garthoff, 'The Soviet SS–20 Decision', *Survival*, 35:3, May–June 1983, pp. 110–19; Stephen Meyer, *Soviet Theatre Nuclear Forces*, Part I, Adelphi Paper 187 (London: IISS, 1983–84).

19. Harriet Fast and William F. Scott, *The Armed Forces of the USSR* (London: Arms and Armour Press, 1984) p. 37. [Hereafter, *Armed Forces.*]

20. Dziak, op. cit., pp. 21–3, 29–34. Scott and Scott, *Art of War*, pp. 4–11.

21. Peter Vigor, *Soviet Blitzkrieg Theory* (London: Macmillan, 1983) pp. 48–67, 102–19.

22. Christopher N. Donnelly, 'Recent Changes in Soviet Operational Strategy' (unpublished research paper of Soviet Studies Research Centre, RMA Sandhurst), pp. 21–8. [Hereafter, 'Recent Changes']

23. Scott and Scott, op. cit., pp. 5–9.

24. C. N. Donnelly, 'The Structure of the Soviet Armed Forces', (Sandhurst: SSRC), p. 7., and 'The Development of Soviet Military Doctrine' (Sandhurst: SSRC) p. 11.

25. Scott and Scott, *Art of War*, p. 7.

26. Victor Suvorov, *Inside the Soviet Army* (London: Hamish Hamilton, 1982) pp. 170–4.

27. Ibid., pp. 52–3.

28. Scott and Scott, *Art of War*, p. 7.

29. Vigor, op. cit., p. 114.

30. Victor Suvorov, 'Strategic Command and Control: The Soviet Approach', *International Defence Review*, 12/1984, pp. 1815, 1818–19. [Hereafter, Strategic Command.]

31. Scott and Scott, op. cit., pp. 17–21.

32. Donnelly, 'Recent Changes', pp. 44–6, 54, 58–9. Donnelly in European Security Study (ESECS), *Strengthening Conventional Deterrence in Europe: Proposals for the 1980s* (London: Macmillan, 1983), pp. 48–50; Victor Suvorov, 'Spetsnaz: The Soviet Union's Special Forces', *International Defence Review*, Sept. 1983, pp. 1209–16; Vigor, op. cit., pp. 122–30.

33. V. Ye. Savkin in Christopher Donnelly, *Soviet Military Doctrine*, pp. 9–13. Suvorov, *Soviet Army*, p. 110.

34. Suvorov, *Soviet Army*, pp. 68–71. John Erickson, 'The Soviet Military System: Doctrine, Technology and "Style"', Erickson and E. J. Feuchtwanger (ed), *Soviet Military Power and Performance* (London: Macmillan, 1979) p. 33.

35. Suvorov, *Soviet Army*, pp. 93–9.

36. Roger Beaumont, *Maskirovka: Soviet Camouflage, Concealment and Deception* (Centre for Strategic Technology, Texas A & M University,

November, 1982), Stratech Studies, SS82–1. Jiri Valenta, 'Soviet Use of Surprise and Deception', *Survival*, 24:2, pp. 51–3. Vigor, op. cit., pp. 144–66.

37. Suvorov, 'Strategic Command', pp. 1817–18.
38. Donnelly, 'Military Doctrine', pp. 11–14. For an overview of pre–revolutionary antecedents to these four principles of military art, see Chris Bellamy, 'Heirs of Genghis Khan: The Influence of the Tartar–Mongols on the Imperial Russian and Soviet Armies', RUSI *Journal*, Mar. 1983, pp. 52–60.
39. Milan Vego, 'Soviet Anti-Submarine Warfare Doctrine', RUSI *Journal*, June 1983, p. 50.
40. Vigor, op. cit., pp. 88–9.
41. Notra Trulock III, 'Weapons of Mass Destruction in Soviet Military Strategy' (Paper delivered to joint RUSI/Boston Foreign Affairs Group Conference on 'Soviet Military Strategy and Western Europe', Nuneham Park, Oxfordshire, 24–25 September 1984) pp. 6–10; Scott and Scott, op. cit., pp. 123–6.
42. Trulock, op. cit., pp. 10–17.
43. Ibid., p. 17.
44. Ibid., p. 21.
45. Ibid., pp. 23–25.
46. Scott and Scott, op. cit., p. 12.
47. Robert P. Berman and John C. Baker, *Soviet Strategic Forces: Requirements and Responses* (Washington, D.C.: Brookings, 1982) pp. 41–6.
48. Douglas M. Hart and Dennis M. Gormley, 'The Evolution of Soviet Interest in Atomic Artillery', RUSI *Journal*, June 1983, p. 26. Berman and Baker, op. cit., pp. 102–4.
49. Berman and Baker, op. cit., pp. 42–6.
50. Ibid., p. 47.
51. Scott and Scott, *Art of War*, p. 158.
52. Ibid., p. 176.
53. R. Malinovskiy, 'Report to the Twenty-Second Congress of the CPSU', cited in Scott and Scott, *Armed Forces*, p. 45.
54. Yosef Avidar, *The Party and the Army in the Soviet Union* (Jerusalem: Magnes Press, 1983) pp. 245–54, 257–74.
55. Scott and Scott, *Art of War*, p. 176.
56. Joseph D. Douglass, Jr., *The Soviet Theater Nuclear Offensive* (United States Air Force: Studies in Communist Affairs, vol. 1) pp. 15–33. Berman and Baker, op. cit., p. 47.
57. As quoted in Trulock, op. cit., p. 41. Marshal Rotmistrov, during the Finnish Army Day reception in Moscow on 4 June 1965 expressed much the same thought. 'As time passes, the threat to the US grows greater, and eventually deterrence will become as binding on the US as on the Soviet Union. Thus, the Soviets with a valid counter-strike capability, will continue to maintain their ability to overrun Europe in 60–90 days either in a nuclear or non-nuclear situation. Thus, Europe will remain hostage to the Soviet Army' Quoted in Phillip A. Petersen and John G. Hines, 'The Evolution of Soviet Military Thought' (Paper delivered to joint RUSI/

Boston Foreign Affairs Group Conference on 'Soviet Military Strategy and Western Europe', Nuneham Park, Oxfordshire, 24–25 Sept. 1984).
58. Erickson, *Soviet Military Power*, pp. 8–12, 41–2. Avidar, op. cit., pp. 275–89.
59. Marshal Rodion Malinovskiy, cited in Scott and Scott, *Art of War*, p. 157.
60. Douglass, op. cit., p. 16. Soviet missile numbers are cited from Berman and Baker, op. cit., pp. 103–4; US missile numbers cited from Hines and Petersen, op. cit., p. 12.
61. Hines and Petersen, op. cit., p. 10.
62. Erickson, *Soviet Military Power*, pp. 8–12, 41–2. Avidar, op. cit., pp. 275–89. Sokolovskiy quote from Petersen and Hines, op. cit., p. 10.
63. Scott and Scott, op. cit., p. 125.
64. Erickson, *Soviet Military Power*, pp. 41, 42–4.
65. Ibid., p. 48.
66. Major-General Lagovskii, writing in *Krasnaya Zveda* (Red Star), 25 Sept., 1969, quoted in Erickson, *Soviet Military Power*, p. 10.
67. Douglass, op. cit., pp. 30, 58–9, 45–67. Erickson, *Soviet Military Power*, pp. 50–1.
68. N. V. Ogarkov entry on 'Strategy, Military' in 1979 *Soviet Military Encyclopedia*, from Petersen and Hines, n. 41, p. 58.
69. A. A. Grechko, 'On Guard Over Peace and Socialism', *Kommunist*, Feb. 1970, quoted in Scott and Scott, op. cit., p. 208.
70. General N. A. Lomov, 'The Influence of Soviet Military Doctrine on the Development of Military Art' in *Kommunist Vooryzhenyk Sil* (Communist of the Armed Forces), Nov. 1967, quoted in William R. Kintner and Harriet Scott, *The Nuclear Revolution in Soviet Military Affairs* (Norman, Oklahoma: University of Oklahoma Press, 1968) p. 156.
71. A. A. Sikorenko, *The Offensive* (Moscow: Voyenizdat, 1970), trans. US Air Force (Washington, D.C.: Government Printing Office, 1974), Soviet Military Thought series no. 1, p. 88.
72. Jeffrey Record, *Force Reductions in Europe: Starting Over* (Cambridge, Mass., Institute for Foreign Policy Analysis, 1980), pp. 22–33. [Hereafter Force Reductions]
73. Berman and Baker, op. cit., pp. 86–9, 91. Erickson, *Soviet Military Power*, p. 41.
74. Berman and Baker, op. cit., p. 136. Record, *TNF Modernization*, pp. 20–3.
75. Garthoff, op. cit., pp. 112–13; Berman and Baker, op. cit., pp. 57–9, 63, 93.
76. Berman and Baker, op. cit., pp. 117–19, 122–5.
77. Dennis M. Gormley and Douglas M. Hart, *Soviet Views on Escalation: Implications for Alliance Strategy*, EAI Paper no. 8 (European–American Institute for Security Research, Summer 1984) pp. 2–4.
78. Scott and Scott, *Art of War*, pp. 207–10.
79. Hines and Petersen, op. cit., p. 46.
80. Scott and Scott, op. cit., pp. 207–8.
81. Petersen and Hines, op. cit., pp. 41–2.
82. Petersen and Hines, op. cit., pp. 42–6, 52–3.

83. Record, *Force Reductions*, pp. 22–33.
84. Petersen and Hines, op. cit., pp. 42–6, 52–3.
85. Christopher Donnelly in *European Security Study*, op. cit., pp. 109–10.
86. Peter Vigor, op. cit., pp. 145–67.
87. Ibid., p. 132.
88. For a catalogue of these measures, see Zyg Ager, 'Political Events Leading up to the Declaration of Martial Law in Poland' in *RUSI/ Brassey's Defence Yearbook* 1983 (Oxford: Brassey's Publishing, Ltd, 1983) p. 3–9.
89. Peter Vigor, op. cit., p. 163.
90. Christopher N. Donnelly, 'The Military Significance of the Polish Crisis', in *RUSI/Brassey's Defence Yearbook* 1983 (Oxford: Brassey's Publishing Ltd. 1983) p. 13.
91. Zdenek Mlynar, *Night Frost in Prague: the End of Humane Socialism* (London: C. Hurst and Co., 1980) p. 186.
92. Peter Vigor, op. cit., p. 83.
93. C. N. Donnelly, 'Recent Changes', p. 19.
94. C. N. Donnelly, *European Security Study*, op. cit., p. 128–32.
95. C. N. Donnelly, 'Recent Changes', p. 60.

CHAPTER 6   THE INVISIBLES OF POWER

1. Similar points have been raised by others, e.g., Richard Pipes, 'Survival is Not Enough: How Vulnerable is the West?', *Survey*, 28:2, Summer 1984.
2. Samuel P. Huntington, *Political Order in Changing Societies*, p. 9.
3. E. H. Carr, *The Bolshevik Revolution*, vol. 1.
4. Richard H. Shultz and Roy Godson, *Dezinformatsia* (Oxford: Pergamon–Brasseys) p. 2
5. Bertram Wolfe, *Three Who Made a Revolution* (New York: Delta, 1964, rev. edn); Adam Ulam, *The Bolsheviks* (New York: Macmillan, 1965); Leonard Schapiro, *The Communist Party of the Soviet Union* (London: Methuen, 1970, 2nd edn).
6. United States Department of State, *Commandante Bayardo Arce s Soviet Speech before the Nicaraguan Socialist Party (PSN)*, Washington DC, Department of State Publication 9422, Inter-American Series 118, March 1985.
7. John J. Dziak in Roy Godson (ed.), *Intelligence Requirements for the 1980s: Covert Operations*, vol. III, pp. 95–7ff.
8. Godson, (ed.), *Intelligence Requirements for the 1980s* vol. I; Godson, (ed.), *Dezinformatsia*, p. 14.
9. Victor Suvorov, *Inside the Soviet Army* (London: Hamish Hamilton, 1982) pp. 92–9; Victor Suvorov, *Soviet Military Intelligence* (London: Hamish Hamilton, 1984) p. 144; Aleksei Myagkov, *Inside the KGB* (Richmond: Foreign Affairs Publishing Co. Ltd, 1976) pp. 26–9.
10. Shultz and Godson, op. cit., pp. 173, 183 – The interviews with Bittman and Levchenko can be found on pp. 165–91.

11. Myagkov, op. cit., p. 21.
12. Shultz and Godson, op. cit., p. 34–5. Myagkov, ibid., pp. 29–30.
13. Robert W. Kitrinos, 'International Department of the CPSU', *Problems of Communism*, vol. xxxiii, Sept.–Oct., 1984, p. 47.
14. Leonard Schapiro, 'The International Department of the CPSU: Key to Soviet Policy', *International Journal* (Winter 1976–77) p. 42. The precise reorganisations and terminologies adopted following the Comintern's dissolution are not fully agreed by Western experts. See Kitrinos, op. cit., pp. 48–9.
15. Kitrinos, op. cit., pp. 47–65.
16. Kitrinos, ibid., pp. 49–52.
17. Shultz and Godson, op. cit., p. 22.
18. Kitrinos, op. cit., pp. 53–65.
19. Kenneth Currie, 'Soviet General Staff's New Role', *Problems of Communism*, Mar.–Apr. 1984, p. 36n.
20. Shultz and Godson, op. cit., p. 112.
21. Levchenko in Shultz and Godson, op. cit., p. 181.
22. Spaulding, op. cit., pp. 52–3.
23. Kitrinos, op. cit., p. 58.
24. Kitrinos, op. cit., pp. 58–9.
25. John Barron, *KGB Today: the Hidden Hand* (London: Hodder & Stoughton, 1983, Coronet edn) p. 272.
26. William F. Scott and Harriet Fast Scott, 'The Social Science Institutes of the Soviet Academy of Sciences', *Air Force Magazine*, Mar. 1980, pp. 60–4. 'The Soviet Academy of Sciences has been especially active in joining non-governmental international organisations. In 1950, it belonged to three, in 1965 to 89, and in 1976 to 155. Soviet scientists are very active in organisations like the UN and UNESCO. They also have increased the number of Soviet scientists holding posts in international organisations from 27 in 1965 to 139 in 1975'.
27. Barron, op. cit., p. 281.
28. Barron, op. cit., p. 265.
29. Kitrinos, op. cit., pp. 62–3.
30. Georgiy Arbatov, *The War of Ideas in Contemporary International Relations* (Moscow: Progress Publishers, 1973) p. 277.
31. Barron, op. cit., p. 286.
32. Sir Clive Rose, *Campaigns Against Western Defence: NATO's Adversaries and Critics* (London: Macmillan/RUSI, 1985).
33. Bittman and Levchenko in Schultz and Godson, op. cit., pp. 174, 184.
34. See the author's 'The Strategic Context of Anti-Nuclear Protest: An Historical Perspective', *Arms Control*, vol. 4, no. 2, Sept. 1983.
35. T. B. Millar, *The East–West Strategic Balance*, (London: Allen & Unwin, 1981).
36. Joe Sobran in *Dartmouth Review*, vol. III, no. 23 (16 May 1983) quoted in Richard Pipes, 'How Vulnerable is the West?' *Survey*, summer 1984, vol. 28, no. 2 (121) pp. 25–6.
37. V. I. Lenin, *Collected Works* (London: Lawrence and Wishart, 1977) p. 277.
38. Quoted in John J. Dziak, *Soviet Perceptions of Military Power: the*

Interaction of Theory and Practice (New York: Crane Russak & Co., 1981) p. 67n.

39. Ladislaw Bittman in Schultz and Godson, op. cit., p. 167.
40. John Barron, op. cit., p. 276.
41. Shultz and Godson, op. cit., p. 77.
42. L. W. McNaught, *Nuclear Weapons and Their Effects*, (London: Brasseys, 1984) pp. 20–2.
43. Barron, op. cit., pp. 268–73.

Bibliography

BOOKS AND MONOGRAPHS

Aims of Industry, *The Challenge of Soviet Shipping* (London: Aims of Industry/National Strategy Information Centre, 1984).

Alexander, A., *Decision-Making in Soviet Weapons Procurement*, Adelphi Paper 147–48 (London: IISS, 1978–9).

Amann, R. and Cooper, J. (ed.), *Industrial Innovation in the Soviet Union* (New Haven, Connecticut: Yale University Press, 1982).

Arbatov, G., *Cold War or Détente? The Soviet Viewpoint* (London: Zed Books, 1983).

——, *The War of Ideas in Contemporary International Relations* (Moscow, 1973).

Ash, T., *The Polish Revolution: Solidarity, 1980–82* (London: Jonathan Cape, 1983).

Avidar, Y., *The Party and the Army in the Soviet Union* (Jerusalem: Magnes Press, 1983).

Barron, J., *The KGB: The Secret Work of Soviet Secret Agents* (New York: Reader's Digest Press, 1974).

——, *KGB Today: The Hidden Hand* (New York: Reader's Digest Press, 1983).

Beaumont, R., *Maskirovka: Soviet Camouflage, Concealment and Deception, Stratech Studies SS82–1* (College Station, Texas: Center for Strategic Technology, 1982).

Beloff, M., *The Foreign Policy of Soviet Russia*, vols I and II (London: Oxford University Press, 1949).

Berman, R. and Baker, J., *Soviet Strategic Forces* (Washington: Brookings, 1982).

Bialer, S. (ed.) *The Domestic Context of Soviet Foreign Policy* (Boulder, Col.: Westview Press, 1981).

Booth, K., *The Military Instrument in Soviet Foreign Policy, 1917–72* (London: RUSI, 1972).

Brown, A. and Kaser, M. (ed.), *Soviet Policy for the 1980s* (London: Macmillan, 1982).

Brzezinski, Z., *The Soviet Bloc* (Cambridge, Mass.: Harvard University Press, 1967).

Byrnes, R. (ed.), *After Brezhnev: Sources of Soviet Conduct in the 1980s* (London: Frances Pinter, 1983).

Carr, E. H., *The Russian Revolution from Lenin to Stalin, 1917–29* (London: Macmillan, 1979).

——, *Socialism in One Country, 1924–26*, vol. III, part 1 (London: Macmillan, 1964).

Charlton, M., *The Eagle and the Small Birds: Crisis in the Soviet Empire from Yalta to Solidarity* (London: BBC, 1984).

Chubin, S., *Soviet Policy Towards Iran and the Gulf*, Adelphi Paper 157 (London: IISS, 1980).

Clubb, O., *China and Russia: The 'Great Game'* (New York: Columbia University Press, 1971).

Dawisha, K. and Hanson, P. (eds), *Soviet–East European Dilemmas: Coercion, Competition and Consent* (London: Heinemann/RIIA, 1981).

Deutscher, I., *Stalin: A Political Biography* (New York: Oxford University Press, 1949).

Djilas, M., *Conversations with Stalin* (New York: Harcourt, 1962).

Douglass, J., *The Soviet Theater Nuclear Offensive* (Washington: United States Air Force).

——, and Hoeber, A. (eds), *Selected Readings from Military Thought, 1963–73, Vol. 5, Part 2* (Washington: Government Printing Office/United States Air Force).

Dziak, J., *Soviet Perceptions of Military Power: the Interaction of Theory and Practice* (New York: Crane Russak/National Strategy Information Center, 1981).

Erickson, J., *Soviet Military Power* (London: RUSI, 1971).

——, and Feuchtwanger, J. (eds), *Soviet Military Power and Performance* (London: Macmillan, 1979).

European Security Study, *Strengthening Conventional Deterrence in Europe: Proposals for the 1980s* (London: Macmillan, 1983).

Freedman, L., *The Evolution of Nuclear Strategy* (London: Macmillan, 1983).

Godson, R. (ed.), *Intelligence Requirements for the 1980s* (New York: Crane Russak, 1983).

——, *The Kremlin and Labor* (New York: Crane, Russak, 1977).

Goldman, M., *USSR in Crisis: The Failure of an Economic System* (New York: Norton, 1983).

Goren, R., *The Soviet Union and Terrorism* (London: Allen & Unwin, 1984).

Gormley, D. and Hart, D., *Soviet Views on Escalation: Implications for Alliance Strategy. EAI Paper 8* (Marina del Rey, California: European American Institute for Security Research, 1984).

Greig, I., *They Mean What They Say* (London: Foreign Affairs Research Institute, 1981).

Haselkorn, A., *The Evolution of Soviet Security Strategy, 1965–75* (New York: Crane, Russak and Co./National Strategy Information Center, 1978).

Holloway, D., *The Soviet Union and the Arms Race* (New Haven, Conn.: Yale University Press, 1983).

Hough, J. and Fainsod, M., *How the Soviet Union is Governed* (Cambridge, Mass.: Harvard University Press, 1979).

Howard, M., *The Causes of Wars* (London: Allen & Unwin, 1983).

Ionescu, G., *The Politics of the European Communist States* (New York: Praeger, 1967).

Isby, D., *Weapons and Tactics of the Soviet Army* (London: Jane's, 1981).

Johnson, A., Dean, R., and Alexiev, A., *East European Military Establishments: The Warsaw Pact Northern Tier* (New York: Crane, Russak, 1982).

Kaplan, S., *Diplomacy of Power: Soviet Armed Forces as a Political Instrument* (Washington: Brookings, 1981).

Kaser, M., *Soviet Economics* (London: Weidenfeld and Nicolson, 1970).

Kozlov, S., *The Officer's Handbook (A Soviet View)* (Washington: Government Printing Office/United States Air Force, 1971).

Laird, R. and Herspring, D., *The Soviet Union and Strategic Arms* (Boulder, Col.: Westview Press, 1984).

Leebaert, D. (ed.), *Soviet Military Thinking* (London: Allen & Unwin, 1981).

Lenin, V., *The State and Revolution* (Moscow: Progress Publishers, 1978).

——, *What is to be Done?* (Moscow: Progress Publishers, 1978).

Luttwak, E., *The Grand Strategy of the Soviet Union*.

Mackintosh, J., *Juggernaut* (London: Secker and Warburg, 1967).

——, *Strategy and Tactics of Soviet Foreign Policy* (London: Oxford University Press, 1962).

Mastny, V., *Russia's Road to the Cold War: Diplomacy, Warfare and the Politics of Communism, 1941–45* (New York: Columbia University Press, 1979).

McCauley, M. (ed.), *The Soviet Union After Brezhnev* (London: Heinemann, 1983).

Medvedev, R. and Medvedev, Z., *Khrushchev: The Years in Power* (New York: Norton, 1978).

Medvedev, Z., *Andropov: His Life and Death* (Oxford: Basil Blackwell, 1984).

Menaul, S. et al., *The Soviet War Machine* (London: Salamander Books, 1980).

Meyer, S., *Soviet Theatre Nuclear Forces, Parts I and II, Adelphi Papers 187–188* (London: IISS, 1983–4).

Millar, T., *The East–West Strategic Balance* (London: Allen & Unwin, 1981).

Mlynář, Z., *Night Frost in Prague: The End of Humane Socialism* (London: C. Hurst and Co., 1980).

Moreton, E. and Segal, G., (ed.), *Soviet Strategy Towards Western Europe* (London: Allen & Unwin, 1984).

Myagkov, A., *Inside the KGB* (Richmond: Foreign Affairs Publishing Co., 1976).

Nove, A., *An Economic History of the USSR* (Harmondsworth: Penguin, 1972).

Oudenaren, J., *The Soviet Union and Eastern Europe: Options for the 1980s and Beyond* (Santa Monica, California: RAND, 1984).

Pipes, R., *The Formation of the Soviet Union: Communism and Nationalism, 1917–23* (Cambridge University Press, 1964).

Plamenatz, J., *German Marxism and Russian Communism* (London: Longmans, Green, 1954).

Porter, B., *The USSR in Third World Conflicts: Soviet Arms and Diplomacy in Local Wars, 1945–80* (Cambridge University Press, 1984).

Record, J., *Force Reductions in Europe: Starting Over* (Cambridge, Mass.: Institute for Foreign Policy Analysis, 1980).

——, *NATO's Theatre Nuclear Force Modernization Program: The Real Issues* (Cambridge, Mass.: Institute for Foreign Policy Analysis, 1981).

Rigby, T., Brown, A. and Reddaway, P. (eds), *Authority, Power and Policy in the USSR: Essays Dedicated to Leonard Schapiro* (London: Macmillan, 1983).

Rose, C., *Campaigns Against Western Defence: NATO's Adversaries and Critics* (London: Macmillan/RUSI, 1985).

Savkin, V., *The Basic Principles of Operational Art and Tactics* (United States Air Force translation, Soviet Military Thought Series 4) (Washington: Government Printing Office, 1979).

Schapiro, L., *The Communist Party of the Soviet Union* (London: Methuen, 1970).

——, *Totalitarianism* (London: Macmillan, 1972).

Scott, H. and Scott, W., *The Armed Forces of the USSR* (London: Arms and Armour Press, 1984).

—— (eds), *The Soviet Art of War: Doctrine, Strategy and Tactics* (Boulder, Col.: Westview Press, 1982).

Scott, W., (ed.), *Selected Soviet Military Writings, 1970–75* (A Soviet View) (Washington: Government Printing Office/United States Air Force, 1976).

Sejna, J., *We Will Bury You* (London: Sidgwick & Jackson, 1982).

Shultz, R. and Godson, R., *Dezinformatsia: Active Measures in Soviet Strategy* (Oxford: Pergamon–Brasseys, 1984).

Sidorenko, A., *The Offensive* (United States Air Force translation, Soviet Military Thought Series 1) (Washington D.C.: Government Printing Office, 1974).

Sokolovskiy, V., *Soviet Military Strategy* (ed. and trans. by H. F. Scott) (New York: Crane, Russak, 1975).

Solovyov, V. and Klepikova, E., *Yuri Andropov: a Secret Passage into the Kremlin* (New York: Macmillan, 1983).

Summerscale, P., *The East European Predicament: Changing Patterns in Poland, Czechoslovakia and Romania* (London: Gower/RIIA, 1982).

Suvorov, V., *Inside the Soviet Army* (London: Hamish Hamilton, 1982).

——, *Soviet Military Intelligence* (London: Hamish Hamilton, 1984).

Talbott, S. (ed.), *Khrushchev Remembers*, vols I and II (Boston: Little, Brown, 1970 and 1974).

Terry, S. (ed.), *Soviet Policy in Eastern Europe* (New Haven, Conn.: Yale University Press/Council on Foreign Relations, 1984).

Tucker, R., *The Soviet Political Mind: Stalinism and Post-Stalin Change* (New York: Norton, 1971).

Ulam, A., *The Bolsheviks* (Toronto: Collier–Macmillan, 1965).

——, *Dangerous Relations: the Soviet Union in World Politics, 1970–82* (New York: Oxford University Press, 1983).

——, *Expansion and Coexistence: The History of Soviet Foreign Policy* (New York: Frederick A. Praeger, 1968).

United States Government, *Soviet Military Power 1985* (Washington, DC: Government Printing Office, 1985).

Urban, M., *Soviet Land Power* (London: Ian Allan, 1975).

USSR, *Constitution (Fundamental Law) of the Union of Soviet Socialist Republics* (Moscow: Novosti Press Agency Publishing House, 1982).

Valenta, J., *Soviet Intervention in Czechoslovakia: Anatomy of a Decision* (Baltimore: Johns Hopkins University Press, 1979).

Valenta, J. and Potter, W. (eds), *Soviet Decision-Making for National Security* (London: Allen & Unwin, 1984).

Vigor, P., *Marxism: Its Influence on Soviet Development* (London: Faber and Faber, 1966).
——, *Soviet Blitzkrieg Theory* (London: Macmillan, 1983).
——, *The Soviet View of War, Peace and Neutrality* (London: Routledge & Kegan Paul, 1975).
Vincent, R., *Military Power and Political Influence: The Soviet Union and Western Europe*, *Adelphi Paper 119* (London: IISS, 1975).
Voslensky, M. (trans. Eric Mosbacher), *Nomenklatura: Anatomy of the Soviet Ruling Class* (London: Bodley Head, 1984).
Wolf, C. et al., *The Costs of the Soviet Empire* (Santa Monica, California/ RAND, 1983).
Wolfe, T., *The SALT Experience* (Cambridge, Mass.: Ballinger Publishing Co., 1979).
——, *Soviet Power and Europe, 1945–73* (Baltimore: Johns Hopkins University Press, 1976).

ARTICLES

Ager, Z., 'Political Events Leading up to the Declaration of Martial Law in Poland', *RUSI & Brassey's Defence Yearbook*, 1983 (Oxford: Brassey's Publishers, 1983).
Bellamy, C., 'Antecedents of the Modern Soviet Operational Manoeuvre Group (OMG)', RUSI *Journal*, vol., 129, no. 3, Sept. 1984.
——, 'Heirs of Genghis Khan: The Influence of the Tartar–Mongols on the Imperial Russian and Soviet Armies', RUSI *Journal*, 128:1, Mar. 1983.
Bildt, C., 'Sweden and the Soviet Submarines', *Survival*, 35:4, July–Aug. 1983.
Blanc, H. 'The Soviet Union, Eastern Europe and the West's Response', *Atlantic Quarterly*, 2:4, Winter 1984.
Brown, N., 'The Changing Face of Non-Nuclear War', *Survival*, 34:5, Sept.–Oct. 1982.
Currie, K., 'Soviet General Staff's New Role', *Problems of Communism*, 33:2, Mar.–Apr. 1984.
Donnelly, C., 'The Military Significance of the Polish Crisis', *RUSI & Brassey's Defence Yearbook*, 1983 (Oxford: Brassey's Publishers, 1983).
——, 'Soviet Operational Concepts in the 1980s' in European Security Study, *Strengthening Conventional Deterrence in Europe: Proposals for the 1980s* (London: Macmillan, 1983).
——, 'The Soviet Operational Manoeuvre Group: A New Challenge for NATO', *Military Review*, 9/1983.
——, 'Soviet Tactics for Operations in the Enemy Rear', *International Defence Review*, 9/1983.
Erickson, J., 'The Soviet View of Deterrence: A General Survey', *Survival*, 34:6, Nov.–Dec. 1982.
Garthoff, R., 'The Soviet SS–20 Decision', *Survival*, 35:3, May–June 1983.
Hacke, C. and Pfeiler, W. 'Soviet Approaches to Limited War', *Soviet Union/Union Soviétique*, 10, parts 2–3, 1983.

Hart, D., 'Soviet Approaches to Crisis Management: The Military Dimension', *Survival*, 36:5, Sept.–Oct. 1984.

Hart, D. and Gormley, D., 'The Evolution of Soviet Interest in Atomic Artillery', RUSI *Journal*, 128:2, June 1983.

Herspring, D., 'GDR Naval Build-up', *Problems of Communism*, 33:1, Jan.–Feb. 1984.

Huyn, H., 'Webs of Soviet Disinformation', *Strategic Review*, Autumn 1984.

Hyland, W., 'Soviet Theatre Forces and Arms Control Policy', *Survival*, 23:5, Sept.–Oct. 1981.

Kitrinos, R., 'International Department of the CPSU', *Problems of Communism*, 33:5, Sept.–Oct. 1984.

Kolkowicz, R., 'The Soviet Union: Elusive Adversary', *Soviet Union/Union Soviétique*, 10, parts 2–3, 1983.

Kushnirsky, F., 'Inflation Soviet Style', *Problems of Communism*, 33:1, Jan.–Feb. 1984.

——, 'The Limits of Soviet Economic Reform', *Problems of Communism*, 33:4, July–Aug. 1984.

Lambeth, B., 'Contemporary Soviet Military Policy', *Soviet Union/Union Soviétique*, 10, parts 2–3, 1983.

Lee, W., 'The Soviet Defence Establishment in the 1980s', *Air Force Magazine*, Mar. 1980.

Lenin, V., 'Left Wing Communism: An Infantile Disorder'.

Mackintosh, J., 'The Soviet Military: Influence on Foreign Policy,' *Problems of Communism*.

Odom, W., 'The Militarization of Soviet Society', *Problems of Communism*, Sept.–Oct. 1976.

——, 'The Party Connection', *Problems of Communism*.

Paul, D., and Simon, M., 'Poland Today and Czechoslovakia 1968', *Problems of Communism*, Sept.–Oct. 1981.

Petersen, P. and Hines, J., 'Military Power in Soviet Strategy Against NATO' RUSI *Journal*, 128:4, Dec. 1983.

Pipes, R., 'Survival Is Not Enough', *Survey*, 28:2(121), Summer 1984.

Ries, T., 'Defending the Far North', *International Defence Review*, 7/1984.

——, 'Sun Tzu and Soviet Strategy', *International Defence Review*, 4/1984.

Rubin, F., 'The Hungarian People's Army', RUSI *Journal*, 121:3, Sept. 1976.

——, 'Security Concerns of the USSR and the Other Warsaw Treaty Organisation Countries', RUSI *Journal*, 128:3, Sept. 1983.

Rumer, B., 'Strategic Imbalance in the Soviet Economy', *Problems of Communism*, 3:4, July–Aug. 1984.

Schapiro, L., 'The International Department of the CPSU: Key to Soviet Policy', *International Journal*, Winter 1976–77.

Scott, W. and Scott, H., 'The Social Science Institutes of the Soviet Academy of Sciences', *Air Force Magazine*, Mar. 1980.

Simes, D., 'The Military and Militarism in the Soviet Union', *International Security*, Winter 1981–82.

Snyder, J., 'European Security, East–West Policy and the INF Debate', *Orbis*, Winter 1984.

Spaulding, W., 'Communist Fronts in 1984' *Problems of Communism*, 34:2, Mar.–Apr. 1985.

Starr, R., 'Checklist of Communist Parties in 1983', *Problems of Communism*, 33:2, Mar.–Apr. 1984.

Suvorov, V., 'Spetsnaz: The Soviet Union's Special Forces', *International Defence Review*, 9/1983.

——, 'Strategic Command and Control: The Soviet Approach', *International Defence Review*, 12/1984.

Tökes, R., 'Hungarian Reform Imperatives', *Problems of Communism*, 3:5, Sept.–Oct. 1984.

Trofimenko, H., 'The Third World and US–Soviet Competition', *Foreign Affairs*, 59:5, Summer 1981.

Valenta, J., 'Soviet Use of Surprise and Deception', *Survival*, 24:2, Mar.–Apr. 1982.

——, and Valenta, V., 'Leninism in Grenada', *Problems of Communism*, 33:4, July–Aug. 1984.

Vego, M., 'Soviet Anti-Submarine Warfare Doctrine', RUSI *Journal*, 128:2, June 1983.

Wädekin, K., 'Soviet Agriculture's Dependence on the West', *Foreign Affairs*, 59:4, Spring 1981.

Ward, R. D., 'The Structured World of the Soviet Designer', *Air Force Magazine*, Mar. 1984.

Index